Why Are So Many Students of Color in Special Education?

Why Are So Many Students of Color in Special Education?

Understanding Race and Disability in Schools

THIRD EDITION

Beth Harry
Janette Klingner

Foreword by Alfredo J. Artiles

TEACHERS COLLEGE PRESS

TEACHERS COLLEGE | COLUMBIA UNIVERSITY

NEW YORK AND LONDON

Published by Teachers College Press, 1234 Amsterdam Avenue, New York,
NY 10027

Library of Congress Cataloging-in-Publication Data

Names: Harry, Beth, author. | Klingner, Janette K., author.
Title: Why are so many students of color in special education? :
    understanding race and disability in schools / Beth Harry and Janette
    Klingner ; Foreword by Alfredo J. Artiles.
Description: Third edition. | New York, NY : Teachers College Press, [2022]
    | Includes bibliographical references and index. | Summary: "Now in a
    third edition, this powerful book describes the school climates and
    social processes that place many children of color at risk of being
    assigned inappropriate disability labels. This edition provides an
    update on the patterns and literature related to disproportionality and
    includes revised recommendations for improving educational practice,
    teacher training, and policy renewal"— Provided by publisher.
Identifiers: LCCN 2022017989 (print) | LCCN 2022017990 (ebook) |
    ISBN 9780807767337 (hardcover) | ISBN 9780807767320 (paperback) |
    ISBN 9780807781210 (ebook)
Subjects: LCSH: Special education—United States—Evaluation. | Children
    with disabilities—Education—United States—Evaluation. |
    Discrimination in education—United States. |
    Minorities—Education—United States. | Educational equalization—United
    States.
Classification: LCC LC3981 .H36 2022 (print) | LCC LC3981 (ebook) |
    DDC 371.9—dc23
LC record available at https://lccn.loc.gov/2022017989
LC ebook record available at https://lccn.loc.gov/2022017990

ISBN 978-0-8077-6732-0 (paper)
ISBN 978-0-8077-6733-7 (hardcover)
ISBN 978-0-8077-8121-0 (ebook)

Printed on acid-free paper
Manufactured in the United States of America

Janette Klingner passed away on March 20, 2014, just a few weeks before the publication of the second edition of our book. Janette's career was marked by integrity, passion, and an intense commitment to the mitigation of social inequities in education and the development of culturally responsive instructional practices for all students. As a friend, Janette was supremely kind and generous with her time and her love, and her departure leaves a chasm in our lives. Her friends, colleagues, and former students take comfort in the fact that her contributions to education will live on.

While I cannot know what Janette's input into this third edition would have been, I know that she would have been delighted to participate, and I believe she would have approved of my revisions. I have used the first person for the sections of the book in which she did not participate (the introductory chapter and the concluding chapter on methodology), and have retained the pronoun "we" throughout the rest of the report, which we wrote together. Our collaboration was precious to me, and I hope this edition will do justice to her memory.

Beth Harry

Contents

Foreword to the Third Edition

Peering Into the Black Box of Race and Ability Intersections
The Promise of Interdisciplinary Equity Analyses

Education is regarded as the quintessential social mobility and justice tool in societies around the world. Trouble arises, however, when education becomes the conduit for the reproduction of societal inequities. There is a longstanding list of educational inequities that affect minoritized groups by virtue of their race, language, ability level, social class, or gender, among others. The quest for educational equity for these groups has proven elusive throughout the history of the United States (Anyon, 2005) and recent work suggests that inequities affecting minoritized groups are not only lingering, but have also deepened in recent years (Artiles, 2019; Bobo, 2011).

Harry and Klingner's book wrestles with these equity challenges. They focus on the racialization of disabilities as a window into the complex equity tensions and dilemmas that become visible when educational policies concerned with access and recognition travel across locales and get implemented in the everyday practices of schools. Despite advances in legislation, federally funded initiatives and monitoring systems, there is still an urgent need for interdisciplinary scholarship on racial disparities in special education to guide policy and practice, and elucidate unsettling evidence that defies simplistic explanations. Indeed, the problem of racial disproportionality in special education illustrates a longstanding puzzle in education equity work: "An interesting paradox in the racialization of disabilities is that the civil rights response for one group of individuals (i.e., learners with disabilities) has become a potential source of inequities for another group (i.e., racial minorit[ized] students) despite their shared histories of struggle for equity" (Artiles, 2011, p. 431).

Harry and Klingner's volume opens a new pathway for the examination of these equity issues in the racialization of disabilities. They report evidence that transcends the traditional focus on either student deficits or professional bias that has characterized this scholarship (Cruz & Rodl, 2018; Waitoller et al., 2010). Their findings challenge us to pursue more nuanced and sophisticated explanations for the racialization of disability. They did not set to hunt for a single cause—for example, child poverty and associated developmental delays or racist teachers. Rather, the research relied on a situated unit of analysis of equity remedies in which multiple factors are examined in tandem. The research team avoided the longstanding "damaged-centered" trope about minoritized communities (Tuck, 2009), and focused instead on the ubiquity of learning in children's lives. This conceptual shift marks a critical move, for it makes visible how children and their families, despite the structural violence under which they live, manage to learn in tight circumstances (McDermott, 2010). This way, kids' and families' agency is restored.

Moreover, Harry and Klingner offer a multidimensional vision of this problem as reflected in the alternative perspectives documented in the study—that is, the perspectives of teachers, administrators, students, parents, and guardians. This is a welcome change from the traditional grounding on what Rosaldo (1993) called "a view from nowhere" that characterizes traditional research on this topic. The result is a more nuanced picture of how the disproportionality problem is experienced by all the actors involved. The study also sheds light on the intersections of race, language, and poverty, and tracks kids' identities while traversing school and out-of-school environments. The identity boxes and essentialist views of culture used in previous studies (Artiles et al., 2010) become fluid and layered in this research. The findings portray students, not as racialized beings, but as active individuals who perform race in social encounters (Carbado & Gulati, 2013).

A unique contribution of this research is the documentation of the problem's trajectories from its precursors—life in general education classrooms—to its outcomes—special education identification and placement. This enabled Harry and Klingner to characterize the phenomenon of disability identification as constituted by a set of representational practices braided with cultural, social, professional, and ideological meanings (Artiles, 2019; McDermott, 1993). The contrast between these official representations and the insights gained from students and their families in and out of school contexts powerfully disrupt cultureless notions of educational competence.

All in all, Harry and Klingner challenge us to rethink our society's equity commitments and to offer educational opportunities to students with ability and racial differences. Using a perspective informed by interdisciplinary tenets about the anthropological, historical, spatial, and sociological nature of human development, the authors grapple with the transformation of the canonical toolkit used to identify ability differences. Their work makes a substantial contribution to a new generation of equity research concerned with the complexities of 21st-century education in pluricultural societies.

Alfredo J. Artiles
Stanford University

Acknowledgments

It has been 20 years since we completed this 4-year ethnographic study of the meaning of ethnic disproportionality in the special education placement process. I am gratified that the book has been received by the field as an effort to enhance our understanding of the role of special education in the lives of students of color. I welcome the opportunity to present this third edition with the aim of accomplishing two goals:

First, to reflect on the importance of our findings in the light of the continuing yet shifting patterns of disproportionality in special education. Second, to locate the study in the landscape of increasingly critical views of the field.

Once more, I must acknowledge the collaborative response we received from the school district. When we initiated the study in 1999, key special education administrators welcomed our request for research on this sensitive and controversial topic. They facilitated our access to schools and responded positively even to our most critical findings. In response to our findings, they took the initiative in reaching out to their general education colleagues in an effort to collaborate to improve the referral process. They also invited our opinions on their revisions of the then Child Study Team, which subsequently became the Student Support Team, introducing new procedures that required specific goals, target dates, and rigorous monitoring of progress for each child brought to the team. We were encouraged by these efforts and continue to be grateful to our school district colleagues for their support of our work. This district can provide a model for others in terms of its collaboration with us as university researchers, as well as collaboration between general education and special education district administrators. It is through such partnerships that special education administrators can position themselves to play a role in developing effective intervention models designed to reduce inappropriate referrals to special education.

I thank our project coordinator, Keith Sturges, and our colleague, Robert Moore, for their extensive help in carrying out this research. Their assistance was invaluable. We would also like to express gratitude for the essential contributions of our research assistants: Elizabeth Cramer, Juliet Hart, Cassaundra Wimes, Sherene McKesey, Patricia Stevens, Josefa Rascón, Thaissa Champagne, Heather Rutland, Aileen Angulo, Tony Ford, Christina

Herrera, Tamara Celestin, and Jennifer Dorce. We could not have collected such an extensive amount of data without their tireless participation in the project. I also thank our consultants, Alfredo Artiles and Lisa Delpit, for their inspired insights and helpful feedback and Alfredo for his foreword to this new edition. Finally, my most sincere thanks to Teachers College Press for its excellent support, and especially to our editor, Brian Ellerbeck, who guided us through the first edition of this book and who invited me to consider writing this third edition.

I dedicate this book to all the racially, culturally, and linguistically diverse students who have experienced less than equitable educational opportunities in U.S. public schools, especially those who have been inappropriately identified as having disabilities. I thank the families who allowed their children to participate and are particularly grateful to those who, by welcoming us into their homes, provided us with a holistic view of their children. I also dedicate this book to the administrators, teachers, and other school personnel who so graciously opened their doors to us despite the sensitivity of the topic. I especially wish to thank Ron Felton and Joe Jackson, the "gatekeepers" whose support made this work possible.

I offer heartfelt appreciation to my husband, Bernard Telson, and to Janette's husband, Don Klingner, as well as our children, Mark Teelucksingh, Heidi Warden, and Amy and John Klingner, who supported us with their love, encouragement, and patience over the years. I also thank Patrice Fenton and Meaghan Chaplin, who were doctoral students at the University of Miami, for their assistance in updating literature for the second and third editions.

Finally, I acknowledge the support of the U.S. Department of Education, Office of Special Education Programs, Grant #H324C980165-99C. I thank our project officers, Grace Zamora Durán and Bonnie Jones, for their unwavering support of our work.

A note on confidentiality. All names of schools and individuals are pseudonyms. In no cases have the real identities of schools or individuals been revealed to school district administrators or to any other persons. However, in hopes of demonstrating the importance of history and social context in research, I have taken the liberty in this edition of naming the city in which the research took place and offering some research-based historical information. I believe that the passage of two decades should provide some distance from the study for any participants who might recognize themselves in it. Moreover, the original consent forms for the study specified that no names of persons or schools would be mentioned but did not specify keeping the name of the city anonymous.

CHAPTER 1

Introduction

What's past is prologue; what's to come, in yours and my discharge.

—William Shakespeare, *The Tempest,* Act II Scene 1

I begin with a simple question: Why a third edition of a book reporting research that was conducted two decades ago? Is this relevant? Nothing can be changed in the data garnered from a 4-year study of racial/ethnic disproportionality in special education in one of the nation's largest school districts. No detail can be omitted, no new information added. So how can this study be relevant in a society which, over those 20 years, has been deeply impacted by innumerable social changes, perhaps most notably the vast sweep of rapidly advancing technology that has brought a world of knowledge to our fingertips while simultaneously challenging our confidence about truth versus fiction, about the borders between public and private information? With that technology has come the ability to see, in real time, the continuing injustices committed against citizens of color—in particular, Black men—and the unsurprising yet shocking backlash against the phenomenal success of the nation's first Black president. Most recently, this backlash has included an increasing effort on the part of those in power to silence the voices of diversity, whether through limited opportunities for voting, restrictions on equity for individuals with diverse sexual or gender orientations, or censorship of knowledge that reveals truths about the trajectory of racism in our nation's past. Complicating this intense landscape has been more than 2 years of a deadly pandemic which, by the time of this writing, had disrupted the education of millions of American children and caused the deaths of over 900,000 Americans and over 5 million people globally (WHO, 2022).

Yet despite all these changes, for better or worse, we carry our history with us. None of the foregoing issues arrived out of nowhere. All were deeply embedded in the social, economic, and political systems on which the nation was built, including the commitment to science that enabled the development of a vaccine to combat the COVID-19 pandemic. It is the notion of the inescapability of an unpleasant past that offends and seemingly intimidates those who shout against Critical Race Theory (CRT) (Crenshaw, 1989; Delgado & Stefancic, 2020; Ladson-Billings, 2021). Most recently, these voices of denial have been fueled by the rhetoric of reckless politicians and conspiracy theorists. Yet the facts are clear for all to see in the overlapping influences on education of race, housing, and the distribution of wealth. A solid body of research has detailed factors such as the history of red-lining in real estate policies that led to the creation of Northern ghettos (Rothstein, 2017; Wilkerson, 2010) and the continuing policy by which approximately half of most school districts' funding is based on local property taxes, allowing for better funding for the schools of the wealthy, while intractable patterns of housing and family income ensure inequities in schooling for children of the poor (Ashby et al., 2020; Kozol, 2006; White et al., 2019). In education, processes of racism and ableism, premised on flawed scientific theories, intersect to sort and limit individuals based on perceived differences (Freedman & Ferri, 2017).

This picture of a nation built on historical oppression and exclusion, however, is complemented by its opposite—the nation's ideal of equality, which pits a humanistic ideology against a history replete with exclusionary practices, yet marked by a continuing struggle to attain the ideal. In education, the Individuals with Disabilities Education Act (IDEA) (1990) and its precursor, the Education for all Handicapped Children Act (1975), represent the most powerful effort to realize that ideal.

Several essential questions highlight paradoxes in the concern over disproportionality. Most frequently cited are the questions: How did this equity-focused legislation come to be interpreted as a source of discrimination and exclusion of students of color (e.g., Reschly et al., 1988)? Why are there disproportionately high rates of such children in special education and why should that be considered a problem (e.g., Heller et al., 1982)? Further, should we even expect "proportionality" in disabilities across all groups and, if so, how might the picture be changed if we used the underrepresentation of White students as the reference point (Cavendish et al., 2018)? Decades of research on these questions have offered only partial answers focusing on a range of answers, most of which we will address throughout this book.

One unusual challenge has been raised recently that seeks to deny that Black students and other students of color are overrepresented in special education (e.g., Morgan & Farkas, 2016; Morgan et al., 2015, 2016). These efforts are mired in doubt because of methodological flaws, including the limited and ambiguous sample on which the researchers based their findings (Collins et al., 2016; Grindall et al., 2019; Skiba et al., 2015). Most important, we note that one premise leaps out of their argument: that poverty, low academic achievement, and income-related family characteristics should predict special education placement. By this premise, these risk factors should result in even greater placement of Black students in special education than was evident in their sample. However, as we will argue throughout this book, if the construction of these disability categories is itself suspect, then to expect high rates of "disabilities" among children who begin at a disadvantage is simply to reinforce and exacerbate the discrimination perpetuated against them. In the case of the high-incidence disabilities, the criterion is a set of school-based skills for which children from middle- and upper-income homes have been well prepared (Donovan & Cross, 2002). Why should a failure to meet these norms be interpreted as disability? The illogic goes something like this: We know that poor Black children are at a disadvantage; therefore, we expect them to perform less well than White children who do not experience those disadvantages; so when they perform less well, we know that that is a disability.

In the research reported in this book, our attempt to address these questions was modeled on the work of Heller et al. (1982), who argued that disproportionality should be considered a problem if inequity existed in any of the processes by which students were initially instructed, referred, evaluated, and placed in special education, and if such placement created additional disadvantage or inequity for students. While acknowledging that many children may have come to school with disadvantageous family or community experiences, our research did not focus on what those were. We asked only if the school experience provided further disadvantage; in other words, did the school alleviate or exacerbate children's learning or behavioral difficulties? Our analysis resulted in a complex picture of many intersecting school-based inequities which, despite the good intentions of many, exacerbated rather than improved children's learning. We concluded that these inequities made it impossible to assume that children's school performance reflected deficits or disabilities within the children themselves.

Current reports of racial/ethnic representation in special education programs show that disproportionality is still with us. I will summarize these patterns in the next section and will detail them further in the subsequent chapter. My purpose in this introductory chapter is to establish the need for an increasingly wide and deep lens for understanding this complex problem. Following Artiles et al. (2016), I will attempt to view our research through a cultural-historical lens that helps us to understand the intractability of the problem of disproportionality yet also to envision the way forward. As stated in the opening quote to this chapter—the past has set the stage for where we are at present, but the future remains in our hands.

In answer to our opening question, then, we reply with a resounding "yes" to the relevance of this study, for three reasons: First, because evidence of disproportionality continues to indicate the arbitrary and socially constructed nature of the disability categories; second, because this study provides a detailed, close-up analysis of all phases of the process, which has not yet been rivaled in the literature; and third, because an increasingly critical and cultural-historical body of literature offers an opportunity to enhance and further theorize the initial conclusions and implications of the study.

In this chapter, I will not reiterate the conceptual, contextual, and methodological details of the study, all of which are provided in Chapter 2. Rather, I will use updated literature to highlight continuities and changes in the landscape of disproportionality since the second edition of the book in 2014, and will reflect further on the findings of this study as seen through a critical cultural-historical lens, with a heightened focus on the intersections between race, socioeconomic status, language, and disability. Toward the first goal, I will begin by describing the shifting, rather than changing, patterns of racial/ethnic disproportionality in both high and low-incidence disability categories, discipline practices, and separate versus inclusive placements. Second, I will draw on critical literature to offer a cultural-historical perspective on the patterns described. I will conclude the chapter with a brief consideration of how a cultural-historical perspective could lead us to deeper study of the nature of disproportionality as we found it in this study.

First, however, I will comment on the first obvious change in this edition—the title of the book.

NAMING COLOR: IS BOB MARLEY WHITE?

Previous editions of this book were titled *Why Are So Many Minority Students in Special Education?* While we understood that many people object to the term "minorities" because it appears to diminish the importance, even the number, of peoples who have been oppressed, we felt that it was well understood globally to indicate the experience of marginalization and would be interpreted as such. We were hesitant to use the term "people of color" because there are minority groups who identify as White who have also experienced marginalization and, contrarily, members of minority ethnic groups, such as many Latinx/Hispanics who do not identify as being "of color."

In any case, where exactly does one draw a line between "White" and "of color"? The American version of the dividing line was created to ensure a binary vision of humanity that would justify and support an economy based on subjugation and enslavement (Freedman & Ferri, 2017; Spring, 2016: Takaki, 1993). This process relied on a concept of "pure" White as a norm against which one's race would be defined. Thus, someone who had just "one drop" of Black ancestry would be known as Black or "colored." A moment's thought helps us to see that had the power been in the hands of the enslaved, a concept of "pure" Black could have been set as the reference point, with the result that anyone mixed with "White" would have been designated "White" or "Whitened," rather than "colored." In discussing this potential reversal with a class of undergraduates, I knew I had reached one mind when a young White student from Georgia brought the house down as he suddenly grasped the concept and exclaimed—"So, I get it! Bob Marley is White!"

Consequently, because of its socially constructed nature, the term "of color" seems to me to have as many limitations as does "minority," and may even serve to reinforce the concept of two different types of people—White and other/of color. The Merriam-Webster dictionary (2022), trying to keep up with the changing terminology, describes the currently popular term "BIPOC" (Black, Indigenous, and People of Color) as an attempt to be "more inclusive," because the histories of Native groups have often not been adequately noted. However, that term is even more ambiguous, seeming to suggest that "people of color" constitute a third group, distinct from the first two.

Adding to this complexity is the need to distinguish between race and ethnicity. Race typically is assumed to refer to physical features that supposedly indicate a "racial" group. Ethnicity refers to tribal, national, or cultural aspects of identity. The conflation of the two concepts is evident in, for example, the assumption that all Hispanics/Latinx are people of color. Many of course, are White. At our University, we had an amusing incident wherein a visiting program evaluator from a northern state expressed confusion at the frequent use of the term "White Hispanic," which she said she had never heard before and which sounded like a contradiction in terms. On the contrary, to locals in this area, this is an important distinction because many people of Hispanic ethnicity are, to all appearances White, which automatically confers privilege (Portes, 2018). Moreover, many of this group identify with the term Hispanic, which points to their European (Spanish) ancestry rather than Latinx, which connotes the brown-skinned, mestizo/indigenous identities more typical of Central and South America. The social and economic nuances of this are obvious to local sensibilities but do not fit the commonplace stereotypes associated with these terms.

Regardless of nomenclature, there is no denying that the social power of centuries of systemic racism continues to divide and exclude (White et al., 2019; Freedman & Ferri, 2017). Research by White et al. (2019) and Ashby et al. (2020), comparing the geographical layout of an urban school district over a period of 80 years, concluded that very little had changed in patterns of housing, socioeconomics, and schooling in terms of racial disparities. Thus, the enduring nature of systemic racism leads me to conclude, although perhaps temporarily, that it is reasonable to use the term "of color" despite its ambiguities and internal contradictions.

In the case of the disproportionate identification of students of color as having disabilities, a look at the statistics erases any doubt that "color" matters. Its reach is long and deep, and as visible in real schools as it is in research and government reports.

THEN AND NOW: SHIFTING CATEGORIES AND DRIFTING STUDENTS, BUT DISPROPORTIONALITY REMAINS

Historically, the disability categories under the IDEA have been sorted into two general groups—"high" and "low" incidence—reflecting the general pattern of greater or lesser numbers. There are four "high-incidence" categories: Intellectual Disability (ID) (previously known as Mental Retardation);[1] Specific Learning Disability (SLD), also referred to as Learning Disability

(LD); Emotional Behavioral Disorder (EBD); and Speech and Language Impairments (SLI).[2] These have been referred to as the "judgment" categories, which depend on clinical judgment rather than on verifiable biological data (Donovan & Cross, 2002), and the controversy around disproportionality has focused on the fact that the risk of identification has been much higher for African Americans and Native Americans in these categories.

Then: Overrepresentation and Variability Over Space and Time

The concern regarding this overrepresentation was first raised by Dunn (1968) and Mercer (1973) and was soon addressed in the courts. In the most famous case, *Larry P. v. Riles* (1979/1984), the courts supported the plaintiffs' charge that the IQ tests being used to place children in the ID category were biased against African American children. While the outcomes of other litigation on this issue have varied (Reschly et al., 1988), the range of cases points to the continuing contentious nature of the issue, which has twice been studied by the National Academy of Sciences (Donovan & Cross, 2002; Heller et al., 1982).

The second crucial point in the history is that there has been tremendous variability in placement rates by state or school district. For example, at the time of the National Academy of Sciences' second study of disproportionality (Donovan & Cross, 2002), the national picture showed African Americans overrepresented in ID and EBD categories but not in LD; yet, the risk index for this group in LD ranged from 2.33% in Georgia to 12.19% in Delaware. Similarly, while the national figures showed no overrepresentation of Hispanics in any category, their rates ranged from 2.43% in Georgia to 8.93% in Delaware. Research by Sullivan (2011), while indicating considerable variability in identification rates over time, found overrepresentation of English learners (ELs) in the categories of SLD and SLI in the state being studied and greater likelihood of restrictive settings than their White peers.

There have also been marked changes in overall rates of usage of these categories over time, most notably a reduction in the use of ID, a dramatic increase in the use of LD with increasing numbers of Black students, and a notable increase in the use of EBD. Donovan and Cross (2002) indicated that from 1974 to 1998, the risk of any student (averaged across racial/ethnic groups) being identified as ID decreased from 1.58% to 1.37%, while, in SLD, the increased usage was referred to as "epidemic" (p. 47), having gone from 1.21% in 1974 to 6.02% in 1998. For EBD, the risk of identification increased from 0.28% in 1976 to 0.93% in 1998. This dramatic state-to-state variability and the changes over time caused Ysseldyke et al. (1992) to observe that the patterns look more like figures from the Dow Jones average than real disabilities among children.

The other nine categories served by the IDEA are referred to as "low incidence," and include Multiple Disabilities, Hearing Impairment, Orthopedic

Impairment, Other Health Impairment, Visual Impairment, Autism, Traumatic Brain Injury, Deaf-Blind, and Developmental Delay. Historically, in these categories there has been no evidence of systematic variation by race/ethnicity (Donovan & Cross, 2002). Currently, however, changes in racial/ethnic representation in some of these categories, and a dramatic increase in the category of Autism/Autistic Spectrum Disorders (ASD) are cause for much discussion.

Now: Nationwide Patterns of Identification and Placement in High-Incidence Disability Categories

The third edition of this book comes more than 50 years after the earliest recognition of the issue (Dunn, 1968; Heller et al., 1982), and 20 years after we completed our research project. Current reports indicate that the patterns of disproportionate identification of Black, Native American, and Hawaiian Native students in high-incidence disability categories of Intellectual Disability (ID), Specific Learning Disability (SLD), and Emotional/Behavioral Disorder (EBD) are still evident in the annual reports of the Office for Special Education Programs (OSEP) (U.S. Department of Education, 2020). Hispanic students are disproportionately represented only in the SLD category. Tables 1.1 and 1.2 show that for both 2018 and 2013 (U.S. Department of Education, 2020; 2015) African American children's risk of receiving labels of ID and ED was approximately twice that of all other groups, with Native American students showing between 1.5 and 2 times the risk of other groups in ID, EBD, and SLD. Hawaiian Native/Asian Pacific Islander students are at similarly high risk for identification in the ID and SLD categories, while Hispanic/Latinx students show disproportionately high rates of placement in the SLD category only. In sum, the reports basically show the same patterns for the high-incidence disabilities over the most recent 5-year period.

Disproportionate identification is accompanied by disproportionately high rates of exclusion in various arenas, such as exclusionary discipline for Black students (Skiba et al., 2014) and disproportionately segregated placements for students designated as EBD and ID, who are disproportionately students of color (Grindall et al., 2019; U.S. Department of Education, 2020). There is no question that inclusive placements have increased significantly for students with high-incidence disabilities since the time of our research (Morningstar et al., 2017; McLeksky et al., 2012). However, McLeskey et al. (2012) in a review of placement rates between 1990–2007, found that, despite significant increases in general class placement and a reduction in pullout services for students with SLD, SLI and other health impaired (OHI), students with the labels EBD and ID continue to experience more restrictive placements than their peers in the other high-incidence categories. In the present study, the pullout model was the normative approach for students

Table 1.1. Exhibit 26. Risk Ratio for Students Ages 6 Through 21 Served under IDEA, Part B, Within Racial/Ethnic Groups by Disability Category: Fall 2013

Disability	Native American or Alaska Native	Asian	Black or African American	Hispanic/Latinx	Native Hawaiian or Other Pacific Islander	White	Two or more races
All disabilities	1.56	0.48	1.42	0.99	1.60	0.91	0.82
Autism	0.88	1.15	0.97	0.75	1.25	1.21	0.91
Deaf-blindness	1.63!	0.88!	0.75	1.03	4.15!	1.13	0.69!
Developmental delay[a]	3.80	0.42	1.68	0.68	2.52	0.92	1.15
Emotional disturbance	1.58	0.19	2.14	0.60	1.38	0.95	1.11
Hearing impairments	1.23	1.21	1.03	1.34	2.81	0.77	0.72
Intellectual disabilities	1.49	0.51	2.26	0.91	1.55	0.71	0.66
Multiple disabilities	1.73	0.63	1.38	0.73	1.88	1.12	0.67
Orthopedic impairments	0.95	0.84	0.83	1.21	1.53	1.00	0.73
Other health impairments	1.32	0.28	1.37	0.60	1.39	1.31	0.92
Specific learning disabilities	1.80	0.32	1.51	1.29	1.91	0.74	0.72
Speech or language impairments	1.32	0.71	1.02	1.06	1.10	1.01	0.85
Traumatic brain injury	1.49	0.54	1.09	0.70	1.60	1.31	0.84
Visual impairments	1.51	0.90	1.12	0.96	1.93	0.99	0.79

! Interpret data with caution. There were 18 Native American or Alaska Native students, 52 Asian students, 10 Native Hawaiian students, and 30 students associated with two or more races reported in the *deaf-blindness* category.

[a]States' use of the *developmental delay* category is optional for children ages 3 through 9 and is not applicable to children older than 9 years of age.

U.S. Department of Education. (2015). *Report to Congress on the Implementation of the Individuals with Disabilities Education Act.*

Table 1.2. Exhibit 27. Risk Ratio for Students Ages 6 Through 21 Served under IDEA, Part B, Within Racial/Ethnic Groups, by Disability Category: Fall 2018

Disability	Native American or Alaska Native	Asian	Black or African American	Hispanic/Latinx	Native Hawaiian or Other Pacific Islander	White	Two or more races
All disabilities	1.6	0.5	1.4	1.1	1.5	0.9	1.0
Autism	1.0	1.1	1.1	0.9	1.3	1.0	1.1
Deaf-blindness!	1.4	1.0	0.8	0.9	1.4	1.1	0.8
Developmental delay^a	4.0	0.5	1.6	0.7	2.1	0.9	1.4
Emotional disturbance	1.6	0.2	1.9	0.7	1.1	1.0	1.4
Hearing impairment	1.4	1.2	1.0	1.4	2.5	0.7	0.9
Intellectual disability	1.6	0.5	2.2	1.0	1.8	0.7	0.8
Multiple disabilities	1.9	0.7	1.3	0.8	2.1	1.1	0.9
Orthopedic impairment	1.0	1.0	0.9	1.2	1.7	0.9	0.8
Other health impairment	1.3	0.3	1.4	0.7	1.2	1.2	1.2
Specific learning disability	1.9	0.3	1.5	1.4	1.7	0.7	0.9
Speech or language impairment	1.4	0.7	1.0	1.1	1.1	1.0	1.1
Traumatic brain injury	1.6	0.5	1.1	0.8	1.2	1.2	1.0
Visual impairment	1.8	0.9	1.1	0.9	1.8	1.0	0.9

! Interpret data with caution. There were 17 Native American or Alaska Native students, 73 Asian students, 164 Black or African American students, 335 Hispanic/Latinx students, 4 Native Hawaiian or Other Pacific Islander students, 767 White students, and 46 students associated with two or more races reported in the *deaf-blindness* category.

^aStates' use of the *developmental delay* category is optional for children and students ages 3 through 9 and is not applicable to students older than 9 years of age. For more information on students ages 6 through 9 reported under the category of *developmental delay* and States with differences in *developmental delay* reporting practices. See Exhibits B-2 and B-3 in Appendix B.

U.S. Department of Education, Office of Special Education Programs. (2020). *Report to Congress on the Implementation of the Individuals with Disabilities Education Act* (for fall 2018).

with SLD and OHI labels at the time of our research, while students with ID and EBD were served predominantly in separate classes or even separate buildings.

To summarize: The shifting patterns of identification and placement described earlier point to the essential instability of these categories and the field's attempt to adjust its definitions to changing social pressures and perspectives (Fish, 2019; Freedman & Ferri, 2017; Ong-Dean, 2009; Sleeter, 2010). Indeed, we may ask whether the traditional distinction between "high-" and "low-" incidence categories continues to be useful. Specifically, the greatest variability has been evident in the categories of ID, SLD, and ASD. A steady reduction in the number of students identified as ID in the last two decades of the 20th century (Donovan & Cross, 2002) has been interpreted as a reflection of social pressure regarding the historical overrepresentation of Black students in that category, yet Black students continue to be overrepresented in that category (U.S. Department of Education, 2015, 2020).

During the latter part of the 20th century, the "epidemic" increase (Donovan & Cross, p. 47) in the SLD category did not show racial/ethnic disproportion. Since then, however, identification of Black students in SLD has increased, showing a risk ratio of 1.5 in 2013 and 2018 (U.S. Department of Education, 2015, 2020). Meanwhile, the category of ASD has shown an increase similar to the "epidemic" proportions of SLD growth two decades earlier. Specifically, a comparison of figures between 2009–2018 (U.S. Department of Education, 2020) shows that the percentage of students between ages 6–21 identified with ASD has doubled while the percentage of those identified with SLD has remained basically the same. Research by Algozzine (2015) and Morningstar, Kurth, and Johnson (2017) report the same pattern, leading Algozzine to compare the trajectories of SLD and ASD and conclude that "ASD is the new LD" (p. 246).

The increasing use of ASD presents a puzzle as it was previously thought of as a low-incidence category that was usually determined by a medical evaluation. Currently, ASD represents 10% of the population of students age 6–21 served under Part B of the IDEA, while ID represents only 5% of the total (U.S. Department of Education, 2020). As we will discuss in a subsequent section, it is debatable whether this trend represents a true increase in the existence of ASD, instability in criteria for eligibility, or a response by professionals to social demands related to a view of ASD as a "high status" disability (Fish, 2019; Ocasio-Stoutenburg & Harry, 2021; Ong-Dean, 2009).

All of the foregoing scholars have interpreted these shifts as a longstanding pattern of preferential use of less stigmatizing and more accommodating categories for higher status groups. Further, Ong-Dean points out that a "high status" category may lose status as school districts become more accustomed to assigning the label to increasing numbers of "low status" students (i.e., students of color and low-income), as in the case of SLD over the years (Algozzine, 2015). The aforementioned pattern of greater exclusion of students with EBD and ID also reflects the "low status" accorded to these categories (Fish, 2019).

Disproportionality in the Low-Incidence Categories

A relatively new phenomenon of concern is evident in recent reports of disproportionately high rates of Native American and Hawaiian Native students in some low-incidence categories (National Center for Learning Disabilities, 2020; U.S. Department of Education, 2015, 2020). Specifically, the most recent report to Congress by the Office for Special Education Programs (OSEP) (U.S. Department of Education, 2020) notes the following risk ratios for Native American and Hawaiian Native students, respectively: developmental delay (4.0 and 2.1), hearing impairment (1.4 and 2.5), multiple disabilities (1.9 and 2.1), deaf-blindness (1.4 for both groups), and visual impairments (1.8 for both groups). The only other groups reporting similar risk ratios in any of these categories are Hispanics (1.4 in hearing impairment) and African Americans (1.6 in developmental delay). The report makes a point of advising caution in interpreting these figures, owing to the very small numbers particularly of Native Hawaiian students; nevertheless, the pattern is cause for concern.

As mentioned earlier, the distinction between low- and high-incidence categories has traditionally been noted because the former represent biologically based impairments that are medically verifiable, whereas the latter represent clinical judgments regarding learning and developmental differences, compared to a normative criterion. The puzzle here is that the potential for errors in judgment based on cultural, linguistic, or contextual differences is what has led to the continuing concerns about disproportionality in the high-incidence categories, but this would not be the case for impairments that are undoubtedly measurable (Donovan & Cross, 2002). Given the traditional interpretation of potential bias in referral and evaluation of students of color for the high-incidence disabilities, we might see this new phenomenon as a puzzle. Does this call for a rethinking of the concept of bias in the identification of disabilities? That is, does it make sense to suspect bias in the case of the "judgment" categories but not in the case of the medically verifiable categories? I believe that the answer to both phenomena lies in our history and I will return to this question in a subsequent section.

To summarize, research since the second edition of this book in 2014 indicates that shifts, rather than changes, in disproportionality continue, and the school-based processes noted in this research continue to be explanatory toward an understanding of disproportionality. Most useful in these studies is the notable emphasis on the historical and continuing roles of culture and context and explicit attention to the role of racism in this history. In the following section, I cite some key exemplars of this body of research in order to illustrate the continuing relevance of the third edition of this book and to enhance our original theorizing from our data.

THEORIZING AND CONTEXTUALIZING DISPROPORTIONALITY

The foregoing statistics and qualitative findings reflect the entrenched nature of cumulative disadvantage experienced by groups of color, particularly Black and Native American students and, in some areas, Hispanic/Latinx students as well. In this section, we seek to view the foregoing patterns through broader cultural-historical lenses.

Intersecting Theoretical Perspectives

Three intersecting theoretical perspectives inform this literature and are helpful in enhancing the interpretations previously offered in this book: First is a cultural-historical view of the impact of beliefs about race and disability (Artiles et al., 2016), which traces the historical roots of public values, laws, and policies, moving analysis from the level of the individual to that of society, and the focus of research from a singular to a collective unit of analysis. Related to this, we also utilize the framework of Disability Critical Race Theory (DisCrit) (Annamma et al., 2018; Connor et al., 2016), which expands and interrelates the basic tenets of Critical Race Theory (CRT) and Disability Studies (DS). At the center of DisCrit is a focus on the processes by which perceptions of disability are created by the intersecting impacts of multiple identity markers that have historically served to oppress and exclude individuals. Thus, this perspective specifies key tenets, which include the interrelationships between racism and ableism, the importance of multidimensional rather than singular constructions of identity, the privileging of marginalized voices, the real-life impacts of socially constructed concepts such as race and ability, the discriminatory effects of legal and historical policies, and the privileging of White interests in disability policies. Across these tenets runs an assumption that activism and resistance are requisite responses to inequity (Annamma et al. 2018). Finally, we cite organization theory as applied to special education by Skrtic (2003), which focuses on how organizational structures arise from, and interact with, the social environment and contribute to the distribution of privilege in the society.

We note these intersecting perspectives to emphasize that they stand as distinct from the traditional construction of disabilities as defined in the field of special education. As will be specified below, numerous scholars have pointed out that attention to racism is largely missing from discussions of disproportionality because research has been driven by the medical model of disability, which interprets learning and developmental differences as indicators of deficits that lie within the individual. In keeping with this medical formulation, research has privileged methods that seek discrete factors that can be counted, measured, and contained within the concept of intrinsic deficit. Thus, researchers have sought to be "race neutral," promoting their definitions and evaluations of disabilities as objective and scientific. The goal has been to measure a child's psychological processing, performance on an IQ test, and mastery of academic skills and information, in order to "prove" that significant distance from a presumed (White) norm indicates intrinsic deficit within the child.

The depth of the belief in intrinsic deficit is best exemplified in the formulation of the SLD category, which specifically requires environmental factors to be excluded as a potential source of a learning disability. Cultural-historical and critical disability perspectives call for exactly the opposite approach—one that "acknowledges the social and historical origins of overrepresentation as related, in part, to the historical legacy of racism in the USA . . . [and as] a social, cultural, and historical issue, rather than just as learning, behavioral and intellectual deficits within students" (Cavendish et al., 2020, p. 4).

Race and Disability: From Parallel to Converging Discourses

Race has been an essential ingredient in the construction of American public education, and inevitably, of special education. The effects of centuries of intense racism can be seen not only in the continuing social, educational, and economic challenges faced by generations of those who were enslaved, but also in the status of conquered indigenous peoples. Spring (2016) and Takaki (1993) explain that, as the European colonial project combined its goal of messianic Christianity with the subjugation of conquered and enslaved peoples, those in power rationalized their actions by creating and perpetuating ingrained beliefs about the inferiority of those groups. Indeed, the histories outlined by Spring and Takaki reverberate across the previously conquered and enslaved communities until today, with the highest poverty rates experienced by Native Americans and African Americans at approximately 20%—more than double the rate for non-Hispanic Whites (U.S. Census Bureau, 2021)—and Native Hawaiians/Other Pacific Islanders at 17.6% and Hispanics/Latinx varying widely from 16% to 26% depending on nation of origin. Takaki further explains how the vilification of dominated peoples and pseudo-scientific concepts of "race" became intertwined with conceptions of disability as the European conquerors propagated their vision of conquered and enslaved peoples as uncivilized and only partially human.

The pattern of exclusion introduced by the eugenics movement blended beliefs regarding the genetics of disabilities with beliefs regarding the racial inferiority of non-White peoples. Using the mental testing movement as the main vehicle for applying the gospel of efficiency to education (Fass, 1991; Gould, 1981), American education became committed to the goal of sorting children. The construction of special education reflected and supported that goal, and by the middle of the 20th century, special classes for "slow learners" were already showing high rates of placement (Gould, 1981).

The Dual Nature of Special Education: New Buildings on Old Foundations

As often happens in history, competing streams of thought ran parallel to each other. Artiles and colleagues (2016) explain that, against the background of the long-term effects of the discriminatory policies of the 19th-century pseudo-scientism of eugenics, special education came into being as a reflection of two competing intentions: discrimination and protection. This insight provides a thoughtful answer to the old challenge mentioned earlier—that the provision of the specialized and costly services of special education should be understood as a great benefit to children, not as a purveyor of discrimination (Heller et al., 1982; Reschly et al., 1988).

As the civil rights movement of the mid-20th century gave fuel to the ideology of protecting rather than discriminating against children with disabilities, a powerful advocacy movement led to the passage of the Education for all Handicapped Children Act (EHA) of 1975. Parallel to this movement, however, was ongoing resistance to the *Brown* desegregation decision (*Brown v. Board of Education of Topeka, Kansas*, 1954), and within two decades, Dunn (1968) and Mercer (1973) had brought to the field's attention a pattern by which supposedly objective psychological testing was resulting in special education classes becoming a vehicle for continued segregation, based on presumed learning deficits (Ferri & Connor, 2005; Freedman & Ferri, 2017). As these placements were challenged in the courts, the blending of special education and minority placements gradually came to public attention (e.g., *Diana v. State Board of Education*, 1970; Dunn, 1968; *Larry P. v. Riles*, 1979; Mercer, 1973).

Artiles et al. (2016) explain how, with the increasing influence and status of the field of psychology, and the increasing bureaucratization of education, the challenge of how to provide protection in the form of needed educational services was met by the professionalization of "boundary work" (p. 782), by which the field demarcated its boundaries, ensured the autonomy and professional authority of practitioners in the field, and determined the definitions of persons designated as having disabilities. As the field of psychology became increasingly influential, its premises and tools became inextricably bound to the processes of schooling. Thus, experts and their technical tools came to define the "objects" of the field—the disabilities that would be addressed in schools. The main tool in this process was psychological and educational testing, which, in the first third of the 20th century, served to reinforce traditional prejudices about the inferiority of non-White "races" (Terman, 1916). Artiles et al. (2016) describe this process as "the colonization of schools by psychology" (p. 786), which came to encompass a "triangle of expertise" (p. 787), which included "the *objects* of study in the field, the evangelism of *experts* . . . and the technical *tools* that experts and their public partners used in practice" (p. 788).

Although the EHA opened the door to all those who had previously been excluded, embedded in the new field of special education was the continuing assumption of deficit that lies at the heart of the notion of disability. As Artiles and colleagues (2016) explain, "The creation of individual rights was layered over the older discourse of problem children as objects of expertise" (p. 791). To this was added the notion of "cultural deficit" and a "culture of poverty," by which children's intrinsic difficulties were interpreted as exacerbated by poverty and family structures perceived as dysfunctional

(Ladson-Billings, 2006). Thus, concepts of race, poverty, and disability were tightly interwoven.

Once a "scientific" labeling process became the dominant mode of interpreting children's learning processes, the discourse of special education labeling came to be taken as truth. Yet, as observed by several researchers, by the end of the 20th century, the subjectivity and instability of these categories was already evident in the extreme variability of identification rates from state to state and even across local school districts (Hosp & Reschly, 2002; Ysseldyke et al., 1992), and in the socially constructed patterns of "shifting" categories and "drifting" students," by which one category's dominance would become replaced by another (Ocasio-Stoutenburg & Harry, 2021). Examples of this include the decrease in numbers in ID and the dramatic increase in numbers in SLD (Algozzine, 2015; Harry & Ocasio-Stoutenburg, 2020; Ong-Dean, 2009; Sleeter, 1986, 2010). Initially, SLD was the category of preference for White students, which gradually gave way to greater numbers of students of color, while percentages of White students shifted to predominance in the ASD category (Algozzine, 2015; Travers & Krezimen, 2018). In addition, White students have been further advantaged by a trend wherein they are twice as likely as Black and Hispanic/Latinx students to be identified as having attention deficit/hyperactivity disorder (ADHD) and to be served under Section 504, which most often provides more inclusive services and more accommodations on ACT and SAT exams than would an EBD designation (Zirkel & Weathers, 2015; Zirkel & Huang, 2018).

Skrtic (1991, 2003, 2005), viewing special education from the perspective of organizational theory, argued that this construction of special education provided the vehicle the society needed to streamline a diverse population. Using the metaphor of a "machine bureaucracy," he described general education as having been charged with the responsibility of preparing the populace to function effectively in the bureaucratic structures of the society, and to do so by creating schools that were a microcosm of that system. As the mental testing movement assisted schools in developing systems for sorting students into perceived homogeneous boxes, special education became the corner of the system that could contain those whose differences were perceived to be too extreme to serve in the mainstream. The challenge of an increasingly heterogeneous student population was met by institutionalizing the concept of individual deficit. Skrtic described special education as "the institutional practice that emerged in the 20th century to contain the failure of public education to realize its democratic ideals" (1991, p. 46).

Thus, with regard to both general and special education, the middle years of the 20th century were marked by competing interests of equity versus exclusion (Tyack, 1993). While racial/ethnic minorities and children with disabilities were relegated to the margins of the educational system, the movement for universal schooling for children with disabilities was fueled by the civil rights movement and deeply influenced by its rhetoric of equality and solidarity. Thus, although civil rights based on race and disability have been envisioned as parallel and mutually supportive movements, we believe it is not farfetched to say that, sometime in the early 1970s, the special education movement and the desegregation movement officially collided. Those whom the society had rejected, and had excluded from its public schools, would meet in the special education system. The concept of deficit, by then an ingrained part of the educational belief system, would become the chief metaphor to encompass difference.

SOCIAL DESIRABILITY AND SHIFTING CATEGORIES OVER TIME

The foregoing analysis of the active social construction of professional roles and disability categories of special education assists us in understanding the shifting and unstable nature of the disabilities described in the previous section. Artiles et al. (2016) state:

> As a boundary object, disability can shift meanings and uses across settings and communities due in part to local contingencies and group interests. . . . For example, federal disability definitions are operationalized in states and school districts with various criteria and assessment and identification tools. (p. 781)

In other words, the disability categories are social constructions that inevitably will change over time and space in response to social perceptions, values, and needs.

Summarizing research on the socially desirable status of different disability categories, Fish (2019) identifies SLI, OHI/ADHD, and ASD as having the highest perceived status, ID and EBD as having the lowest status, and LD as "stratified status." The latter term indicates that some groups benefit more from this designation than others, as the composition of this category has "drifted" from predominantly White and middle class at the onset of the category (Harry & Ocasio-Stoutenburg, 2020; Sleeter, 2010), to increasingly Black, with many low-achieving Black students who do not fit the ID category (Blanchett, 2010).

With the concept of social desirability in mind, we will focus in this section on the two main changes evident in the high-incidence categories: The shift from ID to SLD and the dramatic increase in the use of ASD. In the case of SLD, we will briefly review its history, and will propose that an essential revision of the construct of SLD is on the horizon. In the case of ASD, we will discuss key concerns that have been raised in the literature, which highlight similarities to the way the SLD category has developed over time.

The ID/SLD SHIFT

Intellectual disability is something of an anomaly within the high-incidence categories because the numbers in this category have decreased steadily over the years, with the likely interpretation of shifts in clinical judgment. Consequently, although the numbers are comparatively "low," we treat this category as we would the "high-incidence" categories because the identification of it relies on professional judgment, not biological verifiability. Also, the concept of ID clearly requires greater differentiation and is still specified by IQ scores in some states (Muller & Markowitz, 2004) since intellectual impairments vary greatly in extent as well as in etiology. It has long been asserted that the direction of the ID/LD shift reflects a response to social and political pressure to replace the more stigmatizing label of ID with the less generalized label of LD, which signals deficits in specific areas rather than in overall development (Donovan & Cross, 2002). The "mild" end of the ID spectrum has traditionally been central to the disproportionality debate, as the original observations of Black and Hispanic/Latinx overrepresentation were noted in this category (Dunn, 1968; Donovan & Cross, 2002; Heller et al., 1982; Mercer, 1973). Conversely, the preference for the less stigmatizing LD category led to the suggestion that this category was being used inappropriately in school districts that wanted to avoid the charge of racial imbalance in ID (MacMillan et al., 1998). Whether appropriate or inappropriate, these shifts demonstrate the unreliability of the categories.

The LD Debate: The History

The history of the LD category has been marked by controversy and internal inconsistency from the start, leading educators and researchers to what Gallagher (2010) described as a "state of continual befuddlement." Sleeter (1986), in a scathing analysis of the motivation behind the construction of this category, argued that LD came into being as a result of the 1960s concern with making the United States more competitive in the era of Sputnik. White middle-class families whose children were not proving competitive in that ethos sought the LD label as an alternative to the more generalized, more stigmatizing label of mental retardation. In keeping with this, Collins and Camblin (1983) argued that the underuse of the LD category for Black students reflected a covert racial intent through two mechanisms: First, the exclusionary clause, which excluded consideration of environmental factors (including poverty) and second, by requiring a discrepancy between a student's IQ score and a score on a measure of academic performance. Collins and Camblin argued that cultural bias inherent in IQ tests makes it more difficult for Black students to attain a score high enough to contrast significantly with a low academic level, thus making it less likely that they would meet the discrepancy criterion. Indeed, in Chapter 9, we detail an example of this in the story of Mercedes, who "fell between the cracks" of LD and ID. More recent interpretations have supported this view (Ferri, 2004), contending that this process provided White middle-class students with greater access to the more privileged place within the hierarchy of special education categories, and "allowed racist notions of ability to remain in place . . . since White students might be failing but not for the same reasons as minority, poor, and immigrant students" (p. 511). Further, Ferri questioned whether recent research focusing on dyslexia and other subgroups of LD may serve the purpose of further racial or class resegregation within the category.

To extend this point, we note that the problem with the discrepancy model lay in its two flawed premises: First was the assumption that intelligence is a unitary construct that can be measured by an IQ score (Blumer, 1969; Serpell, 1994), regardless of whether a child has had the opportunity to experience the kind of knowledge being assessed. The depth of this untested assumption about intelligence is evident in a statement by Shaywitz and Shaywitz (2020), who, in trying to explain the concept of "unexpected" reading difficulty, produce a statement so disconnected from social context and so steeped in assumptions that it sounds almost tautological:

> If the child is intelligent, he or she will typically be a good reader, and if he or she is a good reader, the child most often is intelligent. In dyslexic readers, however, IQ and reading diverge, so that reading achievement is significantly below what would be expected given the individual's IQ. These data provide empiric validation of the unexpected nature of dyslexia. (p. 457)

The second questionable premise is the previously mentioned exclusionary clause, which, as Shaywitz and Shaywitz (2020) acknowledge, constitutes "a serious problem that seems to reflect an inherent bias against identifying disabled minority students" (p. 458).

The continuing debate over the validity of the discrepancy criterion for LD (Artiles et al., 1997; Fletcher & Morris, 1986; Fletcher et al., 1998; Stanovich, 1991), and the concern about the manipulation of eligibility criteria (MacMillan et al., 1998), led a symposium of researchers (National Research Center on Learning Disabilities, 2003) to support the Response to Intervention (RTI) model that had been proposed by leading scholars such as Vaughn and Fuchs (2003). With the LD category being described as "an ephemeral construct" (Fuchs et al., 2004), it was evident that the category was up for revision. Since the reauthorization of the IDEA in 2004, the RTI process has leaped from being a recommended alternative, to being a process supported by the DSM-5a (Cavendish, 2013), officially allowed by all the U.S. states and mandated by 14 of them. However, the majority of states permit both RTI and the discrepancy model, leaving the decision to school districts (Zirkel, 2019).

RTI Meets the LD Debate

RTI, also known in many states as Multi-Tiered Systems of Support (MTSS) (Berkeley et al., 2020), offers the prospect of early intervening and increasingly targeted instruction, with systematic monitoring of children's progress. This has tremendous intuitive appeal for special educators who have interpreted overrepresentation as a function of inadequate opportunity to learn (Artiles et al., 2010; Harry & Klingner, 2006; Skiba et al., 2008). In contrast to the static assessment inherent in the discrepancy model, RTI, based on Feuerstein and colleagues' (1981) seldom cited concept of "dynamic assessment," seeks to assess a child's ability by providing instruction that would ensure that the child has had adequate opportunity to learn and then assess the child's growth on the tasks being taught. In a review of studies of RTI, Hoover (2010) cited the positive aspects as: providing a systematic rather than random approach to prereferral interventions, a possible reduction in special education placements, and the provision of immediate rather than delayed assistance to struggling students.

Concerns about the new process, however, were also noted by Hoover (2010), who cited three issues arising in the early research: The inability of RTI to exclude or identify a disability, challenges related to implementation of evidence-based instruction and the provision of needed supports, and clarity regarding the place of special education designation within the tiered RTI system. Moreover, Hoover argued that the success of RTI would require a "systematic paradigm shift" from the old prereferral intervention model to a genuinely targeted approach to prevention. Meanwhile, scholars focusing on the cultures and contexts of learning called for practitioners to investigate "with whom, by whom, and in what contexts" prescribed practices actually work (Klingner & Edwards, 2006, p. 110), and for attention to the larger societal issues that result in overrepresentation of children from poor and marginalized backgrounds (Artiles et al., 2010; Waitoller et al., 2010). Perhaps most eloquent and fearful was the statement by Artiles et al. (2010) that "the anticipated future of RTI is based on a field of analysis narrowed to considerations of ability, stripped of cultural and linguistic resources and mediating forces" (p. 255).

As the process gained momentum nationally, the foregoing concerns have become increasingly evident, the most common being the wide variation across states in policy standards and guidelines for implementation (Berkeley et al., 2020; Zirkel & Thomas, 2010a, 2010b). Most critically, an evaluation of RTI by Balu and colleagues (2015) failed to find any reduction of disproportionality and even found negative effects of Tier 2 or Tier 3 reading interventions for some 1st-graders. Despite some critique of this study regarding flaws in fidelity of RTI implementation within the sample (Berkeley et al., 2020; Fuchs & Fuchs, 2017), these findings have been discouraging.

Changing the mindset of educators regarding the traditional referral and evaluation process has proved to be a key challenge. One pilot study investigating the implementation of RTI in the same school district studied in this book (Cavendish et al., 2016) finds that teachers and psychologists were struggling with exactly the kind of "paradigm shift" referred to by Hoover (2010), and were basically applying traditional models of evaluation and placement to the RTI process. This tendency was aptly illustrated in a study by Orosco and Klingner (2010), which notes a "deficits based RTI literacy model" (p. 276), in which teachers spoke of "referring" children "into" RTI.

Overall, the debate over RTI has proved as contentious as was the original debate about the validity of the SLD category. Citing only a few of the authors of these arguments, the list below represents a continuation and intensification of the initial concerns about its validity and reliability:

- The tendency of school personnel to view RTI as simply a new template for previous special education placement processes, resulting in language such as "referring students into RTI" (Orosco & Klingner, 2010).
- Ambiguity regarding what instructional approaches should be considered as "evidence based" (Kratochwill et al., 2007).
- The assumption that generally effective interventions will be successful with groups that have been traditionally marginalized (Skiba et al., 2006).
- The need to understand the social and historical context of school districts and individual schools that might lead to weak fidelity of RTI implementation (Thorius & Maxcy, 2015).
- The question of whether "slope" or rate of progress is adequately taken into account in determination of an LD (Maki et al., 2020), and whether students placed in different tiers show significantly different rates of progress (Bouck & Cosby, 2019).
- The question of whether the RTI model overidentifies children who are performing low compared to their peers but within their own cognitive ability as measured by an IQ score; that is, this suggests "expected" rather than "unexpected" underachievement, thus "pathologizing the low end of normal cognitive variability" (Kranzler et al., 2019, p. 85).
- The lack of demonstrated success in reading outcomes or any reduction in disproportionality through the use of RTI (Balu et al., 2015; Willis, 2019).
- The need for intensive preparation for teachers in the RTI context, specifically, a racial consciousness that rejects race-neutral assumptions (Sleeter, 2017), collaboration skills across general and special education, and differentiated instruction (Cavendish et al., 2013).
- The need for school psychologists to be trained in the use of RTI for SLD identification, specifically in reading assessment (Barrett et al., 2015; Cavendish, 2013; Sullivan & Long, 2010) and the need for culturally sensitive participation on the part of school counselors (Shell et al., 2019).
- The need to determine whether a "response" should be operationalized by measures of students' average or near average performance or their "growth," and to determine the required extent of that growth (Hendricks & Fuchs, 2020).
- The distinction between the utility of RTI as an effective intervention in contrast with that of a diagnostic tool (Graves & Mitchell, 2011;

Kavale & Flanagan 2007), and the question of whether RTI should replace a comprehensive psychological evaluation as the sole method of evaluation for the determination of SLD (Gartland & Strosnider, 2020; Reschly, 2014).

The RTI/LD Conundrum: Does the Definition Matter?

The final bullet in the list above points to the heart of the issue—the implications of RTI for the validity of the LD category itself, which is defined as a disorder reflecting psychological processing deficits that are "neurobiological in origin" (Gartland & Strosneider, 2020, p. 197). Based on this belief, when an intervention does not work, it is presumed that the problem is a "fixed trait of the child" (Johnston, 2011, p. 517). In challenging this assumption, Algozzine (2015) summarizes research conducted by himself and his colleagues between 1981 and 2000, and laments that their research failed to stem the overwhelming tide of LD identification. Arguing that the issue with children's reading difficulties lies in the absence of "good teaching" rather than a deficit within the child, he describes RTI as "old wine in new bottles" (p. 239).

While RTI was devised precisely to address the absence of "good teaching," it is also tied to the concept of intrinsic deficit; hence, the idea of using a child's nonresponsiveness to "good teaching" as the criterion for SLD determination. But it is the search for intrinsic deficit that continues to present a problem. As Ferri (2011) states, the belief in intrinsic deficit reflects "the intractability of the field's most foundational assumptions" (1). The long history of researchers seeking to prove this premise ranges from early constructions of reading difficulty as a "possible cerebral dysfunction" (Kirk, 1962, p. 263) to recent studies of dyslexia using brain imaging to link reading difficulties to observable brain activity (Shaywitz & Shaywitz, 2020). In the latter publication, the researchers address the question of whether "these changes in brain function and organisation predate the poor reading, or are they the result of poor reading itself?" (p. 459)—in other words, what is the direction of the effect? They answer the challenge with findings from literature suggesting that the patterns are present even before children learn to read. Countering these findings, however, are critiques of the methodology used for these studies (Hruby & Hynd, 2006) as well as sociocultural analyses, starting with Sleeter's (1986; 2010) concerns about the role of race and social class in the construction of LD, to current arguments linking these social constructions to the dominance of "scientific ableism" and "scientific racism" (Freedman and Ferri, 2017, p. 6).

Faith or Reality?

It is remarkable that after some 40 years in the lifetime of the LD construct, the debate over its nature is still continuing (Gallagher, 2010). Compare, for example, the following two statements by leading scholars. First, Gartland and Strosnider (2020), in an "official position paper of the National Joint

Committee on Learning Disabilities (NJCLD)" (p. 195), arguing for fidelity to the original definition of LD, stated:

> Specifically, learning disabilities are defined as neurobiological in origin and involve "psychological processing" deficits. An RTI model implemented as designed should be able to identify students who are not making adequate progress, even with intensive evidence-based intervention. It will not, however, identify the processing deficits that are contributing to the student's failure to learn. (p. 197)

By contrast, Reschly (2014), in reviewing the literature on processing deficits, cites several scholars whose research presented "consistent disconfirming evidence" of this belief, and concludes that the continuing commitment to these constructs is "an excellent example of faith triumphing over reality" (p. 53). While acknowledging several challenges in RTI, Reschly argues that the process should be adequate for determination of an LD if all phases are implemented with fidelity. With this model, he says, comprehensive testing need be added only if screening suggests that there may be competing explanations, such as EBD or subaverage intellectual functioning.

Freedman and Ferri (2017) capture the redundancy and desperation of the supporters of LD. In keeping with Algozzine's metaphor of old wine in new bottles, these authors state:

> Even with the instability of LD as a category, researchers continue to attempt to develop new ways to identify LD and then adjust definitions accordingly. . . . If a particular approach is ineffective, the model places the problem on the student for not responding, rather than the intervention for not being responsive to the student's learning needs. (p. 19)

The range of arguments related to the utility of RTI as a diagnostic tool for LD suggests that this disability construct is once more up for revision. Indeed, we believe that the advent of RTI has brought the field of LD to a crossroad marked by questions that challenge the heart of the LD construct: Does the RTI process provide enough information for a determination of LD as traditionally defined? If so, is the disability designation still necessary for the provision of needed services? Moreover, wouldn't a reliance solely on RTI data negate the traditional definition of LD as an intrinsic processing deficit?

Autism, Other Health-Impaired, and 504 Plans

The category of Autism/Autistic Spectrum Disorders (ASD) poses unique concerns because of its rapid increase in usage and the extreme variability in the characteristics of students assigned this label (Algozzine, 2015; Morningstar et al., 2017; Ong-Dean, 2009; Travers & Krezmien, 2018; White et al., 2019). Based on OSEP data from 2000–2015, Morningstar et al. (2017) concluded that, given the minimal change in the overall numbers of children served under IDEA and the increase in the ASD category, "It is highly likely students with ASD are being re-diagnosed from other high-incidence categories" (p. 9), such as LD, ED, and OHI. Algozzine (2015) and Travers and Krezmien (2018) went further, drawing a parallel between the trajectory of the categories of LD and ASD over the past three decades, with Algozzine (2015) naming ASD as "the new LD" (p. 246).

Besides the shifting criteria for these disabilities, the social and racial associations are evident, with research noting that the ASD category is most accessible to parents with cultural, social, and economic capital (Ong-Dean, 2009; Fish, 2019). Moreover, with higher rates of White students gradually becoming evident in this category (Liptak et al., 2008; Morrier & Hess, 2012), ASD is now the only IDEA category showing overrepresentation of White students in some states (Travers & Krezmien, 2018). Similarly, while students diagnosed with ADHD may be served under OHI and/or Section 504 of the Rehabilitation Act, Zirkel and Weathers (2015) report that White students are twice as likely as Black to receive services with a 504 plan; further, high poverty schools are significantly less likely to have students with 504 plans. This is important because 504 plans typically provide more inclusive services and accommodations than would the competing behavioral category of EBD, in which Black students are known to be overrepresented. Commenting on this pattern, Erevelles (2017) exclaims: "Where are all the Black students with 504 plans?" (p. 122).

The Shift to ASD in This Study

At the time of our study, we did not note any children in general education classes who were being considered for the ASD category, and those who had already been identified were served in separate special education classrooms. At the point of this writing, however, the picture has changed somewhat, with district figures for fall of 2019 showing an increase in overall numbers in this category as well as their increased inclusion in general education classes (Florida Department of Education, 2020). Moreover, a comparison of rates of placement by race/ethnicity in 2009 and 2019 reveals that, in both years, Black students were the only group with a risk ratio that indicated "underrepresentation" in the ASD category: While their risk ratios have risen from 0.68 to 0.81, the risk ratios of the other groups in 2019 ranged from 1.04–1.13 (Florida Department of Education, 2010, 2020). Although these differences are slight, a series of family case studies conducted recently in this community (Harry & Ocasio-Stoutenburg, 2020; Ocasio-Stoutenburg & Harry, 2021) showed that parents were very aware of the social desirability of different categories, with parents describing ID as "the underprivileged label" and ASD as "the big name," "the in-crowd," and "the elite diagnosis" (pp. 102–104).

Emotional Disturbance as an "Ephemeral" but Low-Status Construct

As with the category of ID, the category of EBD is of particular concern for African American and Native American students because they are known to carry the greatest social stigma and the greatest extent of exclusionary discipline and educational placements (Losen et al., 2014; McLesky et al., 2012; Skiba et al., 2014). Yet we would like to adopt the language of Fuchs et al. (2004) to argue that the EBD category is equally "ephemeral" as SLD. The EBD category, similar to the wide range involved in ID, has shifted over time and represents a very variable set of behavioral challenges (Oelrich, 2012) including children who previously would have been designated as "severely emotionally disturbed," which could mean significant mental illness, as well as children whose behavior is seen as "troubled" or even just "troubling" to the teacher (Leone et al., 1990). Further, as Oelrich argued, the exclusion of "social maladjustment" from the definition is confusing because it contradicts another part of the definition that refers to an inability to maintain relationships with peers and adults. Further, many scholars have argued that the cultural nature of behavior makes it difficult to know to whose behavioral norms children are being compared and whether culturally different social interaction styles between teachers and students contribute, at best, to misinterpretations of children's behaviors or, at worst, to culturally biased patterns of discipline (Cartledge & Kourea, 2008; Oelrich, 2012). Inappropriate disciplinary actions may lead to EBD designation (Skiba et al., 2006), and rates of school suspensions and expulsions continue to indicate the highest odds of EBD identification for Black students (Krezimen et al., 2006; Skiba et al., 2014). Moreover, a multilevel analysis of factors related to disproportionality in a large urban school district (Sullivan & Bal, 2013) identified school suspensions, along with race, class, and gender, as strongly related to risk of disproportionality.

In the EBD category, despite the presence of reliable rating scales, subjectivity has been cited as a key challenge in professional practice (Donovan & Cross, 2002; Saeki et al., 2011). Although tiered intervention approaches utilizing the RTI model show great promise for supporting students with behavioral challenges (e.g., Ervin et al., 2007), Algozzine et al. (2012) argued that academic and behavioral challenges must be addressed in tandem and that professional development and a consistent commitment to "adapting interventions and systematically evaluating their usefulness on an ongoing basis is essential" (p. 60) to the success of tiered behavioral interventions. While we do not claim to have conducted a thorough review of this literature, it seems that the literature on RTI for behavioral issues seldom directly addresses issues of culture and social context.

In the state in which this study was conducted, the question of subjectivity was a particular challenge because, as in many states, a determination of EBD depended on projective testing, a process particularly susceptible to the charge of subjectivity and unreliability (Gresham, 1993; Knoff, 1993; Motta et al., 1993). Moreover, the fact that the use of these tests varies widely across states (Hosp & Reschly, 2002) demonstrates that we cannot assume any equivalence among children designated EBD from state to state (Muller and Markowitz, 2004). In sum, Skrtic et al. (2021) describe the classification process as a "status competition," in which White students predominate in categories of ADHD and ASD while students of color are assigned ID and EBD labels.

Low-Incidence Disabilities in Historical Context

As previously mentioned, the low-incidence disability categories have not, historically, been the focus of the disproportionality debate because they are generally indicated by demonstrable impairments in physical, cognitive, or sensory functioning, rather than depending on clinical judgment. Recent reports of racial/ethnic disproportionality, however, raise serious questions about the situation of Native Americans and Hawaiian Native/Asian Pacific Islanders. Disproportionality of these groups, already notable in 2013, has increased at least slightly, not only in the high-incidence, "judgment" categories, but also in biologically based disabilities such as hearing, visual, and orthopedic impairments (National Center for Learning Disabilities, 2020; U.S. Department of Education, 2015, 2020).

Absent an extant analysis, I propose that a cultural-historical view of the issue of the systemic nature of societal inequity can shed light on this disturbing trend. By this perspective we can see that bias can operate in both cases while presenting in different forms. Disproportionately high rates of sensory and other physical impairments could be genetically based, but they could also be the result of systemic biases that are built into detrimental social ecologies or environmental stressors known to plague historically oppressed, low-income communities of color. This kind of bias is based in the histories and current contexts of such groups as well as in the continuing disparities in medical and social services for the poor and communities of color (Centers for Disease Control, 2022; Dr. Gloria Kishi and Dr. Ray Miner, personal communication). In such cases it may be impossible to point to any individual intervention or occurrence that caused the impairment because the bias is larger than the individual. In the clinical judgment categories, bias is also built into historical professional practices but may be more readily evident because the interventions (instruction, referral, evaluation) are conducted by individuals, and research shows tremendous variability across professional judgments as well as across school districts and states.

In sum, I posit that systemic biases may result in inappropriate labeling of those high-incidence learning problems whose etiology is unclear or ambiguous. Systemic bias in social structures may also operate in producing low-incidence impairments that are medically verifiable. I would emphasize, however, that this is an area calling for attention from researchers in the education and medical fields.

Special Education in a Standards-Based Environment

The current policy context of education in the United States adds to this history one more dimension of the sorting-and-classifying paradigm—the use of standardized, statewide testing to determine both teacher and school effec-tiveness. Through the drive for accountability, the movement seeks to ensure that students attain a predetermined standard of education.

The restructuring of the Elementary and Secondary Education Act (ESEA, 1965), in the form of the No Child Left Behind Act (NCLB, 2002), mandated nationwide academic assessment of reading and mathematics achievement from the 3rd to the 8th grade. This mandate represented the good intention of holding all schools to the same high standards, in order to provide all children with the instruction needed to attain high expectations. The downside of this, according to Skrtic (2005), was an "extreme form of bureaucratic outcomes-based accountability" (p. 150), which took little account of students' di-verse languages and cultures. The 2009 revision of the law, in the form of the American Recovery and Reinvestment Act (ARRA), provided the Race to the Top (RTTT) program, which attempted to address the issue of children's differential starting points, by specifying that the evaluation of teachers should include measures of "student growth." In some states this resulted in what is referred to as the value-added model (VAM), by which changes in student achievement from one evaluation point to the next are attributed to teacher effectiveness, and teachers are rewarded or penalized accordingly.

In the state in which we conducted our research, the accountability re-quirement currently includes the VAM for individual teachers. In addition, the "grading" of schools, based largely on the results of standardized test-ing, determines important outcomes such as the intrinsic reward of being highly respected in the community as well as extrinsic rewards of financial and material resources, and the negative sanction of provision of vouchers for students to transfer out of failing schools. Currently, the RTTT program calls for states to include data from special education programs into longitudinal databases.

Despite these efforts, there continue to be loopholes in the accountability process. Until the time this research ended in 2002, although all students had to take the statewide exams, the scores of the students in special education did not "count" in the "grading" of schools. The implication was obvious: It behooves a school aspiring only to a high grade to have as many potential culprits as possible placed in special education at the time of the testing. Shocking as this may sound, it was openly acknowledged by many school personnel in our study. Since that time, the state has mandated that special education students' scores be included in evaluation of schools' effectiveness. However, while hard data are not available, anecdotal reports from district school personnel indicate that the use of waivers to release special education students from the testing has increased.

Overall, there are various ways in which the high-stakes environment is detrimental to students of color: Most noted is a teach-to-the-test syndrome that focuses on the lowest-level cognitive skills, such as formulaic writing, rote learning, how to bubble-in multiple-choice tests, and how to choose an-swers by a process of eliminating obviously incorrect items (Lomax et al.,

1995; McNeil & Valenzuela, 2000; Sacks, 2000). McNeil and Valenzuela's 10-year longitudinal study of the impact of high-stakes testing in Texas shows that these effects were particularly evident in schools with a predominance of African American or Latinx students or both. A study by Skiba et al. (2006) of teachers' perceptions of accountability testing found a strong belief that this testing "creates pressures that increase inappropriate referrals to special education" (p. 1447). Once more, the "machine bureaucracy" (Skrtic, 1991) continues to work to the detriment of students of color.

THE PARADOX OF THE IDEA

An obvious challenge to the foregoing interpretation of special education's sorting process is that the IDEA and its predecessor, the EHA, represent a landmark achievement on behalf of the thousands of children for whom there had been no available schooling prior to 1975. There is no question that this powerful legislation represents the continuing commitment of U.S. society to its goal of equity. It therefore seems paradoxical that the provision of costly and specialized educational services should be interpreted as less than beneficial to children in need.

This longstanding argument was addressed by Reschly et al. (1988), who proposed that the strong objections to special education overrepresentation arise from a reaction against the historical arguments of genetically based racial inferiority as well as from the perception that special education programs may not be beneficial. We agree with these arguments but would take them further. First, as contrasted with compensatory programs such as Head Start, which require only economic eligibility and are voluntarily chosen by parents, special education services can be obtained only through a child's being "proven" to be "disabled." Often, the recommendation is imposed by the school, not chosen by the parents. Further, the stigma that accompanies a disability label is seen as undesirable, particularly by people who are already stigmatized on grounds of ethnicity.

It is not just that members of minority groups, especially African Americans, construe their overrepresentation in disability categories as evidence of continuing stigmatizing and racism, but that the labeling process, with the official sanction of the science of psychology, moves rapidly toward reification. In an ethos in which science rules, what else can such a pattern do but confirm historical stereotypes in the minds of those disposed to clinging to them? Thus, the stigma attached to cognitive or behavioral disabilities battles with the good intention of the provision of specialized services.

Recalling the formulation of the "triangle of expertise" by Artiles et al. (2016, p. 788), it is not surprising that the notion of intrinsic deficit has such sticking power. Labeling theorists (Becker, 1969; Bogdan & Knoll, 1988; Goffman, 1963) have long pointed out that when an official designation becomes "reified," it is interpreted as a definition of the person, overshadowing, even excluding the numerous other traits, abilities, and nuances of the individual. These classifications or labels become, as Goffman (1963) said, the "master status" by which the individual is defined. A poignant study by Banks (2017) of Black male college students with SLD illustrates the continuing oppressions wrought by intersecting stigmatized identity labels. In the United States, while some classifications were developed with the specific intention of separating and isolating, as in the case of the construction of racial categories (Ferrante & Brown, 1998; Rosenblum & Travis, 2000), others have been conceptualized as means of identifying and serving people in need. This is the usual interpretation of the application of disability labels. The paradox arises when the classification system, instead of serving those in need, does them greater harm (Osterholm et al., 2007).

Besides the damage done to the individual by internalization of the label, there is also the limiting effect that the classification system has on professionals' interpretations and insights. These negative effects are particularly likely in the mental health professions because of the overwhelming appeal of science as the basis of psychology and psychiatry, both of which intersect with the conceptualization of special education. This conceptualization becomes doctrinal when endorsed by the *Diagnostic and Statistical Manual of Mental Disorders* (DSM) and accorded the "highest stamp of legitimate authority in the field" (Schwartz & Wiggins, 2002, p. 201). Yet the scientific academy itself is divided on the extent to which we can put faith in the science of these fields (Artiles et al., 2016). Sadler (2002) and his colleagues stated that the DSM-III, "through operationalizing diagnostic concepts into specific criteria," strove to "diminish ambiguities in psychiatric diagnostic concepts" (p. 5). This stripping away of clinical judgment belies the very nature of mental health practice.

To examine the other side of the paradox, we must ask what happens if it is decided that a child who is failing in school is not eligible for special services. Many professionals in our study were adamant on this point: This child would simply "fall between the cracks," and many do. As one psychologist put it, "No LD, no services." In the categorical perspective, special education placement was often seen as the only alternative to school failure—a protective move in favor of a child; or, as the psychologist quoted above said, a move "to save their lives."

Such faith in the efficacy of special education is not borne out by research. Although the literature on special education interventions reports numerous studies of effective practices tested under research conditions, it appears that these practices are not widely disseminated or implemented (Donovan & Cross, 2002). Moreover, postschool outcomes are not encouraging: Data from the National Longitudinal Transition Study (NLTS) of Students in Special Education (SRI International, 1995), reporting on the postsecondary activities of former students who had been enrolled in LD programs, indicated that 73% of these ex-students were working or studying, while only 50% of individuals who had been in EBD programs were employed.

Across these two categories, more than a third of the students did not graduate from high school. Sixteen years later, the most recent version of the NLTS Report (SRI International, 2011) was even less encouraging, showing that only 35.5% of those with LD and 25.8% with EBD were engaged in any form of employment or postsecondary training or study.

One positive finding is that research on outcomes of inclusive placements shows significantly higher academic performance by students with disabilities in regular classes compared to those in separate classrooms (Cole et al., 2021; Gee et al., 2020). As shown in a case study of successful Black students with SLD, this speaks to the promise of inclusion that truly gives all students access to the curriculum (Gatlin & Wilson, 2016). The fact that there is a "crack" between general and special education reflects one of the disadvantages of *either* the "normal" *or* the "disabled" construction of special education. If we understand achievement to exist on a continuum (Donovan & Cross, 2002), why shouldn't special education services be tailored to whichever point on the continuum a child occupies, instead of the child having to be tailored to a set of arbitrarily determined categories? We believe that a well-functioning RTI process ought to be able to address this by tailoring instruction to an individual child's point on a learning continuum.

In summary, there is no escaping the negative implications of the over-representation of students of color in special education. Despite the NAS's acknowledgment that the high-incidence categories represent "artificial and variable" cutoff points on a continuum of ability, it may be only the academics on the academy's panel, and select school district administrators, who understand it in this way. For most teachers, a child so labeled most likely "has a disability," just as, according to one of our study participants, "some children have blue eyes." For the child who is labeled, and the family who must agree to the label and the placement, "to be labeled by mental deficit terminology is . . . to face a potential lifetime of self-doubt" (Gergen, 1994, p. 151). Moreover, the educational system's attempt at the categorization of children has resulted in dilemmas that force professionals to simplify findings, ignoring important contradictions and nuances of children's cognition and emotion. As Gergen (1994) argued, the discipline of psychology has produced a paradoxical situation in which the mental health profession's "prevailing vision of human betterment" has resulted in a "network of increasing entanglements for the culture at large" (p. 143). We concur, and we believe that this paradox and its "increasing entanglements" are well illustrated by the study we report in this book.

FACING RACE IN RESEARCH

A cultural-historical view has implications for research: Specifically, it requires a willingness to see where a so-called unit of analysis fits within a larger picture (Artiles et al., 2016). By this lens, inappropriate designation of disability labels to children of color represents but one detail in the big picture of continuing discrimination that exists in the society as a whole. For example, discriminatory school processes that lead to failure and special education placement include limited curricula offerings, shockingly poor physical conditions, a dearth of highly qualified teachers and myriad other detrimental factors (Brantlinger, 2006; Darling-Hammond, 2012). These factors contribute to what Ladson-Billings (2006) referred to as the "education debt" that implicates everything from housing and urban development policies to health services and wages (Anyon, 1997; 2014; Ferri & Connor, 2014). While one research project cannot attend to all these factors, researchers who seek insight into social processes need to be intentional about investigating relevant and available contextual information.

In bringing this chapter to a conclusion, I offer a brief review of key publications that I believe move us forward in our ability to study the issue of disproportionality within the broadest possible contexts. Across this body of literature lies a direct foregrounding of race and the intersecting power of racism with ableism. Several scholars point to the failure of reform efforts that try to solve the problem of racial disproportionality without directly addressing race (Carter et al., 2017; Ferri & Connor, 2014; Freedman & Ferri, 2017; Tefera and Fischman, 2020). For example, in identifying the root cause of racism and ableism, Freedman and Ferri (2017) argue that we must "go beyond specific outcomes of intersectional identities, to examine the science that constructs identities to begin with" (p. 3). Following this argument, they present a challenge to what they refer to as the "two aims of modern science: (a) finding distinct biological markers of race and (b) discovering biological and neurological origins of learning disabilities" (p. 3).

In the research reported in this book, we clearly saw how unquestioned beliefs about the factuality of learning disability drove professionals to assert that IQ testing is a sure way to "find" a disability, and that the testing "stands on its own." As one teacher said, some children have a learning disability "just as some children have blue eyes." Most participants in the study shared this view, showing no awareness of the historical or current social contexts that influenced children's performance on formal testing. In Chapter 11, our reporting of the psychological evaluation of an African American 2nd-grader reveals how the psychologist made assumptions about the effects of the child's home environment on her behavior, but paid no attention to the influence of the classroom context from which the child was referred. Moreover, there seemed to be no awareness of ways in which the act of testing itself created some of the responses that led to the child being designated as emotionally disturbed.

Studying Context

Tefera and Fischman (2020) typify the theme of the avoidance of race in their consideration of "how and why context matters" (p. 1). Using qualitative interviews, observations, and document analysis to reveal the limitations of color blind or race neutral assumptions and strategies, they explain that the school district they studied had repeatedly been cited for overrepresentation of Black students and had engaged in attempts at reforms which were

> largely symbolic, uncoordinated, and not directly related to addressing racial disproportionality . . . [including] hiring a part-time special education teacher, adopting a computer program to encourage more "appropriate" student behavior, a "homework" room for students with in-school suspension to ensure students stay on track academically, and the development of a voluntary culturally relevant training program for educators. (p. 9)

Unfortunately, the most relevant attempt—the professional development program—failed, because only 20 staff, out of approximately 300 in the district, volunteered to participate every year.

With even greater focus on embedded racism and classism in special education decision-making, some exemplary research has revealed deeply disturbing patterns of decision-making that give a more comprehensive view than those seen in our research. While the research in our study showed vastly different approaches to placement decision-making across 12 schools in one district, Voulgarides' (2018) 2-year observation and interview study investigated team decision-making across three school districts within a state. The study revealed a clear pattern of discrepant team functioning related to the racial identity and socioeconomic status of parents across high-, low-, and mid-SES districts. The powerful influence of parents in the predominantly White high-income district provided a stark contrast to the laissez-faire, disorganized placement processes in the predominantly Black, low-income district, in which parents were often not informed of upcoming meetings.

Going further in the application of a cultural-historical approach to studying disproportionality, Bal et al. (2014) conducted a dynamic intervention using mixed methods in which a collaboration between researchers and district stakeholders resulted in keen insights into historical and current contributors to disproportionality. In reporting this collaborative case analysis, the authors state that the school Leadership Team identified its "instructional core, especially instructional practices and student engagement, relative to the curriculum" (p. 10), as a key source of the problem:

> The Leadership Team engaged in praxis, a deep examination of disproportionality as a complex dynamic systemic problem requiring a systemic transformation effort underpinned by data-based decision-making. . . . [The Team] determined that adaptive solutions were necessary instead of continued reliance on purely technical solutions such as compliance activities (e.g., procedural checklists, new documentation systems, evaluation guidelines, brief professional development seminars from external experts . . .). (pp. 9, 10)

Perhaps the greatest impact of the studies by these researchers (Bal et al., 2014; Bal & Trainor, 2016) is their demonstration that a collaborative approach to research can move the field beyond understanding, to action that makes a difference. In pursuit of this goal, Bal and Trainor (2016) proposed a rubric for "expanding the field's dominant empirical paradigm and increasing reflexivity and responsivity in knowledge production" (p. 319). This work helps point the way forward for researchers. For example, in our study, while the district leadership did respond to our findings by modifying some aspects of their referral process, I believe that a logical next step could have been a similar collaborative investigation with school and district personnel into the process involved in modifying their approaches.

Systemic Racism and Classism: Same as It Ever Was

While politicians express panic over rising critical voices, researchers are making the meaning of systemic forces in education increasingly clear. A line of research by Ashby et al. (2020) and White et al. (2019) elevates the foregoing arguments to the macro level, taking into account historical policies and practices over a period of 80 years. These scholars' geospatial analyses of historical red-lining practices in an urban school district in 1937 as compared with 2015 demonstrates the "persistence of racial segregation that is enacted systematically and systemically via special education placements, disability categories, and geography" (White et al., 2019, p. 453). This study, entitled *"The same as it ever was,"* methodically lays out the long reach of historical racism, classism, and ableism: In mapping present-day demographics and special education placements onto the school district data from 1937, the researchers reported "stark spatial and statistical disparities in the assignment of disability categories and rates of inclusion for students based on race and socioeconomic status" (p. 460).

Their key findings are particularly instructive, even shocking: Specifically, the racial and socioeconomic composition of neighborhoods that determined redlining in 1937 was essentially unchanged, with neighborhoods that were graded "A" 80 years ago continuing to be composed of 91% upper-income and White families, while 75% of the "D grade" neighborhoods were of lower income and hypersegregated racially. Further, the patterns illustrated how, over eight decades, neighborhood housing, socioeconomic status, and race intersected with disability labels and inclusiveness in special education placement:

> Black students were less likely to be labeled with Autism than White students . . . and Black students with Autism, ED, and ID were more likely to be taught in low inclusion environments than their White peers with the same disability labels. . . . Very few White students were taught in low inclusion environments and they were geographically represented in formerly A/B graded areas, with just a few outliers in D graded areas. Conversely, students with autism who were taught in

segregated educational environments were primarily students of color and represented in formerly C and D graded schools. (p. 464)

Another study by this team in the same school district (Ashby et al., 2020) applied the geospatial methodology to the study of a "Small Schools Plan," by which a group of elementary schools were reconfigured into K–8 school buildings, eliminating the only traditional middle school in one quadrant of the city—which happened to be in a more affluent and highly educated neighborhood. While the students with disabilities who attended the new schools benefited from more inclusive placements, the reform effort also resulted in the K–8 schools becoming "whiter and wealthier than district average," producing "enclaves of privilege" within the school district (p. 407).

Overall, scholars using a cultural-historical lens, including geospatial analysis, are increasingly successful in demonstrating the entrenched effects of history, geography, and social policies, including parents' opportunities to choose schools for their children (Waitoller & Lubienski, 2019), school transfers and closings (Waitoller & Radinsky, 2017), and the school-to-prison pipeline (Annamma et al., 2014). Such patterns of equity/inequity exemplify Tate's (2008) concept of "geographies of opportunity" (p. 29).

RTI as a Systemic Challenge: The Strain of Shifting Concepts

A cultural-historical perspective on RTI goes beyond technical implementation issues to the larger challenge of change in existing cultures of schools. Thorius and Maxcy (2015) offered an insightful analysis of why the hopeful implementation of the RTI process has struggled. Citing the work of Welner (2001), these researchers illustrated how four historically laden processes can combine to limit success: Inertial forces, based on "deeply embedded cultural practices of schooling in the local site; technical forces, the organizational and operational functions of a school; normative forces, which reflect the "prevailing beliefs about people's inherent worth and capacities," and political forces, by which power imbalances influence concerns and practices of stakeholders (p. 119). Studies by Cavendish and Espinosa (2013) and Cavendish et al. (2016) in this school district during the advent of RTI reflected several of the features noted by Thorius and Maxcy (2015). Cavendish and Espinosa (2013) noted that school personnel, lacking adequate preparation and guidance, experienced the "strain of the shift" (p. 191) from previous practices and beliefs embedded in the medical model to the instructional focus of RTI. The authors called for intensive teacher preparation that would address historical notions of race, culture, and disability.

In terms of current practice in our school district, I will comment here only on the minimal information gleaned anecdotally and through examination of district documents on RTI. The official approach is clearly stated in the district's RTI implementation manual as the MTSS (Miami–Dade County

Public Schools, 2021). Based on a problem-solving model, the guide provides timelines and checklists for all steps of the process. At tier 3, an SST meeting should be scheduled "to review the tier 3 data and determine if psycho-educational evaluation is appropriate" (p. 47). A request for evaluation may be initiated by a parent or "informed by the data collected after conducting interventions with fidelity" (p. 61). The guide further specifies that the MTSS process and the evaluation to determine eligibility are distinctly separate procedures. The guide specifies in the parental consent form that a team that includes an evaluation specialist will conduct appropriate testing.

This information promises to attend to the concerns expressed by some researchers (e.g., Gartland & Strosnider, 2020) regarding the possibility of RTI data being used to supplant the traditional psychological evaluation. Moreover, the manual is accompanied by numerous forms with detailed checklists regarding implementation of various steps in the process. However, anecdotal information raises questions as to the fidelity of implementation of the official approach.

A 4th-year doctoral candidate who is now in her 13th year as a special education teacher in the district, with 5 years as a staffing specialist, states that, in practice, the current process in the district is open to tremendous variability and subjectivity. This source explains that the determination of SLD is most often done based on the records of the RTI interventions, rather than by a formal evaluation. Further, when an evaluation is conducted, in her words:

> RTI is the guiding force of SLD eligibility. A formal evaluation with academic testing cannot stand in the place of RTI. I am not able to make an SLD placement decision without all three tiers of RTI data present. The evaluation for SLD consideration can also simply be a review of RTI data as formal academic testing is not necessary for SLD eligibility. Some school psychologists, however, will also administer academic testing such as the KTEA-III (if we're lucky!). (Personal communication, Meaghan Chaplin)

THE POWER OF A CULTURAL-HISTORICAL FOCUS:
QUESTIONS ARISING FROM OUR STUDY

The research reviewed in this chapter prompts me to consider aspects of our research that would benefit from a deeper cultural-historical analysis. An outstanding study by sociologist Alejandro Portes (2018) provides the background for an investigation of relationships between the city's history and present-day special education processes. Portes provides an intriguing view of this unique "minority-majority" city where a predominant immigrant group has succeeded in replacing the original White power structure in a process of "acculturation in reverse" (p. 56). Below, I summarize some key points from this history and suggest ways in which they could inform a deeper understanding of the key questions of this study.

Acculturation in Reverse

As Thorius and Maxcy (2015) caution, "macro-level special education policies . . . do not enter into neutral local educational environments" (p. 117). That the ground is not neutral in this relatively young city has been carefully documented by Portes (1993, 2018) in his vivid portrait of the deep divisions and alliances that have brought the city from one "on the edge" to a precarious global stature. Portes' history (2018) traces the unusual success of Cuban immigrants in replacing the previously White power structure, not only numerically but politically and culturally. Despite continuing to hold considerable economic power, the White (non-Hispanic) population decreased from 65.7% in 1970 to a mere 12.2% in 2020, while Hispanics increased from 27.6% to 69% over the same period, while also accruing political dominance and economic leadership in the city. While Portes notes that the Hispanic population is now more than 50% non-Cuban, "other" Hispanics represent disparate profiles, such as upper income professional and business people from South American countries, as compared with lower income populations from Central American countries.

Portes (2018) explains that the steady stream of Cuban refugees throughout the second half of the 20th century came with significant political and economic support by the U.S. government. However, the educational and economic outcomes differed greatly for the first wave of political refugees (pre-1980) who were from the elite classes of the island as compared to the second wave, who were predominantly economic refugees. Portes points out that the predominantly White racial appearance of both groups afforded them additional social status. Nevertheless, those from the second wave have continued to maintain a working-class profile, including a family income at the low end of the spectrum and on par with that of non-Hispanic Blacks. Portes relates this disparity in income to the reduction in U.S. federal support for the second wave and the fact that the children of the first wave attended private religious schools established by the elite group while the children of the second group predominantly attended public schools, often in poorer parts of the city. Notwithstanding these "bifurcated" outcomes within the Cuban immigrant population, Portes states emphatically: "If non-Hispanic Whites represent the mainstream of the American population, then that mainstream has disappeared in Miami. . . . The mainstream in Miami is now resolutely Hispanic" (p. 23). The truth of this statement is evident in the widespread use of Spanish throughout the city and the high status accorded the language. He refers to this phenomenon as "acculturation in reverse" (p. 56).

Meanwhile, the city's traditional racial hierarchy was maintained, in which Black populations, both native and immigrant, remained at the bottom of the social and economic ladder. The Black population, increasing from 15% to 20% between 1970 and 2020, represents several groups, most notably African Americans whose historical ties to Jim Crow America continue to result in negative social and economic outcomes. Haitian immigrants, the majority of whom are native speakers of Haitian Creole, comprise the next largest Black group in the district, while English-speaking West Indians (pre-dominantly from the Bahamas, Jamaica, and Trinidad) make up the balance.

The schools we studied reflected this history. Specifically, I believe that a close-up investigation of the histories of Black and immigrant groups in this school district would provide us with deeper interpretations of the key themes of our findings: school and teacher quality, cultural assumptions about children and families, instruction and classroom management, special education referral, evaluation, and placement processes. Further, it would be instructive to note the breakdown of nationalities among Black and Hispanic students placed in special education. Below, I propose a couple of questions that could contribute further to our understanding of the trajectory of special education placement among "students of color" in this school district.

Does the Mainstream Matter? Racial/Ethnic Disproportionality in the Context of Reverse Acculturation

> What could we learn from a cultural-historical and geospatial analysis of race/ethnicity in the city's public schools? Specifically, how does a milieu of reverse acculturation affect special education placement of students of color?

I believe that the history and current racial/ethnic and economic milieu of the city is relevant to our findings regarding Black students. One clear pattern in our data was that

> schools serving the poorest, Black neighborhoods had the most extremes in quality of instruction and classroom management. . . . Ethnicity . . . seemed to be a key factor within the low-income populations, with the highest poverty Black schools tending to be worse off than the highest-poverty Hispanic schools. (Harry & Klingner, 2014, pp. 76–77)

With this in mind, I note that the two schools with the most detrimental practices were in a historically Black neighborhood that fits exactly the description of the decimation of Black culture through urban redevelopment policies implemented in the middle of the 20th century (Rothstein, 2017; White et al., 2019). The construction of a major interstate highway in 1957 cut directly through Overtown, a neighborhood that boasted successful Black-owned businesses and was a nationally known center for Black arts and music (Florida International University [FIU], 1998). The FIU report states that this neighborhood now has the highest poverty and crime rates in the city and explains:

> The expressway and urban renewal projects displaced close to 12,000 people and . . . from 1960–1970 the community lost 51% of its population and 33% of its businesses. . . . In addition to the severe loss of residents and businesses, the community's internal circulation system was left in shambles, the vacant space under

the elevated expressways became a wasteland and haven for undesirables, and home ownership dropped from 12 percent to 5 percent from 1950 to 1970. (p. 2)

We came to know parts of this neighborhood well as our sample included schools located in the area. One child, whose story we tell in Chapter 11, lived just a block from the "wasteland" underneath the highway.

Diversity and Social Status Among Low-Income "Students of Color" in the School District: The Green Acres/Creekside Contrast

What could we learn from a cultural-historical, comparative ethnographic exploration of two schools serving two groups of low-income immigrants of different race, language, ethnicity, and nationality?

Another finding in our data that points to differing quality of schools within low-income populations is the clear contrast between two schools, referred to in the study as "Green Acres" and "Creekside." Both schools served low income populations of recently immigrated students, the former being predominantly from Central America and the latter from Haiti. The quality of instruction and overall organization from the front office to each classroom at Green Acres was so outstanding that we referred to it as the anomaly across the 12 schools. Although instruction was in English, Spanish was spoken casually throughout the school and in meetings with parents of children referred to special education. In this school the vast majority of teachers were of Hispanic ethnicity and the principal told us that the school was full of excellent teachers because she had "good eyes" in the selection process and was able to hire "people that I know in our community" (p. 36).

The exact opposite was true at "Creekside," where an energetic African American principal said she struggled to get high-quality teachers because she had minimal autonomy in hiring. Teachers in this school seemed to be a balanced mix of Hispanic, White, and Black, a few of whom were Haitian. Despite the predominance of Haitian Creole–speaking children, this language was seldom heard, either in the front office or in the classroom. Our data pointed to the influence of the principal at Green Acres, who was anomalous in having been in that position for 12 years, as compared to a turnover rate of 2–4 years at Creekside and the other schools serving Black children. We could not discern what social and political influences made the difference in these two schools but I would venture that a close cultural-historical analysis would have produced revealing information.

The foregoing reflections on the continuing effects of historical systems point to the dilemmas related to the traditional model of neighborhood schools. White and colleagues (2019) state: "Because of housing segregation resulting from redlining and other forms of color lines (including infrastructure), neighborhood schools tend to reinscribe and deepen hyper-segregation" (p. 469). School choice, however, is not a simple matter for parents, who must juggle numerous concerns, including safety, distance, available cur-ricular programming, and race/ethnicity of the student body (Waitoller and Lubienski, 2019). White et al., recommend that school zoning practices should be examined from a DisCrit perspective that would include critical spatial analysis, which takes into account the sociohistorical contexts that have set the trajectory of current neighborhood characteristics.

"HUMAN VARIATION RATHER THAN PATHOLOGY"

As we will argue throughout the book, we support the view of Reid and Valle (2004), who called for a reconceptualization of SLD "in terms of hu-man variation rather than pathology" (p. 473). The variability in patterns of disability designation over time and place, and the intense debate over the meaning and identification of SLD support the perspective that the categories are reliant on definition and interpretation, which, in turn, are influenced by social and political agendas of various states, groups, and individuals. The literature reviewed here strongly supports the main argument of this book—that the high-incidence categories do not necessarily reflect real disabilities within children.

Since the time of this study, there has been one ominous outcome of the 2004 revisions of the IDEA, which underscores the social and political nature of disproportionality: The 2004 authorization specified State Performance Standards by which states are required to report "significant" disproportion-ality, but left it to the states to determine the criterion for "significance." Between 2005 and 2008, across states the minimum criterion set was 2.0, the mean was 2.75, with a range of 2 to 5 (Albrecht et al., 2012; U.S. Government Accountability Office, 2013). Since a risk ratio of 1 indicates equal risk for a group as compared to others, these criteria mean that all states find it ac-ceptable to have a racial/ethnic group represented in special education at any-where from twice to 4 or 5 times the rate of their presence in the general population. How can this be acceptable?

NOTES

1. Although only 17 states subcategorize ID according to level of severity (Muller & Markowitz, 2004), IQ scores at the higher end of this category represent the "high-incidence" side of the ID spectrum.

2. While disability terminology varies across states, in this book, we use those terms that are most commonly known.

CHAPTER 2

Overview

Racial/Ethnic Disproportionality in Special Education

In many schools across the United States, February is the month for honoring the history of the people who became American by virtue of forced emigration from Africa to the New World. It is the month for teaching about the accomplishments of African American heroes and martyrs, for learning that, because of their courage in the face of overwhelming oppression, the ideals of equality and freedom that once were a reality only for some are now a reality for all. As part of this project, many children all over the country are introduced to Martin Luther King Jr.'s famous statement of his vision of racial equality and brotherhood, and many are required to write their own versions of Dr. King's dream.

Matthew was an African American 2nd-grader in a school where almost all the children of his ethnicity were bused from a low-income neighborhood "on the other side of the highway," into a school in a wealthy, predominantly White neighborhood where high academic achievement on the annual statewide tests earned the school an A in the governor's school-evaluation plan. The children in Matthew's class were given a dittoed sheet with a silhouette of Martin Luther King Jr. in the top right corner and six or seven lines on which to write their "dream." In a neat, slanted script, Matthew wrote:

> I have a dream that there will be no more wars. There will be no more fighting, throw away the drugs. I have a dream that one day there will be no more rich people poor people. We will all be equal. I have a dream that we will all wear helmets with our stoooters and bikes.

Matthew's identification of helmets as an indicator of social status in his community gave our research team a fascinating insight into the sensitivity of an 8-year-old. We believe that it tells us more about Matthew than did his label as a child with "emotional disturbance."

RACIAL/ETHNIC DISPROPORTIONALITY IN SPECIAL
EDUCATION PROGRAMS

When this research project began in the 1998–1999 school year, Matthew was one of the 1,111,650 African American children served in special education programs across the United States. A National Academy of Sciences (NAS) study of racial/ethnic representation in special education (Donovan & Cross, 2002) indicated that, in that year, across racial/ethnic groups and high-incidence disability categories, this number placed African American children at the greatest risk of receiving a disability label—a risk index of 14.28% as contrasted with 13.10% for Native Americans/Alaska Natives, 12.10% for Whites, 11.34% for Hispanics, and 5.31% for Asians.

The risk estimates reported above were most commonly in use at the time of the first writing of this book. The risk index is essentially the percentage of students in a given ethnic group who are placed in special education. Since that time, scholars have preferred to use a risk ratio, which is arrived at by a two-step process wherein the within-group risk ratio is calculated for a racial/ethnic group and is then compared to the rate within other racial/ethnic groups. At the time of this writing, the most recent publication of the Office for Special Education Programs' (OSEP) was the 42nd Annual Report to Congress on the Implementation of the Individuals with Disabilities Education Act, 2020 (U.S. Department of Education, 2020). To briefly recap the data reported in Chapter 1 for the fall of 2018, the report cites a risk ratio of 1.9 and 2.2 for Black students in the Emotional Behavioral Disability (EBD) and Intellectual Disability (ID) categories respectively, and 1.5 in Specific Learning Disability (SLD). Native American students were also overrepresented in these categories, with risk ratios of 1.6 in both EBD and ID, and 1.9 in SLD. The only overrepresentation for Hispanics was in the LD category, with a risk ratio of 1.4. Across all categories, White and Asian students continued to show placement rates either approximately proportionate to their presence in the school population or disproportionately low.

Coming Back to Matthew

Matthew's school, which we will call Sunnybrook, was a microcosm of the national picture on ethnic disproportionality in special education. African American children represented approximately 17% of the student population. They represented, however, approximately 35% of those served in special education classes for children with LD. Since Sunnybrook's special education program served only children designated as having LD, those designated as having EBD or ID were transferred to a school that offered self-contained classes for children with these disabilities.

When Matthew was referred for evaluation, the decision on his disability designation seemed to have been a toss-up for either a learning disability or an emotional disturbance label. Although his reading and math skills were measured as being almost on grade level, and his composition and spelling were quite competent for an 8-year-old, Matthew's grades were generally at the bottom end of his high-achieving class. Further, his mood swings from emotional outbursts to silent withdrawal made him a difficult child to handle in a 2nd-grade class of about 28 children. Knowing that Matthew had witnessed a death in the family, the school had provided counseling, which, according to the teacher, did not seem to help. When his African American classroom teacher initially referred him for evaluation, the referral papers cited "learning problems." However, the psychologist conducting the assessment reported no evidence of learning disability but found Matthew eligible for services under the category emotionally disturbed.

The school to which Matthew was transferred served a population with similar racial and socioeconomic demographics, but at least 80% of the students in the EBD program were Black. Before the end of his 3rd-grade year, Matthew had become "a star" in this structured behavior modification program, almost always earning his full quota of behavior points and maintaining an academic level above those of most of his peers. His mother, who described Matthew as having a "bad temper," had accepted the placement but disliked the separateness it imposed on her son, and she wondered when the school would decide that he was doing well enough to go back to the regular class in his old school. When our research efforts ended in 2002, Matthew, then a 5th-grader, was still doing very well in a self-contained class for children with emotional disturbance, and there was no talk of his return to the mainstream.

This brief summary presents only the kernel of Matthew's story, but it is sufficient to highlight the main purpose of this book. We will demonstrate that what has come to be known as the disproportionate representation of minorities in special education programs is the result of a series of social processes that, once set in motion, are interpreted as the inevitable outcomes of real conditions within children. These social processes do not occur by happenstance, or by the good or evil intentions of a few individuals. Rather, they reflect a set of societal beliefs and values, political agendas, and historical events that combine to construct identities that will become the official version of who these children are. In special education, the construct of disability has become the overriding metaphor by which differences in students' behavior and school achievement are explained. This metaphor comes to be taken for a reality, which, all too often, is treated as permanent. It should not be surprising that race has become intertwined with the construction of special education, since race has been an essential ingredient in the construction of all aspects of American life. Moreover, as Goffman (1963) argued, it is all too easy for categories that are understood as deficient to become associated with one another. But we will come to that theme later.

To those who would say that Matthew's placement was the natural outcome of his own learning and behavioral patterns, we suggest that, had any of the circumstances of his situation been different, the outcome might have been different, and instead of being seen as a "disabled" child, Matthew might have been seen as a "normal" 8-year-old in need of continued counseling and an emotionally supportive school environment. We believe that Matthew's official identity was negatively affected by several social and personal inter-sections , including, his "racial distinctiveness" (Fish, 2019) as a low-income, African American child in a wealthy, high-achieving, predominantly White elementary school; a raising of the bar for acceptable achievement among his high-income peers; the competition among schools to earn a high rank in the state's testing system; the requirement of a specific deficit label in order for children to qualify for special education services; and the separateness of the general and special education programs.

This is not to say that Matthew had no problems. Rather, it is to say that, once the discourse of disability was set in motion, Matthew's problems came to be defined as a disability, and that disability as a fact. The concept of disability became reified—made into a "thing" that belonged to Matthew, a thing that would be very difficult to discard.

A common objection to this interpretation of events might be the ques-tion, "But are you saying Matthew did not have a disability? Or, Is there no such thing as a disability?" We would answer that there is an infinite range of abilities among individuals and that, while there are certainly individuals whose capacities are more limited than the average, it is society's decisions related to such individuals that determine whether they will be called dis-abled. This is particularly true of the high-incidence, "judgment" categories for which Matthew was considered. We do not argue that there are no dif-ferences in performance and ability among children. Our concern is with the "human responses to those differences" (Connor et al., 2016, p. 18).

CONSTRUCTING DISABILITIES IN SCHOOLS

A cultural-historical perspective on the issue of disproportionality calls on researchers to expand their conception of the "unit of analysis" from the in-dividual to the broader social and historical context (Artiles et al., 2016). In addition, disability critical theory (DisCrit) (Connor et al., 2016; Annamma et al., 2018) encourages us to identify the many intersections of identity that place an individual or social group at increased risk of experiencing further exclusion or oppression in social contexts. A DisCrit lens requires us to understand that one of the main tasks of special education has been to engage in "boundary work" (Artiles et al., 2016) that seeks to define and categorize what are really the "shifting boundaries between normal and ab-normal, between ability and disability" (Connor et al., 2016, p. 18). Guided by these perspectives, our study sought to elevate the voices of those expe-riencing the effects of arbitrary identity boundaries and to examine those experiences within the complex social, cultural, and historical contexts that created them.

Our focus in this book is on the high-incidence disabilities whose determination depends on clinical judgment rather than hard data. These categories stand on the "soft" side of science and that very "softness" provides the key to their analysis. Effective clinical judgment requires an understanding of the contexts in which children learn, the affective as well as the cognitive processes that influence their learning, and the cultural predispositions that prepare children for formal, academic education. In short, many intangibles that defy measurement and enumeration are essential ingredients of these "disabilities."

The "softness" of the high-incidence categories points also to the role of culture in how cognitive competence and incompetence are defined. As Cole (1996) noted, psychological theories of learning tend to assume that culture is irrelevant to the process of knowledge acquisition. This view ignores the considerable body of literature that demonstrates cross-cultural differences in the structuring of knowledge (Rogoff & Chavajay, 1995). Moreover, many studies have shown differential cultural interpretations of a wide range of impairments, including deafness, blindness, physical deformities, epilepsy, mild intellectual disabilities, learning disabilities, and emotional disturbance (for a comprehensive review, see Kalyanpur & Harry, 2012).

This is not to negate the role of biology. Indeed, the very notion of intersectionality means that everything in a person's experience is interconnected, including the biological features. Artiles et al. (2016), questioning the dichotomous formulation of "soft" and "hard" sciences, highlight the need to seek an "integrated understanding of the interplay of biological and cultural notions of disability that torque and traverse other identity markers (e.g., race and class)" (p. 810). Later in this book, as we consider the nature of psychological evaluation, we characterize that practice as being centered on a dilemma of being "between a rock and a soft place."

High-Incidence Disabilities as Points on the Continuum of Learning and Behavior

Over the course of two decades, the NAS (Donovan & Cross, 2002; Heller et al., 1982) convened two panels to study disproportionality. The work of both these panels is very relevant to our study. The second NAS panel (Donovan & Cross, 2002) approached the issue by seeking data in all possible environments that could contribute to disproportionality. Despite recording a host of potential social, environmental, biological, and educational contributors, the report nonetheless emphasized that the high-incidence disabilities cannot be assumed to represent intrinsic deficits in children. We quote the report at length because it points to the essential ambiguity in what is generally interpreted as a firm set of categories:

The historical concept of a student with a disability or of a gifted student suggests that the characteristics of concern are within the child—an individual or fixed-trait model of ability—and that the student with a disability or a gift is qualitatively different from peers. However, for the high-incidence disabilities with which we are concerned, as well as for giftedness, both of these propositions are called into question. . . .

In terms of cognitive and behavioral competence, students fall along a continuum . . . there is no black and white distinction between those who have disabilities or gifts and those who do not. At the far ends of the continuum there is little dispute about a child's need for something different. . . . But as one moves away from the extremes, where the line should be drawn between students who do and do not require special supports is unclear. *A variety of forces push on the lines from opposing directions.* . . .

We have argued that where along the continuum of achievement the lines are drawn for specialized education is artificial and variable. Perhaps of greater concern, however, are *factors that affect where a student falls along the continuum.* For students having difficulty in school who do not have a medically diagnosed disability, key aspects of the context of schooling itself, including administrative, curricular/instructional, and interpersonal factors, may contribute to their identification as having a disability and may contribute to the disproportionately high or low placements of minorities. The complexity of issues of culture and context in schools makes it nearly impossible to tease out the precise variables that affect patterns of special education placement. (pp. 25–27, emphasis added)

This statement leads us directly to the main purpose of our book: to delineate the "factors that affect where a student falls along the continuum" of student achievement, and to elucidate the "variety of forces [that] push on the lines from opposing directions." We argue that the process of determining children's eligibility for special education is anything but a science. Rather, we agree with Skrtic (1991) that it is the result of social forces that intertwine to construct an identity of "disability" for children whom the regular education system finds too difficult to serve.

The ambiguities inherent in converting a continuum into categorical sets are intensified by the social nature of the processes used to determine disabilities. The classic 5-year ethnographic study of decision-making in special education by Mehan et al. (1986) demonstrates that decisions arrived at in special education conferences were essentially a "ratification of actions taken earlier" (p. 164). Acknowledging that schooling does "sort and stratify . . . students in such a way that differential educational opportunities are made available to them" (p. 171), Mehan and colleagues argue that this is not a simple process of reflecting students' measured abilities or their background characteristics. Rather, they emphasize that every act of evaluating a student, whether face to face or through committees' decisions and reports, constitutes a step in the creation of the student's "social identities" (p. 175). As each step builds on the next, the social identity of the student becomes reified and the evidence is perceived as more and more credible.

This book has a great deal in common with that of Mehan et al. (1986), and we acknowledge the influence of their work on ours. Our study cannot lay claim to the level of ethnographic intensity involved in that study, since we tended to take a broader rather than a deeper look at processes across 12 schools, and since our data collection did not include videotaping. Nevertheless, our goals and methods were similar but for one crucial concern: Mehan and his colleagues did not focus particularly on the role of race/ethnicity in special education decision-making. This book does.

A PROCESS APPROACH TO UNDERSTANDING RACIAL/ETHNIC DISPROPORTIONALITY

In studying racial/ethnic disproportionality, we focused on the complex processes that led to special education placement. Our research was modeled on the recommendation of the NAS's first study of disproportionality (Heller et al., 1982). That report began by stating that one cannot assume that ethnic disproportionality in special education is a problem, since it could be that certain groups of students need special education in disproportionate amounts. Thus, the panel argued, to know whether or not the pattern is problematic, we must ascertain the adequacy and appropriateness of all phases of the placement process: early instruction, prereferral activities, the decision to refer, and the process of assessment. Finally, we must know whether the outcome of the process—placement in a special education program—was beneficial to the child. If we find bias or inappropriate practice at any phase of this process, then we must treat disproportionality as a problem.

This approach begins its examination at the level of the school and asks two questions: first, whether the school provided adequate opportunities for children to progress and, second, whether it engaged in biased or discriminatory practices in making decisions about the evaluation and placement of children who were not progressing adequately. It does not ask whether the child came to school with a disability. It does not ask whether the child was predisposed, by virtue of prior exposure or experience, to have a disability. It simply asks whether the school did its job.

This is an important distinction for two reasons. First, in the deficit-oriented culture described by Gergen (1994), the presupposition of intrinsic deficit tends to trump all other reasoning. School personnel are heavily influenced by this thinking, if only because they operate under a legal framework that requires professionals to seek, find, and serve students with disabilities. Second, when deficit interpretations are being applied to members of a group that has historically been viewed through the lens of deficit, the deck is powerfully loaded. As critical race theorists have asserted, racism is "normal, not aberrant, in American society" (Delgado & Stefancic, 2000, p. xvi). For many people, blaming the victim is as natural as breathing.

"Risk" in Schooling

Studies of risk have focused on the long-term impact of early home experience. For example, Sameroff and colleagues (1993) found that IQ scores are
quite stable across time and are negatively affected when a child has been
exposed to multiple risk factors in the home. Using a composite score that
included 10 home-based risk factors, the studies found that the combination,
rather than any one factor, accounted for depressed IQ scores at ages 4 and
13. Similarly, the research of Blair and Scott (2000) demonstrated strong
correlations between pre- and perinatal risk factors and special education
placement.

Strangely, these studies did not look at what happened at school during
the years from age 4 to age 13. They did not ask how school experiences may
have contributed to depressed IQ scores remaining depressed or to special
education placement. This is particularly ironic when it is obvious that IQ
tests are focused on the kinds of learning acquired in school. According to the
NAS (Donovan & Cross, 2002), these should be considered "tests of general
achievement, reflecting broad culturally rooted ways of thinking and problem
solving" (p. 284). If much of the IQ test score reflects learning and experience, and school learning in particular (for example, vocabulary and analytic
thinking), and if these children are exposed to poor schooling, then their ability to increase their scores on these tests will be further limited.

This gap in conceptualization of the problem is glaring, and Keogh (2000)
has called for a better understanding of "risk and protective influences in
schools" (p. 6) as well as in families. As we will show throughout this book,
the presence of multiple family- and community-based risks tends to increase
the likelihood of *school-based risk*, which appears in the form of poor teachers, overcrowded classrooms, negative social-class and ethnic biases, and a
host of other detrimental influences. Thus, "risk" cannot be considered without attention to risks induced and exacerbated by poor schooling. Schools
are a huge contributor to what Tate (2008) called the "geography of opportunity" (p. 397). O'Connor and Fernandez (2006) take this point further by
including in the concept of "risk," the very norms and benchmarks by which
school success is measured. In a rebuttal of the NAS's (Donovan & Cross,
2002) focus on poverty as a contributor to disproportionality, O'Connor and
Fernandez argue:

> It is the normative culture of school that places poor children at risk by privi-
> leging the developmental expressions more likely to be nurtured among White
> middle-class children. In the process, the developmental expressions that are
> more likely to be nurtured among poor minority youth are marginalized and are
> positioned to produce low achievement. (p. 9)

Researchers have noted the difficulty in teasing out the school-based factors
that affect where students fall along the continuum. For example, a line of

work by Oswald and colleagues (1999) display the complex interplay between numerous key variables, such as size of ethnic group in a district and high- versus low-poverty conditions. Noting that Black and Hispanic students were more frequently labeled LD in high-poverty districts but more frequently labeled ID in low-poverty districts, the authors concluded that the ID label was inappropriately applied. Conversely, MacMillan et al. (1998), in a study of LD labeling, find that the LD label was inappropriately applied to Black students who had in fact qualified for ID. The NAS report (Donovan & Cross, 2002) argues that the latter trend could represent a competing hypothesis to explain the findings of Oswald and his team.

Studies using statistical multilevel modeling have presented more nuanced analyses of the roles of race, socioeconomic status (SES), gender, and school disciplinary practices (Shifrer et al., 2010; Sullivan & Bal, 2013). While Shifrer et al. emphasize that overrepresentation was entirely explained by low SES, Sullivan and Bal noted a broader set of effects, namely, male gender and free/reduced lunch (FRL) status, and race, as well as school disciplinary policies. Black males were at the highest risk for placement in categories of SLD, ID, EBD, Other Health Impaired (OHI), and Speech and Language Impaired (SLI). Despite the detailed analysis accomplished, the researchers explained that it was "impossible to identify the mechanisms by which the observed gender, race, and SES effects operate" (p. 490).

A helpful line of research on risks in schooling has been provided by scholars examining differential patterns of disciplinary practices and their relation to EBD identification. Focusing on Black students, this research shows that disproportionately punitive practices are most notable in schools with high Black enrollment (Artiles et al., 2012; Rocha & Hawes, 2009; Welch & Payne, 2010; Skiba et al., 2014). In examining this trend, the latter authors highlight a complex interplay of types of infraction, student characteristics, and school level characteristics. Significant among the latter factors was principals' discipline philosophies. Further, noting that a higher enrollment of African American students in a school predicts more punitive and exclusionary practices, the researchers dispelled the idea that this reflected more problematic infractions by this group of students. Rather, their data indicated that White students were more often referred for demonstrable offenses, such as smoking or vandalism, while African Americans were referred more often for behaviors reflective of subjective judgments, such as disrespect, excessive noise, or threat. The researchers conclude that "systemic school-level variables appear to contribute to disproportionality in out-of-school suspension far more than either type of infraction or individual demographics" (p. 664). Pointing to the need for greater research on this topic, Skiba and colleagues (2014) state:

> The assumption that Black students from more disadvantaged backgrounds are at greater behavioral risk and will hence require tighter controls and supervision may lead to an a priori inclination to impose more restrictive and punitive

measures as black enrollment increases, regardless of the actual individual or behavioral characteristics of the schools' Black students. (p. 661)

Shores, Kim, and Still (2020) echo these findings, concluding that school-level decisions result in clear disparities between Black and White students in disciplinary actions, grade level retention, special education placement, and access to advanced level courses. The researchers describe the overall outcome pattern for Black students as "cumulative categorical inequalities" (p. 2111). While also noting the interaction of family income and education with these patterns, the researchers found that:

> in districts where Black students are the worst off socioeconomically, school districts increase the educational disadvantages Black students face, as they are more likely to be disciplined, retained, classified into special education, or excluded from GT or AP courses. (p. 2122)

The likelihood of bias in these patterns is inescapable. However, absent a qualitative investigation, we cannot know how bias in placements operates, whether through individual decision-making; group pressure; or institutionalized forces built into the fabric of the education system, or even the society as a whole. As Mehan et al. (1986) observed, the creation of official student identities does not occur solely in face-to-face interactions. The same is true of racism or any type of bias. Bias is often inherent in social situations: in funding patterns, organizational arrangements, personnel hierarchies, and numerous other structural aspects of any social organization. There may be in an institution not one individual who professes or explicitly displays bias, yet all members may be, by virtue of uncritical participation in the system, purveyors of biased practice.

Cumulative Risk

As the report in this book will show, our data are fully consonant with the interpretation that schools exacerbate the challenges faced by Black students in low-income districts (Shores et al., 2020; Skiba et al., 2014). In keeping with the call by Artiles et al. (2012) for a range of research methods that can explore the complexity of factors at play in the identification of EBD, our study showed the power of close-up qualitative methods to attend to that complexity. Indeed, the issues identified in the literature regarding EBD and discipline were vividly on display in our data.

First, the most exclusionary disciplinary practices were noted in predominantly Black schools, where "zero tolerance" policies resulted in even kindergartner and 1st-graders being suspended from school for offenses like fighting. One child, Robert, whose behavior in his 2nd-grade classroom we had noted as primarily out-of-seat and distractible, was placed on a half-day suspension that lasted for a period of 5 months. On his return to full-day placement, Robert displayed new, more aggressive behaviors. When our research assistant asked him why he was behaving so aggressively, he replied, "I'm a gangsta—tha's why!" (Harry et al., 2007, p. 21). We believe that Robert had begun to redefine his identity in response to the exclusion he had experienced.

Second, the processes in referral of the four children labeled EBD were the most problematic in terms of dubious subjective and stereotypical decision-making by professionals. We came to this conclusion because we engaged in in-depth observation of these children's functioning in the classroom and at home, as well as repeated interviews with their parents, their general education and special education teachers and, for Robert and Kanita, the psychologists who conducted the evaluations. Three of these cases were marked by professionals' expressed assumptions about "dysfunctional" family settings, which contrasted greatly with information we gathered through home visits and interviews. Moreover, referral processes totally excluded any information on dysfunctional classroom instruction, weak behavior management, and peer bullying and teasing, all of which were observed in our data.

In all four cases, the designation of EBD resulted in the students being removed not only from general education but moved to different schools that provided an EBD program. Robert, whose initial evaluation as having attention deficit/hyperactivity disorder (ADHD) was in synch with our observations of him in the classroom, was re-evaluated as EBD and sent to a separate school serving only students with that disability. About 5 years after the end of the study, Robert's mother reported that he had been "running with some bad kids" and was caught shoplifting, as a result of which he was sent to a residential program for youth with behavior disorders.

Special Education as a Support Rather Than an Alternative

As special educators, we are all too aware of the history of exclusion and oppression that brought special education services into existence. We believe that special education has a role to play in supporting and assisting children and youth whose needs make them more vulnerable to the competitive contexts of schooling and less receptive to run-of-the-mill, generic instruction in an education system whose mainstream caters to the middle. Therefore, we continue to believe that the individualization espoused by special education is desirable and necessary in education. We continue to believe that, for purposes of practicality, school systems will need to conform to specified guidelines regarding which children should be afforded the individualized supports of special education.

We do not believe, however, that it is necessary for guidelines for eligibility to be based on a belief system that constructs arbitrary borders between normalcy and disability. Like Artiles (2003), we believe that to continue to do so is to continue to stigmatize, alienate, and underestimate children, in particular, children whose families and communities are already underestimated and marginalized. Children should be able to obtain specialized services by virtue of their level of performance in the academic tasks of schooling, not on the basis of a decontextualized testing process designed to determine an underlying "deficit." We do not believe that it is necessary to conduct such testing in order to determine a child's educational needs. As argued by Johnston (2011) and Hoover (2010), the RTI process ought to provide the avenue for tailoring instruction and prevention to individual children's needs, rather than functioning as the lever for identification of disabilities. Moreover, to accomplish the latter, RTI needs to be conceptualized as social justice rather than a technical endeavor (Artiles et al., 2010).

This book points to the fallacies involved in relying on the disability construct for the provision of special education services. In exposing these fallacies, we propose reforms that we believe are feasible and that would allow the field to avoid the negative outcomes too frequently associated with the reified views of cognitive and behavioral "disabilities." We conclude this chapter with a brief introduction to the way we approached our study of the processes involved in overrepresentation.

THE SCHOOL DISTRICT OF HYPHENATED IDENTITIES

The school district we studied presents a portrait of dynamic multiculturalism in a city that defies the country's centuries-old tradition of defining people by race. While the predominant ethnicities present in the public school system in 1999 were officially classified as Black (34%), Hispanic (51%), and non-Hispanic White (15%), these labels have little meaning in the context of the tremendous racial, ethnic, and linguistic variability within all groups.

The majority of those choosing "Hispanic" ethnicity are of Cuban origin, while other South and Central American nations are also well represented, such as Nicaragua, the Dominican Republic, Mexico, and Peru. Racially, Hispanics in this region may appear to be either "White," "Black," or any racial mixture, and many self-identify as White. However, since official racial/ethnic classifications allow for "White" and "White-non-Hispanic," those choosing White on official documents tend to be mainly people of Anglo American or Jewish origin. The official classifications also allow for "Black" and "Black-non-Hispanic," so Black American and Caribbean populations who do not identify as Hispanic may select "Black," and may speak Haitian Creole, French, English, or any of the varieties of English spoken in Caribbean islands such as Jamaica or Trinidad/Tobago. Asians and Native Americans represent a tiny minority who mostly select those racial/ethnic categories.

Race/ethnicity language and socioeconomic status (SES) are the key variables that differentiate the county's public schools, since, as in many localities across the United States, ethnic minorities of low income tend to cluster in neighborhoods. Of course, within all ethnic groups there is variability in SES levels. However, non-Hispanic Whites and Cuban origin immigrants from the first wave of political refugees from the island hold the highest economic status, with non-Hispanic Blacks and second wave Cuban economic refugees, fall at the lower end of the economic spectrum (Portes, 2018).

Most schools in the sample tended to reflect the income levels of their neighborhoods. For Matthew's school, however, this was modified by the presence of a desegregation order that was in place throughout the duration of the study, but has since been withdrawn. Matthew's school, described at the beginning of this chapter, still participated in the busing of African American students into a school in an upper-income, predominantly White and Hispanic neighborhood.

Special Education Placement Patterns in the School District

In the two decades since the completion of this research project, the overall numbers in the school district have changed considerably. Hispanic students have increased from 51% in 1999 to 72% in 2019, while Black students have decreased from 34% to 20% and White students from 15% to 7%.

The patterns of relative disproportionality among ethnic groups, however, remain similar. At the time of the study, special education placement in this school district reflected the nationwide and state figures, showing that Black students were overrepresented in the ID and EBD categories at all three levels. Hispanic students were slightly overrepresented only in the LD category at the district level. We will keep the table that we used in the first edition of the book (see Table 2.1), although the numbers at that time were

Table 2.1. Percentages of Students in District, State, and Nationwide Special Education Programs by Ethnicity and Years (1999 and 2007)

	DISTRICT						STATE					
	Black		Hispanic		White		Black		Hispanic		White	
Year	1999	2007	1999	2007	1999	2007	1999	2007	1999	2007	1999	2007
ALL	34	26	51	62	15	9	25	23	15	25	17	46
ID	60	52	35	43	6	4	48	48	11	16	31	33
EBD	46	49	40	41	13	8	37	39	9	13	25	44
SLD	33	27	54	64	13	8	25	24	13	25	17	47

	NATION					
	Black		Hispanic		White	
Year	1999	2007	1999	2007	1999	2007
ALL	17	17	17	21	66	56
ID	31	13	31	7	58	7
EBD	25	11	25	5	66	7
SLD	17	44	17	54	67	40

not reported as risk ratios, but were inferred by comparing the percentage of a group in the school district as a whole to that group's percentage in each disability category.

Since the first edition of this book in 1999, official reports have utilized risk ratios, so we will show, in Tables 2.2 and 2.3, the comparative risk ratios

Table 2.2. Florida Department of Education State and School District Risk Ratios for Students Placed in Exceptional Education (2009)

The risk that students of a given race will be identified as a student with a disability or a student in selected disability categories when compared to students of all other races. A risk ratio of 1.0 indicates the students of a given race are equally likely as all other races combined to be identified as disabled. A risk ratio of 0.00 indicates that either the race of interest or the sum of all other races is equal to zero. In calculating risk ratios, students reported as multiracial are prorated across other racial/ethnic categories. The data are presented for all students with a disability; students who are identified as ID, EBD, or SLD; and students who are identified as having autism spectrum disorder (ASD), speech or language impairments (SI-LI), other health impaired, or homebound or hospitalized (OHI-HH). The data are presented for the district and the state as reported in **October 2009** (survey 2). An asterisk indicates less than 30 students of a specific race/ethnicity with the given disability.

	ID		EBD		ASD	
	State	District	State	District	State	District
White	0.68	0.66	0.95	0.90	1.27	1.41
Black	2.29	2.37	2.07	2.73	0.68	0.66
Hispanic	0.67	0.52	0.48	0.43	1.00	1.16
Asian/Pacific Islander	0.51	*	0.12	*	1.13	1.53
Native American/ Alaska Native	0.80	*	0.78	*	0.90	*

	SI-LI		OHI-HH		SLD		All Disabled	
	State	District	State	District	State	District	State	District
White	1.35	1.11	1.51	1.72	0.98	0.76	1.07	0.92
Black	0.96	1.19	0.81	0.53	1.04	1.02	1.13	1.16
Hispanic	0.71	0.84	0.77	1.27	1.08	1.12	0.88	0.93
Asian/Pacific Islander	0.76	0.88	0.32	*	0.30	0.33	0.49	0.51
Native American/ Alaska Native	1.07	*	1.11	*	1.04	*	1.01	*

Table 2.3. Florida Department of Education State and School District Risk Ratios for Students Placed in Exceptional Education (2019)

The risk that students of a given race will be identified as a Student with Disabilities (SWD) or a student in selected disability categories when compared to students of all other races. A risk ratio of 1.0 indicates the students of a given race are equally likely as all other races combined to be identified as SWD. The data are presented for all SWD who are identified with the following exceptionalities: ID, EBD, SLD, ASD, SI-LI, OHI, or HH student. The data are presented for the LEA and the SEA as reported in **October 2019** (survey 2). A blank cell indicates less than 10 students of a specific race/ethnicity with the given disability.

| | SEA | | | | | | |
	ID	EBD	ASD	SI-LI	OHI-HH	SLD	SWD
White	0.78	0.94	1.05	1.29	1.24	0.88	1.02
Black	2.03	2.21	0.84	1.04	1.00	1.32	1.20
Hispanic	0.72	0.49	1.06	0.76	0.87	1.01	0.90
Asian	0.64	0.11	1.07	0.60	0.26	0.28	0.49
Native American/ Alaska Native	1.09	1.03	0.88	1.12	0.89	1.19	1.05
Native Hawaiian/ Other Pacific Island	0.66	0.55	0.81	0.96	0.54	0.68	0.73
Two or more races	0.85	1.42	1.06	1.09	1.01	0.89	0.99

| | DISTRICT | | | | | | |
	IND	EBD	ASD	SI-LI	OHI-HH	SLD	SWD
White	0.71	0.71	1.13	1.01	0.94	0.66	0.82
Black	2.78	3.44	0.81	1.17	0.79	1.22	1.22
Hispanic	0.45	0.36	1.13	0.89	1.29	0.98	0.92
Asian	0.53		1.04	0.75	0.23	0.34	0.53
Native American/ Alaska Native							0.70
Native Hawaiian/ Other Pacific Island							0.90
Two or more races		1.94	0.73	0.78	0.85	0.87	0.89

between 2009 and 2019. These two points of comparison reveal similar patterns for Black students and interesting patterns in the categories of ASD and OHI for White and Hispanic students. Specifically, over the 10-year period, Black students' risk of placement in ID increased from 2.37 to 2.78, and in EBD from 2.73 to 3.44; Hispanics' representation in most categories remained lower than 1 across the 10 years, with the exceptions of ASD, where they showed a risk ratio of 1.16 and 1.13 in 2009 and 2019, respectively, and in OHI a small increase from a risk ratio of 1.27 in 2009 to 1.29 in 2019. Hispanics in this district also showed a decrease in SLD placement from 1.12 to 0.98 over the 10-year period. Placement patterns for White students in this district are similar to those of Hispanics, with risk ratios below 1 in all categories except ASD, which changed from 1.41 in 2009 to 1.13 in 2019, and in OHI a decrease from 1.72 to 0.94 over the 10-year period.

To summarize, over the last 20 years, Black students in this school district have continued to be overrepresented in the categories of ID and EBD at 2–3 times their rate in the general student population, while Hispanic and White students have shown only minimal disproportionality in ASD and OHI. The category of SLD does not appear to be disproportionately used for any groups, with placement rates hovering just below or just above 1 for both Hispanic and Black students.

It is beyond the scope of this edition to delve into potential explanations for the relative patterns across these three racial/ethnic groups in the school district. However, as explained in Chapter 1, it is worth noting that, in general, while the local Black (African American and Caribbean, including Haitian) populations generally hold the lower end of the economic and political spectrum, Hispanics in this geographical region represent a relatively high status group generally perceived as racially White with considerable political representation and middle- to upper-level income. The historical context of this relates mainly to the preferential treatment given to Cuban immigrants for approximately 60 years, because of U.S. opposition to the Castro regime. A close examination of which Hispanic groups predominate in special education programs would help to shed light on Hispanic representation in this school district and state.

The Research Process

Our sample of 12 schools was carefully selected to represent at least some of the complexity of the school district, including a range of racial/ethnic populations, a range of socioeconomic levels, and differential rates of special education referral and placement. After consultation with the administrators of each of five geographical regions in the district, and meetings with principals of schools suggested by the administrators, we selected the 12 schools.

Envisioning children's school experiences as affected by a series of concentric circles (Strauss & Corbin, 1998), we designed the research as a funnel, beginning with the issue at its broadest level, including figures on nationwide, statewide, and districtwide patterns of ethnic distribution of students in special education. We then narrowed our focus to the school district and the rates of special education placement in various regions of the district, and then to the rates at particular schools. From there we moved into the center of the circle, investigating processes within the 12 schools, and, ultimately, to a focus on 12 individual children.

Table 2.4. School Demographics: Percentages by Race/Ethnicity, FRL, and Disability

School	Ethnicity of Students			Free or Reduced-Price Lunch	ID	EBD	LD
	W	B	H				
Bay Vista	8	1	90	68.7			6.6
Sunnybrook	55	17	23	18.5			4.1
Clearwater	3	92	3	70.1	0.2		4.1
Blue Heron	7	4	92	65.6		5.8	12.5
Green Acres	2	0	98	88.9			5.3
Centerville	0	99	1	97.1	7.0		9.8
Palm Grove	0	89	10	98.9	0.5		6.8
Creekside	0	92	8	97.2	0.1	0.01	3.5
Esperanza	6	11	82	89.6			4.2
Beecher Stowe	1	69	29	98.4	2.6		4.2
Mabel Oakes	2	56	42	99.0		0.1	4.4
South Park	2	79	19	98.3	0.5	0.3	5.8

Note: W = White; B = Black (African American as well as Haitian, Jamaican, and other Caribbean); H = Hispanic (various countries of origin); ID = Intellectual Disability; EBD = Emotionally Disturbed; LD = Learning Disabilities.

Table 2.4 shows the three types of ethnicity patterns and special education placement rates across the 12 schools that we selected. Four of the schools were predominantly African American, four were predominantly Hispanic, and four included mixtures of African American, Hispanic, and White. We also took account of SES, by including one school that served a high-SES White and Hispanic population with a minority of low-income African Americans bused to the school, and one that served a low- to middle-SES African American population (as contrasted with the schools that served African Americans of low-income to poverty levels). With regard to placement rates, we note that the absence of a percentage under the categories ID and EBD at some schools indicates that these programs were not offered at those sites.

We began by developing a broad picture of the 12 schools through interviews with school personnel, observations of all K–3 regular-education classrooms, and of a sample of support and placement conferences. The research funnel narrowed further as we selected two classrooms in each school to observe intensively, focusing on those children about whom teachers were concerned and who might be referred to the special education process. We observed these children in various school settings and observed support and placement conferences and psychological evaluations, wherever possible. At the end of our intensive data collection in these 24 classrooms, we conducted a round of exit interviews with the teachers. In the third year, we followed students into their postevaluation placements, whether in general or special education, and also observed in all the special education classrooms in their schools. Finally, we identified 12 students for whom we developed intensive case studies.

Overall, our data amounted to 272 audiotaped, open-ended or semi-structured individual interviews with students, parents, and school-based and district personnel; 84 informal conversations; observations of 627 class-rooms; 42 child study team (CST) meetings; 5 psychological evaluations; 15 special education placement meetings; 14 other meetings; and observations in 15 home and community settings relevant to target students. Interview length ranged from 20 minutes to 2 hours, classroom observations ranged from 30 minutes to a full day, and CST and other meetings lasted from 5 min-utes to more than an hour. The documents we examined included individual education plans (IEPs), students' work, psychological and other evaluations, school district guidelines and policies, and extant data on special education placement in the school district.

The main project lasted 3 years. In the fourth year, we conducted quar-terly visits to schools to monitor the progress of the 12 case study students. Additionally, the case studies of three students placed in EBD programs were extended in a fifth year through the doctoral research of one of our students (Hart, 2003). We draw on all these sources in this book.

ORGANIZATION OF THE BOOK

We have organized our discussion to reflect the funnel-like process of our research, moving from broad to more individualized portraits of schools, school personnel, children, and families. In Chapters 3 and 4, we describe the overall structural and administrative features, as well as personal and contextual biases, that operated in these settings. In Chapter 5, we explore the general climate of classroom instruction and the provision of opportunity to learn. In Chapter 6, we begin our close attention to individual cases by contrasting school personnel's constructions of families' identities with the voices of family members themselves. In Chapter 7, we describe the decision-making policies and contexts that determined special education eligibility, and in Chapter 8, we discuss how these applied to English language learn-ers. In Chapters 9, 10, and 11, we provide a close-up view of the process of disability assignment to individual children, and in Chapter 12 we address the question of whether special education placement provided beneficial out-comes. In Chapter 13, we offer solutions that we see as strong alternatives to the current special education model. Finally, the book closes with an epilogue on our research methods.

In view of the large body of research findings, we note here our con-cern with the challenge of selecting, for the purposes of this book, only the most salient exemplars of the broad-based issues we studied. We assure our readers that our findings are grounded in ethnographic data too extensive to be reported within the confines of one book (for further detail, see Harry et al., 2005).

OUR PREMISE

We approached our very complex data with one guiding premise: We could only conclude that special education placement was appropriate if children had received adequate and appropriate opportunity to learn within supportive environments and had been placed through a fair and well-reasoned referral, assessment, and placement process. We found that this was by no means the case. The caveats to our conclusions are obvious: First, we could not study every case in the 12 schools; second, we did investigate some students whose placement process was appropriate and helpful.

To summarize here what we will explain in detail throughout the book, we found a host of explanations that competed with the belief that special education placement reflected genuine learning and behavioral deficits that required such placement. In many cases, there was simply no way of knowing how children would have fared in more effective educational circumstances in the regular classroom or with a more systematic and appropriate referral process.

There are many reasons that this conclusion is important. First, the belief that school-based disabilities reflect real impairments further fuels beliefs about the inferiority of any groups who seem to "have" these impairments in greater proportions than do other groups. On the symbolic level, there is no escaping that a label of disability carries a stigma; to add this to already existing historical prejudices against certain groups is to add insult to injury. The second reason to be concerned and to understand the social nature of disproportionality is that the benefits of special education placement continue to be questionable (Kavale, 1990; Reschly, 2000).

This book offers a unique view inside the assumptions, policies, and practices that characterized special education decision-making in one of the nation's largest, most diverse school districts. The power of our findings lies in the voices and actions of school personnel, family members, and children. It lies also in the complex portrait of the social pressures and realities of schools operating under political mandates that sometimes work against children's best interests. By exposing the human and social processes at work in the designation of disability, we dispute the belief that the overrepresentation of minority groups in special education can be assumed to reflect real disabilities within children.

CHAPTER 3

School Structure

Institutional Bias and Individual Agency

> So many principals! Each has worked an average of 3 years, and then they
> retire. One received a promotion, and then retired. The 12 years that I've been
> here, I've seen three principals retire. I think this one will be the fourth.
>
> —School counselor

As we enter the third decade of this 21st century, the concept of systemic or structural racism is in the forefront of public conversation. I believe that, for those who have traditionally wielded power, the resistance to this notion reflects a fear of having that power undermined by revelations of its history. But the evidence of these processes is incontrovertible and resonates throughout societal systems, not the least, the education system. Further, taking too deep a historical view of current policies and practices may mean questioning the belief in social mobility, which lies at the heart of American democracy.

Schools have been envisioned as the main vehicle for ensuring a meritocracy based on individual ability and hard work. Social reproduction theory, however, as articulated by Bowles and Gintis (1976), argued that structural features of schools ensure that schooling tends to reproduce rather than change the societal status quo, by preparing children to function at the same societal level from which they came. Researchers such as Kozol (1991, 2006), Oakes (1985), and Anyon (1981, 1997) have provided portraits of schooling that demonstrate social reproduction in action through inequitable funding patterns, institutionalized low expectations resulting from tracking, and the provision of differential curricula according to the social class level of students.

As cited in the opening chapter, research by scholars using geospatial analysis (White et al., 2019; Ashby et al., 2020) demonstrate the effects on education of endemic social class and racial discrimination in housing over a period of 80 years. Thus, it is evident that many decisions and outcomes are somehow larger than the individual, operating through a force that seems designed more to serve bureaucratic and organizational ends than to advance individual ones. Yet it is individuals who make decisions, and critics have argued that the structural view inherent in social reproduction theory is too deterministic, ignoring the power of individual agency (Brantlinger, 2001) and the influence of family social and cultural capital (Lareau & Horvat, 1999). Thus, certainly, some children will beat the odds. Structuralism, however, can also be countered for good or bad by the actions of leaders, as in the case of school principals' influence on disciplinary practices in their school buildings (Skiba et al., 2014).

Our research certainly supported the argument that children from higher-SES contexts will usually get better schooling than those from low-SES contexts, and that density of Black student populations in a school is related to increased exclusionary practices (Shores et al., 2020; Skiba et al., 2014). We identified school quality in terms of administrative decisions regarding scheduling, instruction, discipline policies, and interactions with parents, as well as in terms of teacher quality, which we determined through classroom observations and objective criteria such as the percentage of teachers with advanced degrees. State ratings of the schools also provided a more global sense of achievement. The only exception to the social reproduction pattern was Green Acres, an excellent school serving a Hispanic population of whom 89% were on free or reduced-price lunch (FRL). Across the other 11 schools, higher socioeconomic status (SES) was consistently associated with better school quality. At the lowest end of the pattern were those schools in which low-income Black children predominated. Social reproduction theory was chillingly reflected in the following statement of a special education teacher referring to a student at a school that served low-income Black and Hispanic students:

> She's lumped in with the dregs of society. . . . She doesn't understand what school is for. . . . We create blue-collar here at this school. If I could teach her social skills to get a job and not get fired, that's a goal—entering the labor force.

Despite the presence of social reproduction processes at work in these schools, our most important finding defied all simplistic assumptions about the overrepresentation of Black and Hispanic students in special education: *We learned that special education placement showed no systematic relationship either to school quality or to children's own developmental or skill levels.* Rather, it reflected a multiplicity of influences, including structural inequities, contextual biases, limited opportunity to learn, variability in referral and assessment processes, detrimental views of and interactions with families, and poor instruction and classroom management. Overarching all these was the power of each school's ideology regarding special education, which we came to refer to as the school's "culture of referral."

All of these contributing factors will be discussed as the book proceeds. In this chapter, we describe the structural inequities we noted in children's schooling and grapple with the elusive line between structural and individual responsibility. We will be concerned with those aspects of school structure that seemed to be within the purview of the school and school district administrators. When a child entered a school building, what policies and practices would be in place to support that child's advancement? Who would be the child's principal? Who would teach the child? Which peers would be in the child's classroom? What instructional programs would be used to assist the child? How would the child learn how to behave? What would happen if the child misbehaved?

SCHOOL LEADERSHIP: ASSIGNMENT OF PRINCIPALS TO SCHOOLS

Beecher Stowe Elementary, located in the heart of the old city center, served a low-income, predominantly African American population. Besides the counselor quoted at the introduction to this chapter, who said that he had seen four principals assigned in 12 years, another teacher who had taught for 22 years at Beecher Stowe reported that he had worked under a total of eight principals during his time. This school, serving the neediest of children in the school district, had a pattern of constant change of leadership.

It was not only the inner-city schools that suffered from such discontinuity. The pattern was frequent across the 12 schools, and while teachers sometimes expressed dismay at the lack of continuity in leadership, principals' comments tended to be rather noncommittal, suggesting either acceptance of or resignation to a fact they saw as beyond their power. The principal at South Park, another inner-city school serving a mixture of African American and Hispanic students, was a 30-year veteran and had served as an assistant principal (AP) for 12 years "all over the district." In one year, she had been moved to temporary AP appointments six times. When asked about these moves, she replied:

> As an administrator, you have to be willing to serve in any capacity— wherever you're needed. . . . You know, tomorrow they might call and say, "I need you to report to the region office," and when you get there they would say, "Give me the keys to your building, because you are going over here." But I've had a very positive attitude about that.

Not only was the leadership of these two schools very changeable, but so were the faculty. The percentage of new teachers at Beecher Stowe and South Park in the 1999–2000 year was 17% and 25%, respectively. Such faculty instability has been cited as a key variable in school risk (Keogh, 2000).

At the other end of the spectrum was Green Acres, a school serving a population that was 99% Hispanic; 89% of these students received FRL. This school ran exceedingly smoothly and efficiently under the leadership of a principal who had been there for 12 years and a new faculty of only 4%. In between these two extremes were variable leadership histories, but it seemed that most schools had had several changes. Frequent moves of APs were also common across the schools. At Mabel Oakes, which served a low-income Hispanic and African American population, there were three different APs during the 3 years of our research.

We do not know how these decisions were made. We learned only that, despite an apparently stringent screening process, the selection of applicants for administrative positions was influenced by unwritten policies such as asking the district superintendent whether he or she had anyone particular in mind for a position, and seeking ethnic and gender diversity among school administrators. Beyond these official guidelines, we had no way of knowing the inside details of the process or how any of the principals we met were selected.

What was clear, however, was that some, though not all, principals exerted tremendous influence over decisions at their schools, including hiring practices, discipline policies, student retention procedures, class size and scheduling, visitor policies, tolerance of interruptions, resource allocation, and curricular decisions. Variability in all of these was evident across our 12 schools. We focus on the decisions that seemed to have the greatest direct impact on children—the hiring and assignment of teachers. We then discuss other variables prominent in our data: discipline policies, scheduling, and interruptions.

TEACHER QUALITY: HIRING AND RETAINING GOOD TEACHERS

Perhaps the most important responsibility of the principal is to hire teachers and assign them to classes. Yet finding and retaining qualified teachers is a challenge in urban schools (Ansell & McCabe, 2003; Darling-Hammond, 1995; Oakes et al., 2002; Pflaum & Abramson, 1990), which typically have higher numbers of inexperienced, uncertified, temporary, and substitute teachers (Hardy, 1999). Whereas administrators in wealthier schools tell of having "stacks of résumés" to look through, principals in high-poverty urban schools relate how difficult it is to attract teachers to their schools—they must take whomever they can get (Krei, 1998). Retaining good teachers is equally challenging. Urban schools typically have high turnover rates as novice teachers gain experience and request transfers to schools that they consider more desirable. Though a few districts have attempted to alleviate disparities in teacher quality by providing monetary incentives to keep teachers at urban sites, these efforts usually are insufficient (Ferguson, 1991; Jacobson, 1989; Krei, 1998). Krei (1998) noted that, in some districts, issues of teacher quality are further complicated by principals in wealthier schools who transfer teachers deemed unsatisfactory to high-poverty urban schools rather than going through the process of dismissing them.

It is our position that these hiring decisions are but one set out of a complex array of interrelated factors that affect the special education referral process and ultimately the disproportionate representation of culturally and linguistically diverse students in special education.

District Data on Teacher Qualifications

District data on teacher quality across our 12 schools indicated a clear bias against the higher-poverty schools, in particular, those serving Black populations. With advanced degrees (master's, specialist's, or doctoral) being employed as a measure of teacher quality (a commonly used indicator in federal reports), Table 3.1 shows two main patterns and one anomaly. Using FRL as an indicator of SES, we can divide the schools into two main groups—eight with more than 86% FRL, and four with 70% or less FRL. In the higher-income group (Group A), the percentage of teachers having master's degrees ranged from 39% to 47%. With the exception of Green Acres, which we refer to as the anomaly, the range in the lower-income group (Group B) is from 21% to 36%. At Green Acres, 54% of the faculty had master's degrees. This percentage was 18% higher than the highest of the other low-income schools, and 33% higher than the lowest school. It was also 7% higher than the percentage in the school serving the most affluent population. Green Acres was also different from other Group B schools in that 98% of the students were Hispanic, whereas the other low-income schools either had predominantly Black or mixed populations.

We observed all K–3 classrooms in the 12 schools and analyzed teacher behaviors in terms of three dimensions of teacher quality: instructional skills, classroom-management skills, and socioemotional behaviors. Our analysis, which preceded any checking of data on teachers' qualifications, was very much in line with the discrepant teacher quality outlined above. In the schools in Group A and in Green Acres, teachers' instructional skills were consistently average to high, and it was rare to see a classroom where behavior was out of control or where instruction seemed haphazard, based on rote learning, or inappropriate to children's needs. By contrast, in Group B, teacher skills were very variable, with marked extremes of high and low as well as many in between. For example, in one such school, of 18 K–3 classrooms observed, we rated five very good, six average, and seven very weak. In another, of 12 classrooms observed, we rated five very good, two average, and five very weak.

Since we have grouped the schools according to FRL, which is a feature of the children, not the teachers, a reasonable question to ask would be whether the children themselves, because of poor behavior or poor academic readiness, might account for the impression of classroom quality. Our observations indicated quite certainly that this was not the case. In subsequent chapters we will detail the tremendous variability in child behavior in response to the skills of teachers. As one excellent kindergarten teacher in one of the poorest neighborhoods stated, "When you close the classroom doors, the children in this neighborhood are no different."

Table 3.1. Student and Teacher Data

| | STUDENTS | | | | | | TEACHERS | | | | | | | |
| | Ethnicity (%) | | | | | | Ethnicity (%) | | | | | | | |
	White (Non-Hispanic)	Black (Non-Hispanic)	Hispanic	FRL (%)	LEP (%)	Mobility Index	White (Non-Hispanic)	Black (Non-Hispanic)	Hispanic	Master's Degree (%)	Specialist (%)	Doctorate (%)	New to School (%)	Average Years of Teaching Experience
GROUP A														
Bay Vista	8	1	90	68.7	27.2	21	5	22	73	44	5	0	10.3	10
Sunnybrook	55	17	23	18.5	5.8	10	36	31	33	47	7	2	12.0	11
Clearwater	3	92	3	70.1	2.0	22	38	41	21	43	14	0	15.2	15
Blue Heron	7	1	92	65.6	31.3	23	24	36	40	39	5	0	19.4	10
ANOMALY														
Green Acres	2	0	98	88.9	50.0	22	12	25	63	54	9	0	4.5	12
GROUP B														
Centerville	0	99	1	97.1	0.5	47	44	36	20	36	10	0	17.1	11
Palm Grove	0	89	10	98.9	27.3	42	36	36	26	35	4	2	11.8	13
Creekside	0	92	8	97.2	43.2	41	36	34	25	35	6	0	8.5	9
Esperanza	6	11	6	86.6	46.2	26	9	28	63	27	3	0	16.7	8
B. Stowe	1	69	1	98.4	13.9	43	30	25	45	21	5	0	17.0	10
M. Oakes	2	56	2	99.0	26.1	50	38	23	39	32	9	0	16.9	8
South Park	2	79	2	98.3	8.3	44	18	30	53	21	2	0	25.0	8

Note: FRL = Free or reduced-price lunch; LEP = Limited English Proficient; Mobility Index = Rate of student mobility in school (turnover)

Limitations to Principals' Selection of Faculty

Principals were not necessarily to blame for the patently unfair pattern of teacher quality. Although a senior district official told us that principals had "sole control" over the hiring of teachers who had satisfied the district-level screening, there were two exceptions to this: First, there was a desegregation requirement that between 24% and 36% of a faculty must be Black; second, it was mandated that district personnel decide where to assign "surplused" teachers (usually less experienced), who were released from a school when the student population had declined.

Regardless of policy, it seemed that some principals had more autonomy than others. When the principal at Green Acres was asked how she came to have such an excellent cadre of teachers, she confirmed that she was able to handpick her teachers, exclaiming, "I think I have pretty good eyes!" For the most part, she listed the usual criteria one would expect, such as applicants' previous experience and behavior management strategies. However, one comment she made suggested that there may be more informal, more personalized aspects of the selection process: "I guess it has to do with the hiring of the people that I know in our community. We have a lot of children that do not speak English and you know [who can] do the best for those children." The phrase "our community" was not explicitly explained, but, since she followed it with a comment about English language learners, we interpreted it as probably meaning that she sought teachers who would be compatible in terms of ethnicity and language—Hispanic teachers. However, it was not just an ethnic match that made this faculty look so good, since in the other schools we saw as many weak Hispanic teachers as we did weak teachers of any other ethnicity.

In contrast, other principals in high-need schools said they experienced many limitations in their ability to choose, including inadequate applicant pools. New teachers often avoided inner-city schools, not responding to phone calls from principals at schools they considered undesirable. Geographical location was another limitation. Most of the schools serving very-low-income populations were in the older parts of the inner city, where few teachers lived. One principal explained that commuting was a source of stress that often resulted in teachers moving as soon as an opportunity arose that was nearer to their homes, leaving the principal to settle for teachers "who are not even mediocre [but] the bottom of the barrel!" These teachers then required a great deal of professional development and might still turn out to just "not have the capability."

Assignment of Teachers to Classes

Once teachers are hired, the next level of decision-making is to determine which students will get the best teachers in the school. A central issue is whether to group children by ability, and if so, which teachers to assign to higher and lower levels. Some principals believed in ability grouping and others did not. In one school that had two pre-K classes, these children, thought to be more promising because of their pre-K experience, were kept together throughout kindergarten and into the 1st grade before they eventually were spread out. Many of them, reportedly, turned out to be the "top students." This school also grouped children according to ability in math and in writing. In two other inner-city schools, the principals told us they sorted classes by ability, since they believed that this allowed teachers to tailor their instruction appropriately, rather than losing children at either end of the spectrum.

The principal at Green Acres, however, reported not using ability grouping, with two exceptions. First, students in the lower ESOL (English for speakers of other languages) levels were grouped for self-contained classes. Second, students who had to be pulled out for special education classes were clustered into certain classrooms, no more than four in each room, so that the special education students would be "easy to pull and schedule." After placing these two groups of children, the principal then tried to "balance" the placement of children so that all the rest of the classes had "high and low" children. Our observations suggested that this process worked well: We saw no classrooms that had an overabundance of children with learning or behavioral difficulties. In another school with relatively high achievement, the presence of a magnet program meant that those children were grouped together, but, otherwise, grouping was heterogeneous. Our observations suggested that heterogeneous grouping was fairer to the lower-performing children, and, if the teacher had good organizational and instructional skills, better for all.

In decisions regarding which teachers were assigned to particular groups of children, again the policies varied. Several principals preferred to place teachers at the grade level at which they would be most comfortable. One principal explicitly stated that she tried to place her best teachers in the grades that were most affected by high-stakes testing. Some teachers believed that the principal used class assignment to reward or "punish" them. In one school, according to a teacher, her "punishment" was being assigned many ESOL students in her class even though she was not ESOL endorsed. For those who were ESOL endorsed, however, being assigned to a predominantly ESOL class was appreciated by teachers who perceived that the Hispanic children were easier to manage than were African American children.

In some schools, it was evident that the strongest teachers were assigned to the higher-achieving students. For example, in one inner-city, predominantly African American school, we noted that weak teachers tended to be placed in classes in which children with challenging behaviors, low academic achievement, or both were clustered. One such teacher was constantly moved over a period of 2 years—from her 1st-grade assignment, which she had had for many years, to a troublesome 2nd-grade class, to an alternative-education class. When, in the following year, she was moved to a gifted class, the pattern had become incomprehensible to us. In the third year, she enrolled in a graduate program in special education and was immediately assigned to a special education class. With regard to her 2nd-grade class, the teacher told us that "almost half" the class had been referred for testing or were already receiving special education pullout services. She said that across the 2nd grade, one teacher had the high-achieving children, one had half and half, and she had all the difficult children. She said that this arrangement, made by the principal, had overridden a more heterogeneous proposal from the teachers. She felt that there was favoritism and punishment involved in the decision. Our observations of the three classrooms confirmed that both the children and the teachers had been "tracked" by ability.

Firing

Terminating ineffective teachers was a complicated process. Within a probationary period of 97 days, a new teacher could be terminated by the principal, who was required to evaluate the new teacher during this period. According to a senior official, "all kinds of help were available" to support new teachers and, after the 97-day period, terminating a teacher took "a lot of process and documentation." This was evident in the number of weak teachers we saw who had been teaching for many years.

Generally, we could not tell whether principals did not know, did not care, or could not do anything about the many ineffective teachers we observed. One inner-city principal, when asked what she could do about a teacher who was really struggling, offered some insights into the dilemmas she faced:

> [They've] got to go! . . . One teacher in particular I had to weigh the
> good with the bad. This person lacked the classroom management but
> she makes up for it with what she does with those children in the arts.
> And I had to make a decision, do you keep the teacher and try to deal
> with her classroom management in order to allow these children to
> experience something that they will not be able to experience? Or, do
> you immediately jump in there and then you don't have that particular
> teacher because there is a shortage because there is nobody else to take
> her place, or one who has the same problem? But, nevertheless, enough
> is enough and that person has been given notice. . . . You have to want
> to do it and you have to be willing to take the heat and get beat up and
> the whole bit.

Principals shared with us how constrained they felt in their ability to dismiss incompetent teachers. One principal explained:

> Many teachers just can't work in this [urban] environment. Then you
> have some teachers who have been here for 25 and 30 years. Some
> have been here for so long, when you go into their class [you see that]
> they know how to do just the minimum. So now I'm glad that we have

this new observation [system] . . . that has certain standards. Even though I am not going to able to get rid of [teacher's name], this gives me ideas on how I will be able to work with her before we put her on prescription and then you have to go through that process. . . . You just keep plugging away and at the end of the year you do have the option of hiring a 3100 [a teacher on temporary assignment] to come in to replace them. But it is a year or 6 months that you have to go through.

This principal went on to say that there used to be a time when "if a teacher had a problem, and they really needed to get rid of them, then they put them in the inner-city schools where they had to suffer." We assumed that this policy was no longer in place.

These comments point to the difficulty of getting and retaining good faculty. As we will detail later, our observations showed that there were many teachers who simply should not have been in the classroom. On the other hand, teachers' most common complaint was lack of support from their administrators, particularly support for discipline problems.

DISCIPLINE POLICIES

The variability in discipline policies and in children's behavior across schools was staggering. Clearly, the question arises of whether the problem lay mainly in the children or in the schools' response to them.

The school we opened this chapter with, Beecher Stowe, located in the poorest of the inner-city neighborhoods, cited the most problems with discipline. In this area we had two schools, both of which we cited as having many leadership changes. School personnel who knew the neighborhood well offered the opinion that the children's circumstances were really getting worse. In one school, the counselor, an African American man who expressed great commitment to the community, noted: "The children have such anger. This anger and bad attitude are everywhere." Our observations in both these schools showed behavior problems in some classes, but not all. In a later section, we will detail our findings regarding classroom management, making the point that when we see, within one school, classrooms with dramatically different types of behavior, although the children are all coming from the same neighborhood, it seems more likely that the issue is management rather than the children themselves. Further, when we see a group of children actually change their behavior as they move from one teacher to another, we are even more certain of the importance of teachers' skills.

Regardless of whether individual classroom teachers are able to bring out the best in children, the policies of any school's administration are at the center of the issue. Some teachers placed the responsibility squarely in the hands of the administration. In the case of beginning teachers, this was particularly troubling, since new teachers' contracts required that they stay at their first appointed school for at least 3 years, in an attempt to encourage greater commitment to staying in inner-city schools. Lack of support from school administrators made this outcome unlikely. One new teacher in an inner-city school had a class of 30 children, 9 of whom she described as "EBD kids." She felt as though she had been thrown "into the lion's den," but she would not send children to the office, because "nothing happens." She exclaimed:

> I wasn't trained to deal with these kinds of problems. I never had any problems compared with this, even though I did some [field experience] in an inner-city school. . . . They just don't send you. I wanted to go [to the inner-city schools]. The first day was terrible. I left crying. I just hadn't understood the need, how there can be so much need here, and I'm from Peru, a third world country. Many of my parents [here] don't work. My kids who are behavioral problems are always here because it is the only way they eat. I want to help. Something needs to be done. I have to give the students crayons and pencils because they don't have anything.

In an almost identical statement, a first-year teacher at another school said her primary need was

> more administrative input. More support for beginning teachers. You need your back rubbed. If you've been called a White cracker bitch, you shouldn't see that child walking the hallways. At the beginning, I was fighting. I was not very popular. . . . These kids are all smart. They're not special ed. They are bright kids. They just need discipline.

The counselor in this school, an African American man, said that more needs to be done to retain new teachers such as the former speaker. He said:

> Too many wait 2 years, then transfer. If they wait it out, it's gonna get better. What I learned in school [college], I had to throw it out! . . . Some years ago they used to give extra pay for working in this area . . . "combat pay."

Another teacher in this school felt she had very few options: "They told me not to put students in the corner, have them write lines, or send them out of the room. . . . And if we contact parents, when they go home, they get beaten." She said the school had started indoor suspension and after-school detention but, shaking her head, she added that a student in her class *liked* to go to after-school detention and deliberately pulled a fire alarm to get placed there. Another teacher told us, "What they really need to do is bring in someone from boot camp, and pay them a regular teacher's salary, and have them instill some discipline in the students." This school employed security guards who were called when students misbehaved, but they didn't always come to the classroom right away, and they didn't seem to be a deterrent to negative behavior. The view was that security needed to be stronger. One teacher described her administration as follows:

> You go to the office with a complaint and they are like cockroaches. You know, when you first cut on a light, the cockroaches run everywhere. That's what the administration does when you come to them, they'll do nothing. They don't want to hear anything from you. I have never seen anything like this school and its administration. I'm not happy. I feel like I'm being wasted here. It's hard dealing with the disciplinary measures. I'm primarily isolated. We have to handle everything ourselves. "See no evil. Hear no evil. Speak no evil."

In the two inner-city schools frequently cited above, the most troubling aspect of the administrations' response to discipline was the excessive reliance on out-of-school suspension.

Out-of-School Suspension

Elaine, a mother who attempted to be an advocate for her children, exclaimed in frustration to the principal at her son's school, "Every little thing he does, you all throw him out." Table 3.2 shows the district's report of rates of

Table 3.2. Suspensions by School

	Number of Students Suspended	Total Number of Students
GROUP A		
Bay Vista	1	1,379
Sunnybrook	8	828
Clearwater	12	658
Blue Heron	8	550
GROUP B		
Green Acres	9	1,160
Centerville	34	417
Palm Grove	2	820
Creekside	20	780
Esperanza	7	1,183
B. Stowe	101	806
M. Oakes	44	1,036
South Park	102	603

suspension in our 12 schools. At South Park and Beecher Stowe, suspension was the discipline policy of choice, showing rates that were totally out of line with the norms for the other schools: 102 children suspended out of a total of 603 students, and 101 children out of a total of 806. This was particularly distressing because for these children, being out of school meant being in the very detrimental environments so derogated by school personnel.

Many teachers were very vocal on this issue. Several felt that they had very few options for controlling behavior. One teacher said, "Some students get suspended all the time, but it doesn't work. How they handle discipline doesn't work." Another teacher said she tried to handle discipline problems on her own and not send students to the office. Although three of her students were out on suspension, she had not suspended them—other teachers or administrators had. She explained that she did not suspend kids, because "they just go home and get into more trouble. It is not a punishment for these kids."

SCHEDULING AND INTERRUPTIONS: "WE'RE THE ONES WHO MAKE THEM HYPER!"

The proliferation of programs at some schools was a matter of great prominence in our observations. With the best of intentions, several of the schools serving the neediest children were detrimentally affected by this problem. In some cases, the programs that contributed to an impression of overall curricular fragmentation were, in themselves, excellent programs or represented some very convincing educational philosophy. The difficulty, it seemed, was in the implementation and coordination with other potentially good programs.

Four of the inner-city schools were using Success for All (SFA) as their reading program. This program requires that children receive reading instruction in small groups of peers at their own level. Therefore, for approximately 2 hours every morning, the children went from their homerooms to another classroom for this instruction. While some teachers liked SFA and some did not, we noted that the more "special" programs there were in a school, the greater the frustration that was expressed, even by many who liked SFA. Other "special" programs included physical education (PE), music, and art. Also, in three of these schools, children had to go to different rooms for language programs, including ESOL, Curriculum Content in the Home Language (CCHL), or Home Language Arts (HLA). One teacher exclaimed:

> I've never had such a bad schedule. I don't have time to teach. I have them for less than 30 minutes, then they go to PE. Just when they have settled down and are working well, it's time for them to leave again. Then they come back for 10 minutes, then they go to lunch. Then they come back and go to Spanish (for an hour on Mondays and Fridays, and half an hour on Wednesdays). Then they come back at 2:00. We're the ones that make them hyper!

Our observations absolutely corroborated the statement that constant movement contributed to the children being "hyper." In schools with a high population of recently arrived immigrant children, it seemed to us that what they needed most was stability—a teacher who would get to know them well so that they could become socially and linguistically confident and able to focus on their work. It was obvious that homeroom teachers had little opportunity to get to know students personally or even to be sure of their academic levels. In one 1st-grade classroom, we had direct evidence that a child's reading and math levels were quite unclear to the teacher. The researcher gave a child initial prompts with the first set of sums on a test sheet, then sat and watched him do all the rest correctly. The teacher expressed surprise at the level of his work, saying that the teacher for the HLA program (using Haitian Creole) did most of his math with him. In the 3rd-grade classroom of an otherwise excellent teacher, we saw her giving a child manipulatives to add and subtract, while, in the HLA classroom, taught by the same Haitian Creole speaker, we observed the same child doing complex multiplication on the blackboard and getting all the answers correct.

It was ironic that this type of "hyper" scheduling occurred most often in the neediest schools. It seems that principals were trying to find a "magic bullet" for their children but, in so doing, failed to note the lack of coherence that resulted from "overdosing." In contrast, we once more cite Green Acres, where SFA was not included, but the high ESOL population was also served by an array of language programs. However, the scheduling was done so that the teachers, rather than the children, did most of the moving. In this school, there was a much greater sense of stability and continuity, although the ESOL teachers were sometimes noticeably weaker than the classroom teachers.

Another contributor to a hyper feeling in some schools was the high tolerance for interruptions, whether from intercom announcements at any time of the day, people stopping by to chat, or students switching classes. As with all other features, this varied widely from school to school. At several schools, interruptions to instructional time seemed to be pervasive, perpetuated by administrators, and accepted by many at the school as normal practice. These disruptions reduced instructional time. Most problematic seemed to be students going to and returning from special education classes. For instance:

> Students continue to come in. One boy shouts loudly, "Hey, Elton!"
> The teacher asks, "Why are you late?" Then she asks, "Why did she
> keep Robby?" Another student responds, "She didn't keep Robby." As
> it turned out, Robby wasn't there because he was wandering the school
> grounds, mad about something that had happened in the previous class.

Another program that proved quite disruptive showed the irony of too many uncoordinated efforts to boost the performance of children in inner-city schools. This was an individualized computer curriculum program that required children to do half an hour a day working on the computer at their her own level. The individualization required by this program, however, was effective only in the hands of very organized teachers, since they were required to monitor students on the computers at the same time that they were trying to teach. Students cycling on and off the computers seemed to give the message that the teacher's instruction was not important. Many teachers were unsuccessful in catching students up or in structuring the flow smoothly.

There was much coming and going to and from classrooms in many schools. Teachers were called out of the room for child study team (CST) meetings or placement conferences, sometimes without prior notice. People entering classrooms during lessons included, for example, the counselor, security guards, parent volunteers, parents, paraprofessionals, other teachers, other school support staff, other students, and computer repair people. Some of these interruptions were to pick up children for various reasons, or to borrow materials, but at other times the visitor simply had a comment or question, such as, "Did anyone in here go to the Girl Scout meeting on Wednesday?"

Other than during SFA, when there seemed to be an effort not to interrupt instruction, intercom announcements were common and occurred at varied times. At some schools we noticed a policy that instruction could only be interrupted over the intercom at set times, such as at the end of the day, but this did not appear to be the case at several inner-city schools. Overall, in the better schools, there was less of a tendency to use the intercom for unnecessary announcements and much less coming and going. This was clearly a matter of administrative policy, since it varied from school to school even in the inner-city schools.

CONCLUSIONS

There is no underestimating the importance of school leadership. It has long been demonstrated that strong leadership is a key element of effective urban schools (Edmonds & Frederickson, 1978; Jackson et al., 1983; Scheurich, 1998; Weber, 1971). The principal's beliefs, values, educational philosophies, and interpersonal as well as management skills have a great influence on the climate and culture of a school (Skiba et al., 2014).

We did not note any particular pattern in the skills of principals. Some of the least effective schools had principals who were energetic and imaginative. However, it was evident that some of these schools experienced the highest turnover in administrators. Certainly, our data on the schools that served predominantly poor, Black populations supported research showing disproportionately punitive and exclusionary practices in such schools (Artiles et al., 2012; Losen et al., 2014; Rocha & Hawes, 2009; Welch & Payne, 2010; Skiba et al., 2014). This meant that the most vulnerable children were placed at increased risk by virtue of inequitable hiring practices, assignment of weak teachers to weak students, retention of extremely weak teachers, homogeneous classroom groupings, unsupportive discipline poli-cies, and poorly coordinated curricular programming. All of these factors were to some extent within the realm of individual principals' agency.

At Green Acres, individual agency was evident. With a strong princi-pal, high-quality teaching, and positive personal interaction with parents, the children of low-income, immigrant families did well, special education place-ment rates were moderate, and the school consistently earned a B or A on the state grading system. At another school with a similarly high percentage of non-English speaking, immigrant children—Haitian rather than Hispanic—we saw a high-energy, enthusiastic African American principal struggling to increase educational outcomes in the midst of a faculty of whom perhaps one-third were effective. This principal told us she could not choose her fac-ulty, while the principal at Green Acres did.

What accounts for this discrepancy? It is possible that it could reflect different policies across the school district's administrative regions, or social capital in terms of who knows whom in the school district. The influence of social capital could also be related to the differential power of Hispanic versus Black populations in the school district (Portes, 2018). Our research could not answer this question but left us continuing to mull the dilemma of structural versus individual agency. On the one hand, we concur with Brantlinger (2001) that structural theories make it appear that external forces are in control, while "agency and deliberate intention remain invisible. Yet if there are no intentions, there is no responsibility and no possibility for change" (p. 12). Nevertheless, there is no escaping the fact that administra-tive power that comes from the top of a school district may reinforce social biases toward one group or another. While research by Bal et al. (2014) dem-onstrated that a dynamic intervention with school district stakeholders could result in structural change, we also note that this effort had support from the top leadership in the district.

In concluding our discussion of how school structures affected children, we reiterate that there was no clear-cut connection between structural issues and special education placement. The fact that poor Black children received the least adequate schooling did not mean that they were necessarily at greater risk of special education placement, since placement rates in these schools ranged from 3.5% to 9.8%. Nevertheless, the structural issues outlined in this chapter point to an accumulation of detrimental policies that combined to limit children's achievement. In some cases, this pressure pushed children at the border further toward the special education end of the performance spectrum. However, *whether or not children would be placed depended more on the context of each school than on the child's own performance.* In the following chapter, we consider the roles of race and culture in these children's educational contexts.

CHAPTER 4

Cultural Consonance, Dissonance, and the Nuances of Racism

I guess you're looking for racial bias in referrals. But all the students here are Black!

—School administrator

In the era of Black Lives Matter and the intense backlash against Critical Race Theory (CRT), the notion of systemic or institutional racism is an anathema to many who fear that their history will define them in negative ways. In the foregoing chapter, we discussed the pros and cons of structuralism versus individual agency. In this chapter, we reiterate: To say that discrimination is systemic or "institutional" is not to say that individuals bear no responsibility for it. In the case of schools, it is in the privacy of the classroom that each individual teacher bears the responsibility of being the mediator of the larger ecology. In this chapter, we ask: How does institutional racism play out in the classroom?

One of the first reactions we received from school personnel in many schools was exemplified by the quotation that introduces this chapter. Many school personnel believed that the concept of overrepresentation was not relevant in schools where Black or Hispanic students predominated.

Reflecting on this statement brings us to a deeper understanding of the complexity of racism. The commonsense notion behind school personnel's view was that racially discriminatory practice cannot be found within a racially homogenous population. Certainly, in the absence of a second ethnic group it is not possible to say that one child was referred over another because of race. However, it is still possible that professionals' views of a child may be influenced by aspects of the child's racial identity that become interwoven with historical stereotypes of low intelligence, stigmatized behaviors, poverty, or detrimental family circumstances. In such a situation, the issue becomes the rate of referral to special education in a school rather than disproportionality in that school. A high rate of referral may be related to prejudices based on combined racism, classism, or cultural hegemony. Further, the possibility of racism becoming internalized by its victims has long been noted

(Clark, 1965; Delgado & Stefancic, 2000), with the implication that individuals may engage in race-based discriminatory practice against members of their own group.

Our findings were not identical in all schools. In some schools we saw clear-cut examples, even patterns, of educational practice that seemed to be affected by racist or classist preconceptions. However, in most schools the findings were ambiguous, even contradictory, as we observed across and within classrooms. Thus, as we discuss various aspects of this theme, we will offer vignettes illustrating different findings, but only in rare cases will we argue that any one of these represented a general pattern.

RACISM AS A STRUCTURAL ISSUE

CRT is not new. The essential insight that the historical legacy of racism is so deeply built into the nation's social structures and policies that it operates as an often-unrecognized insidious ideology has been explained by scholars too numerous to mention (e.g., Bonilla-Silva, 1996; Crenshaw, 1989; Delgado & Stefancic, 2000; Ladson-Billings & Tate, 1995; Ladson-Billings, 2021). It is no wonder that the current furor over the concept comes as a surprise to many scholars and teachers who have been introducing their students to this concept for decades.

Indeed, it is well known that, despite our nation's official ideology of equity, data on inequity in public services, including education (CDC, 2022; Darling-Hammond & Post, 2000; U.S. Department of Education, 2001) and health (National Academy of Sciences, 2002), indicate the ongoing impact of the legacy of racist beliefs on the social, political, and economic structures of the society. As Tate (2008) observed, the very location into which a child is born presents him or her with a "geography of opportunity" that sets the stage for success or failure. How does this legacy become perpetuated in schools?

Essed (1991), arguing that the distinction between individual and institutional racism is a false dichotomy that obscures the role of individual agency, proposed the term "everyday racism" as the intersection of microsociological and macrosociological dimensions of racism. Practices and meanings that have developed as a result of "socialized racist notions" (p. 52) become normative within our daily routines and appear as the "common sense . . . rules for perceiving and dealing with the other" (Bonilla-Silva, 1996, p. 474).

The idea that racist practice may be so interwoven into the affective landscape of classrooms as to be hard to isolate and document gives rise to several questions: Exactly how do racist attitudes infiltrate the classroom? Is there an important difference between personally held prejudice and discriminatory practice? Does the "whiteness of teacher education" matter (Sleeter, 2017)? If a teacher holds racist beliefs, will it be evident in the kinds of decisions she makes about children? Will it be evident to the children themselves? Will it

affect their performance? Irvine (1990) answers these questions in the affir-
mative, stating:

> Part of the puzzle of black non-achievement has to be related to this predicament:
> Some teachers are in classrooms with black and low-income students whom they
> prefer not to teach and, even worse, do not like as individuals. (p. 48)

There have been many approaches to explaining how negative attitudes
affect students. The "self-fulfilling prophecy" (Merton, 1948; Rosenthal
& Jacobson, 1968) argues that children respond to teachers' expectations
of them. Ogbu (1987), Fordham (1988), and others have interpreted low
achievement of Black students as a form of resistance and withdrawal by the
students themselves. Spencer (1995) has argued that student resistance must
be viewed in terms of normal responses of youth at different developmental
periods, and Steele's (1997) research has demonstrated that perceived "stereotype threat" can depress Black students' academic functioning and test
scores. A study by Jussim et al. (1996) goes further, suggesting that Black students' academic performance is actually more vulnerable to negative teacher
perceptions than is the performance of their White peers. In a well-controlled
study of 1,664 6th-graders, these researchers found that teacher perceptions
had a negative impact three times greater on the test scores and grades of
Black students than that on those of White students.

Beyond personal interactions and perceptions, a large body of literature
has focused on culture and cultural hegemony as the mediators of discriminatory practices. Thus, Gay (2010) makes a subtle distinction between attitudes to race and to culture, arguing that "while most teachers are not
blatant racists, many probably are cultural hegemonists. They expect all
students to behave according to the school's cultural standards of normal-
ity" (p. 46). Gay proposes that the goal should be "culturally responsive caring" by teachers who are at the same time "academic task-masters" (p. 75).
Recent iterations of culturally responsive pedagogy (e.g., Ladson-Billings,
1994) have called for culturally sustaining approaches that explicitly value
and extend, rather than replace, children's home cultures (Paris & Alim,
2017). Pressing further into a critical perspective, Hernandez et al. (2022)
relate special education disproportionality directly to general education
pedagogy, which they propose should foreground a culturally responsive
education systems approach. Moreover, scholars in Disability Studies (DS)
have pointed to the hegemony of ableism in all aspects of the school experience, resulting in deleterious outcomes, especially for students who experience multiple stigmas based on intersections of race, gender, and ability
(Boskovich et al., 2019).

As we searched for examples and counterexamples of biased practice,
we treated issues of cultural hegemony in curriculum content as beyond our
scope. We focused instead on the cultural contexts of schools, interpersonal
communications, and referral practices.

Cultural Hegemony as a Contextual Bias

The concept of cultural hegemony (Gramsci, 1971) means that the cultural style, beliefs, and practices of the mainstream of a society infiltrate the values and behaviors of all sectors of the society and are valued and privileged above all others. Thus, public contexts explicitly and implicitly favor the dominant culture, which, in the case of the United States, is derived from what Spindler and Spindler (1990) called the "referent ethniclass"—or White, middle-class Americans. This is certainly the case in schools. We refer to these biases as contextual to distinguish them from the specific actions of individual faculty and staff.

The hegemony of this group means that a bias in its favor is built into most public situations, resulting in a sense of cultural consonance for some and dissonance for others. Let us consider the meaning of *cultural consonance* for a moment. We could define it as a comfort level that does not require one to change one's accent, one's language, one's tone of voice, or one's laughter, or as an environment where language preference, customs, and interaction style are shared and implicitly valued by all. It is natural for most of us to prefer such a setting, although members of many minority groups, through necessity, develop skills in becoming "border crossers" (Giroux & McLaren, 1994). As the notion of "White privilege" suggests (McIntosh, 1989), the opposite is not necessarily true, in that most White middle-class Americans can choose not to cross over into minority cultures.

Although we noted nuances of cultural difference in the public areas of schools in which Hispanic or African American students predominated, it was clear that middle-class Anglo American culture was the expected currency of classrooms. It was also clear that students most familiar with this culture were at an advantage affectively, if not cognitively. Arising from this fact is the question: Is cultural consonance between teachers and students a requirement for success in schools? Our answer is no, since we saw effective and ineffective teachers of all ethnicities working with diverse groups of children. The counselor in one of the predominantly Black, inner-city schools was adamant on this point, exclaiming:

> The best-qualified teacher should be the teacher for the job. There's a teacher who's been called all kind of White names, but she was good. . . . If you care enough about the kids, you're gonna do the job. . . . But a workshop isn't really going to do it. It has to be your heart. It has to be strong.

We do believe, though, that cultural consonance was a plus, once the basic requirements of good teaching were met.

Understanding across cultures can be hard to accomplish in the face of the U.S. history of racial oppression. An African American community involvement specialist at the same school as the counselor cited above felt strongly that there needed to be more African American teachers at the school, because other teachers could not understand the community as well. She said:

> I think that basically it is because they are different. I mean if they were to just study Black culture, maybe they would understand. And there again, I came up during the time of Dr. Martin Luther King. I know what it is to be segregated. I know what it is to be looked down upon because of my race. I remember when I first started, when the Whites didn't want us there but they had to because of the law. . . . If they could truly, truly, truly know and get down with our culture and understand what poverty really is, what kind of fights there are for you. And we shouldn't have to fight, I was born here. They just get more things just given to them and we have to fight. And don't get me started there!

As noted in the introductory chapter, the last sentence underscores the fact that racial tensions in this study ran in many directions (Portes, 2018). A notion of "people of color" as a generalized group, distinct from Anglo American Whites, does not work in this community, since many Hispanics in the region generally do not see themselves, and are not seen as, "people of color." This teacher's reference to a privileged "they" who, implicitly, were not "born here," represented a theme of resentment common among African Americans in this city—a belief that immigrants, particularly from Hispanic countries, tend to get preferential treatment and allowances that are not available to Black populations. Also, because many Hispanics in the area have a combination of Caucasian features, relative wealth and status, or both, they tend to be accorded a higher place in the community's ethnic ranking. This was explicitly stated by a Black faculty member in a predominantly Hispanic school, who spoke of the difficulties experienced by students who were not Hispanic, such as an African American girl who was suffering from low self-esteem because she "does not look like" the rest of her classmates. This teacher spoke also of racial bias among her colleagues. She said:

> Here they make sure that you understand the distinction, you're Black. And this is a White person, a Hispanic, and I feel we need to get away from that. And when I came in one day in that class, one adult told me, "I'm having a problem, this Black kid has been disrespectful," and I was very upset. And, I cannot hide my feelings when I'm upset and I said, "I'm sorry, but this Black kid has a name." Let's call him by his first name. So, already you can see, if the person is talking to me as an adult and using that, what happens when I'm not around in that room?

Although we saw many Hispanic and other teachers who related very well to African American children, information from several schools indicated that many teachers had a preference for the ESOL group. The comparison between African American and Hispanic children was not only offered by non-Black personnel, however. An African American faculty member who had been moved to a predominantly Hispanic school described her 5th-graders as being "super innocent . . . like babies . . . with their Barbies and their . . . Pokémon cards." By contrast, she said, 2nd-graders in the African American neighborhood "knew about drugs . . . about sex . . . about guns."

Teaching the Culture of Power

While the negative aspects of inner-city communities are clearly detrimental to many children, our observations of strong teachers in the inner-city schools showed that children being "street smart" or "too grown" did not mean they could not be taught the behavioral and academic skills needed for school success. In the face of much discussion over the extent to which success in school requires that students meet the expectations of the dominant culture (e.g., Fordham, 1988; O'Connor & Fernandez, 2006; Ogbu, 1987), we concur with Delpit (1988), who argued that explicit inculcation of the "culture of power" is needed, along with strong support of the children's home cultures and languages. Thus, the children are given access to the cultural capital that will contribute to their success in the mainstream. In the following chapter, we will offer an exemplar of this process—a strong African American teacher in a predominantly African American school who argued that teaching the culture of power was exactly her purpose in explicitly teaching acceptable school behaviors to her kindergartners.

DOCUMENTING BEHAVIOR AND INTERPRETING RACISM

While there was ample evidence that race and culture were inextricably woven into the fabric of the school contexts we observed, personal racial bias in classroom practice was not easy to document. Perhaps it was the tightness of the weave that made it difficult for us to isolate racism from all the other "isms" that pervaded our interviews and observations. In our research we looked for bias in terms of negative or positive preconceptions or preferences expressed by teachers as well as in terms of negative or positive relationships with students. We sought examples of behaviors that appeared to reflect these essentially intangible aspects of classroom interactions.

We found that relationships were easy to document, whether positive or negative. Positive relationships could be seen in the physical affection between a child and teacher; smiles or laughter that produced a good feeling in the classroom; or a teacher who would take an angry or sad child aside and counsel her gently, out of earshot of the other children. Negative relationships were evident when a teacher insulted children and their families to their faces or in front of the entire class, and in the angry or defiant expressions on children's faces when that teacher addressed them. In all schools, both positive and negative relationships were evidenced between teachers and children of their own ethnicity, as well as across ethnicities. However, it was much harder to determine whether racial or social-class bias motivated these relationships. We will use one classroom as an example of how difficult it can be to determine the presence of bias, despite teachers' explicit statements and researchers' nagging intuitions. The story is also an example of the possibility of a teacher being able to practice professionalism despite the presence of personal biases.

AN EXEMPLAR: "VERY GOOD, MAH MAN!"

Ms. Q, a White, Hispanic teacher in an inner-city school, was potentially a strong teacher. However, a tendency to be unduly harsh undermined this impression. She described the African American children and their community in extremely derogatory terms, stating, for example, that her 1st-graders did not know "how to walk, how to sit in a chair." Concluding her list of deficiencies, she exclaimed: "It's cultural!"

We observed Ms. Q's classroom twice toward the end of our first (academic) year of research. Seeing her getting inches away from a child's face and reprimanding her in an extremely loud and harsh voice for some minor infraction, we had to assume that her negative attitude to this child and others had been building throughout the year. On the second occasion a few weeks later, a visitor joined our observation and expressed shock at Ms. Q's harsh manner with the children, noting that she seemed either to not like teaching or not like the students. Ms. Q seemed unhappy and angry.

In the fall of the following year, Ms. Q was a changed person. She greeted us with smiles, exclaiming delightedly that she was happy that she had been assigned "the ESOL [infusion] class." The class included approximately one-third Hispanic students, whom she described as "generally calmer and better behaved." Certainly, in our eight observations of this classroom, we saw that Ms. Q's relationships with the group as a whole were much better than with the previous year's class, and we noted her strong instructional skills. Indeed, both the children and the teacher were "calmer and better behaved."

Despite Ms. Q's characterization of the superior behavior of the Hispanic children, our observations showed that the troublesome children were as often Hispanic as African American. Two Hispanic boys, Juan and Francisco, though reasonably compliant under Ms. Q's firm hand, would literally run wild in the less structured setting of the music class, tormenting the teacher and instigating others to do the same. One or two other children stood out, such as Jimmy, an African American boy whose family problems were severe and who would act out occasionally, and Tomás, a Hispanic boy who tended to be a bit hyperactive when he was bored. Andre was an African American boy about whom the teacher complained consistently. This was a puzzle to us, since in four out of five observations where he was a target focus (unknown to him), we found him very attentive and eager, shooting his hand up to answer, but seldom being called on by the teacher.

Ms. Q's greater empathy for the Hispanic children was evident in the way she interpreted their difficulties. For example, after describing Juan as "a very angry child" and Francisco as having behavior problems but "very manageable," she said she "feels bad" for these two, because they may have a learning problem and the bad behavior may be a result of frustration. She did not express such feelings of sympathy for any of the African American children with behavior and academic problems, although they were all lower academically than Juan and Francisco, yet generally better behaved. In fact, Juan's Scholastic Aptitude Test (SAT) scores were above those of the group generally—at the 62nd percentile in math and 25th in reading; Francisco's scores were at the 21st percentile in math and 17th in reading. Andre and Jimmy, whom Ms. Q described as having behavior problems, had much lower scores—both around the 2nd percentile in reading and the 10th in math, indicating that their learning needs were greater than those of both the Hispanic boys.

Despite this evident ethnic preference, Ms. Q's feelings did not seem to affect her referrals. This teacher was one of the three highest-referring teachers across the 12 schools; the other two were Anglo American teachers, also in predominantly Black schools. However, we noted that Ms. Q used the CST process as a supportive as well as an evaluative mechanism. That year, she referred 18 students of varying ethnicities, about half of whom were found eligible for special education services. At the CST conferences, with the exception of negative interactions with Andre's mother, Ms. Q treated the parents with respect and seemed to use the committee for the benefit of the children, often by seeking parents' cooperation through daily or weekly home-school contracts. One such case was Jimmy, about whom Ms. Q was concerned because of his mother's alcoholism, but whom she did not feel needed special education placement. We concluded that, while we did note ethnic bias in Ms. Q's interactions with the children, she did engage in an equitable and helpful referral process.

Despite this teacher's strengths, however, in our classroom observations we noted a steady undertone of cultural bias or what might be termed "micro-aggressions" (Pierce, 1970). Our final illustration of this is of a particularly subtle form, whereby the teacher's attitude seemed to be condescending toward the child's ethnicity and or language. In the example we give here, this might not be evident to anyone who has not experienced such condescension, but we believe it would be understood by people who have. Ms. Q, who normally spoke in Standard English to her class, became effusive when an African American boy who seldom participated gave a surprisingly good answer. She exclaimed: "Good! Very good, mah man!" The switch to an approximation of African American vernacular was out of place and made the two researchers present feel distinctly uncomfortable. Both researchers were Black and their immediate exchange of glances confirmed that their gut reactions had been identical.

To be clear on this example, the impression of condescension did not come merely from the fact of a Hispanic teacher's using a Black vernacular phrase. It was that this was so unusual for Ms. Q, so out of character, that it came across as contrived. By contrast, in a classroom in another similar school, we noted an excellent Hispanic kindergarten teacher whose regular repertoire of interaction included terms of endearment commonly used by African American teachers, such as *baby* and *honey*. These expressions seemed natural to the teacher in the context of affectionate and caring relationships with her students. We believe that these two groups of children would know the difference.

PERCEIVED RACIAL BIAS IN CLASSROOM ARRANGEMENTS AND REFERRALS

Our sense of "easy to spot but hard to prove" bias was frequently triggered in schools in which African American students were in the minority, whether among Anglo American or Hispanic peers. In such classrooms, it was common to see an African American, usually male, student seated separately in the classroom, often at the teacher's desk or at the back of the room. This child might be the only, or one of a couple of, African American children in the room, so this seating arrangement was very noticeable. We were not always aware of what behaviors had earned the children this distinction, but we did see some classrooms where the children so seated did, indeed, display behaviors that the teacher found troubling. Occasionally, though not usually, the teachers in these rooms were African Americans.

The best exemplar of this pattern was Sunnybrook, the school that Matthew attended. African American students from a relatively low-income neighborhood were bused into this affluent, predominantly Anglo American neighborhood and constituted approximately 17% of the student population. The distinction between the two groups was marked by common references to students being from either "east or west of the highway." As we will detail later in the book, the high achievement of the majority of students made that of the African American students seem lower than it would have seemed at low-income schools. The same was true of their behaviors, which were perceived by school personnel as less compliant and more troublesome. The principal of this school commented on the fact that such judgments are relative to local norms and expectations.

The teachers whom we observed intensively in this school were both very strong, one an African American and one an Anglo American. In observing their classrooms, we detected no differential behavior toward the children based on ethnicity. However, all of the six referrals from the latter teacher's class were for African American children. Three of these were found eligible for special education—one as ID and two as LD. Unfortunately, we were not able to gain permission to examine the level of these students' work. The other three did not go to testing—one because the parents did not sign consent, another because it was agreed to get the child into tutoring and monitor her progress, and for the third we do not know the outcome. The

African American teacher referred two children, Austin and Matthew, both also African American, who were found eligible for LD and EBD respectively. We will report on these cases in detail in our later discussion of the construction of these disabilities.

Despite an initial welcome from this school's administration, as our research progressed, we had considerable difficulty obtaining access to detailed records of placement rates. All indications were that this was a school where much more intensive research was needed to ascertain the reasons for the disproportionately high rate of placement of Black students. Indeed, we noted an approximately equal distribution of White students and Black students in the school's LD classrooms. This balance led one of the special education teachers to say that the numbers were not disproportionate, since they were equal. Clearly this teacher had not reflected on the meaning of the term, for Black students represented 17% of the school's population, but approximately 50% of her class. In reflecting on our findings, we felt frustrated at our inability to adequately probe the processes in this school. Not only was the pattern similar to research finding that Black overrepresentation was evident in predominantly White high-income districts (Fish, 2019; Oswald, Coutinho, Best, & Singh,1999), but, we believe, the presence of court-ordered school desegregation was also salient. Eitle (2002), in an analysis of survey data on 1,203 school districts nationwide, found that Black overrepresentation in special education programs increased in districts that were operating under court-ordered desegregation. Eitle concluded that the pattern reflected "alternative forms of segregation" (p. 599) being practiced by school or school district administrators. Whether or not the discriminatory effect was intentional in this school, we agree with Fish that the context of a forced racial mixture had many disadvantages for Black students, one of which could have been increased likelihood of special education placement.

RACE/ETHNICITY IN TEAM MEMBERSHIP, REFERRALS, AND TEACHING STYLES

In most schools, faculty membership on the CSTs was ethnically diverse, revealing an attempt to reflect the mixture of the student population. However, since district policy required that membership include an administrator and a counselor, ethnicity could not be a criterion for these two key positions. Additional members were usually a general education teacher, the referring teacher, and other ad hoc members according to the case being considered. Some schools included the psychologist as a regular team member.

In one inner-city school serving a student population that was 99% African American, three issues related to teacher ethnicity came to our attention. One was the complaint of an irate parent that the CST comprised only White members. The administration explained that this was coincidental, since the requirement is that the AP, counselor, and psychologist serve on the

CST. All three happened to be White. The fourth team member had to be a teacher, and the teacher thought most appropriate by the administration was a reading specialist who also happened to be White. After the parent's challenge, however, the administration changed the CST composition to include an African American teacher who was much respected in the school as an excellent teacher.

The second issue related to ethnicity at this school was the fact that most special education referrals came from White teachers. Some personnel believed that this reflected Black teachers' lack of confidence in the special education system, while others argued that it might be related to a third issue—differential behavior management styles.

The question of behavior management was particularly interesting because it reflected the notion of cultural fit with African American students' behavioral styles (Gay, 2010). Further, Neal and colleagues (2003) found that White teachers interpreted African American students' culturally based movement styles as indicative of aggression, low achievement, and potential for special education referral. We heard this opinion from an African American professional in this school who believed that the expressive verbal and physical interaction style displayed by many African American children tended to intimidate some Anglo American teachers and that the children, perceiving this, acted out as a result. She was speaking in general, not just regarding this school. However, our observations of 11 of the 16 general education classrooms in this small school did reveal differential classroom management styles that, to some extent, seemed to relate to teacher ethnicity. Specifically, what we refer to as the "passive" style was displayed only by Anglo American teachers.

Authoritarian Style

There were three teachers, one African American, one Hispanic, and one White, whose management styles were characterized by a stern authoritarianism. The White teacher ran a calm, very structured classroom in which students typically scored well, although we noted a great deal of negative ignoring of a child who was working well but whose grooming left much to be desired. The Hispanic teacher's class was generally chaotic. She made sporadic efforts to use positive reinforcement such as stickers, but mostly resorted to yelling and threats. The African American teacher used an overly rigid structure and constant yelling. The researcher commented in her notes that, while in this room, she felt as though she was in "boot camp."

Authoritative, but Friendly

Five teachers (four African American and one Hispanic) displayed this approach, four very effectively and one moderately so. While none were effusive in their manner, all used a lot of verbal praise and enforced clear standards for behavior. Their instructional approaches varied, but all included explicit instruction, consistent monitoring of seat work, and relevance to children's lives and interests. Overall, these teachers were effortless in their reinforcement of behavior and their quietly authoritative handling of their students. The children had no doubt about who was in charge. Two African American teachers in this group had the reputation of being excellent teachers, and both demonstrated what Ladson-Billings (1994) has referred to as a key feature of effective teachers of inner-city children—an explicit affiliation with the community, even the neighborhood of their students. One of these teachers told us that she works in this school to "give something back to the community," while the other spoke of her willingness to go directly to students' homes to talk with parents when issues arose, a strategy which, she said, "the White teachers won't do!"

Passive Style

Teachers exhibiting this style made little effort to impose authority on the class. All three teachers who fitted this pattern were Anglo American. At the most extreme end was a music teacher, whose total neglect of classroom management resulted in chaos, which will be described in the following chapter. The behavior in the classrooms of the other two teachers was not as extreme, but the teachers' management styles were characterized by minimal or no intervention related to troubling behavior. One of these began her lesson with a creative approach—using a puppet that initially gained the children's attention and enthusiasm—but her ignoring of two disruptive individuals gradually led to total inattention and finally a chaotic environment. At the end of the lesson, the teacher, who had started with a friendly and relaxed style, was visibly angry. The other teacher was Ms. E, whom we observed twice, once in a 1st-grade class in the spring and then in the subsequent fall when she was assigned to a 2nd-grade class. In both classrooms, this teacher showed a low-key, friendly manner toward the children but made no effort whatsoever to curtail the early signs of disruptive behavior. Rather, she ignored these signs, allowed the behavior to escalate and spread to other members of the class, and then demonstrated an expression of resignation and frustration that she had been assigned a class with all the troublesome children. A brief excerpt from the 2nd-grade observation will illustrate this point:

> The children work quietly for about 10 minutes, moving from one worksheet to the next, while the teacher circulates looking at work. Larry enters the room. He never really settles down. Within minutes, he starts playing with his chair, rocking and balancing it. Next, he goes over to a girl who is standing next to her chair, and he whisks her chair away, grinning. The girl responds with a show of annoyance but is smiling. The teacher is standing quite close to them but with her back to them as she looks at a child's work. She does not turn around

or show any awareness of Larry's behavior. A boy in a green shirt gets up and starts to walk around. He goes and sits on the high stool at the blackboard in the front of the room and looks around the room with a grin. Soon he gets down from the stool and starts a slow chase after Larry. They make it through a couple of rows of desks and then the teacher looks up and says the boy's name softly. He sits down for a few minutes. Larry is still walking around . . . the noise level is gradually rising. . . . The boy in the green shirt gets up and starts to chase after Larry until he gets to the row where the teacher is standing and she reaches out and stops him by putting an arm gently on his shoulder. She tells him to go and copy his homework from the board. He goes to his desk and, standing, copies the work neatly into his notebook. . . . By now all the children in the room are talking to each other, moving around, and the general sense of disorder is escalating steadily. . . . When the children leave for their Spanish class, the teacher turns to us with a resigned expression and says, "You see what I mean?"

Ms. E's tone of resignation indicated a pervasive sense of low expectation for her students. As one of the highest-referring teachers in the school, she had, in the previous year, referred almost half her class. She told our team that she did not believe in the "cooperative consultation" (prereferral) process, because she believed in handling the children's problems by herself until she was sure they really needed to be evaluated. She believed that the children in the school were becoming steadily "worse" because of their detrimental home and community settings. Thus, she felt that the team should "trust" her judgment and that her referrals should go forward to evaluation.

From these observations, we cannot come to any conclusions about ty-pologies of behavior management according to teacher ethnicity. However, this limited, but in-depth, view offers examples of concerns frequently ex-pressed in the field about low expectations and about cultural mismatch in behavioral management, particularly in reference to the difficulties of some Anglo American teachers in handling behavior issues with African American children. We are not suggesting that teachers' ethnicity needs to be matched to that of their students. Rather, we concur with scholars such as Gay (2010), Cartledge and Kourea (2008), and Ballenger (1992), who argue that caring, responsive teachers can become aware of different cultural patterns in chil-dren's behavior and can learn strategies and approaches that may work better with either individuals or groups.

Most important to this discussion is the role of poorly managed class-rooms in referrals to special education. As we will note at length in our chap-ter on decision-making at the conference table, Ms. E's total lack of behavior management was never mentioned when her referrals were brought to the CST conference. One of her students was Kanita, a child found to "qual-ify" for emotional disturbance, whose case we will describe in detail in later chapters.

CROSSING THE BIAS BARRIERS

To what extent did the various kinds of bias we have noted show up in most classroom interactions? We cannot generalize across classrooms or schools. We saw examples of them all. However, we also saw examples of many teachers who successfully crossed the barriers of bias. There was no single route to this success, since these teachers represented a range of teaching and personality styles. Perhaps the only common thread we could feel sure of was that these teachers expected the children to work and to succeed, yet they were capable also of a light touch that reached out to the children as people worthy of respect. They seemed to illustrate Gay's (2010) model of "warm, demanding, academic task-masters" (p. 75). The following examples will illustrate.

In one classroom in a predominantly Haitian American school, a veteran Anglo American teacher was simply a very good teacher, despite the fact that she was a very high referrer. She was strict, but she tried to be fair. Laughing at herself as an old dinosaur who couldn't understand the children's complicated schedules, she would give the children the responsibility of telling her when they had to go to some special program. She was humorous and entertaining while also being very serious about the children's learning. She cared if the children did well and they knew it. Despite the complaints of many teachers that the SFA materials were boring and repetitive, this teacher made wonderful use of them, and she adapted some of the SFA strategies to the skill levels and interests of her students (for more detail on this, see Klingner et al., 2006). For example, she explained that the SFA "jump in reading" is supposed to have children "jump in" spontaneously to read aloud. Her children, she felt, were not ready for that, so she modified the activity by moving quickly around the room, touching children on their shoulders to indicate their turn to read. As she chose the children, she would put on a comical facial expression and wiggle her legs to indicate her own excitement at deciding which child to call on. The children giggled and became very excited waiting for their turns. Every child was called on.

A Cuban American teacher in a predominantly African American school used humor and her own natural spontaneity to build wonderful relationships with her students. For example:

> She encourages them to think of a special day in their life. She breaks out singing the song "Unforgettable." Then she goes around the classroom brainstorming with the class. The students give examples of special days in their life. She encourages everyone to volunteer an answer, reminding them that it won't be wrong—she just wants them to think.

In a school that served a very-low-income community of African American and Hispanic students, negative comments from faculty often suggested biases against the former group. In the class of one of our selected teachers, a lively Anglo American New Yorker, we saw no sign of negative interactions with any children. Her natural humor and strong relationships with the children made behavior management seem easy, as in the following example:

> While they worked on their assignment, the students spoke freely, but quietly. (They seemed to know the limitations for acceptable activity.) A few students who had questions about their assignments or who sought approval for their work went to the teacher while she helped an African American girl whose hair was braided and beaded. . . . Other students followed suit and, after a few minutes, seven students surrounded her. She said to the class in a direct but soft voice, "Now listen. How many teachers and how many students are there here?" "One and thirty-two," called out most of the students in unison. Then, she asked the class, "Can I talk with each of you at the same time?" All, almost all, said, "No." One boy, Osvaldo, however, said, "Yes." The teacher heard him and responded, "Well, Osvaldo, it may seem like that to you, since I'm always talking to you." The whole class roared with laughter, especially the teacher and Osvaldo.

In a predominantly African American inner-city school, where negative stereotypes of children's families were openly expressed by faculty of all ethnicities, the researcher sometimes sought refuge in the class of an outstanding African American teacher who addressed her boys and girls with the titles *Mr.* and *Ms.* Halfway through an excellent math lesson, we could feel the sense of solidarity occasioned by the teacher's spontaneous shift from Standard English into an African American tone and accent as she exhorted her class to keep their attention focused: "Y'all wit me?" she challenged, to which the students chorused a rousing, "Yeah!"

CONCLUSIONS

Our classroom observations do not give us clear-cut answers to the question of whether racial bias against particular groups contributed to ethnic disproportionality in special education. The subtleties of racism are difficult to document, and though we could detect it in various "moments of exclusion" (Lareau & Horvat, 1999) that we observed in schools, we had no direct evidence of its contribution to disproportionality, since there was no clear pattern, across schools, of referrals by teacher ethnicity.

Yet we could see clearly that racial bias was present in the nuances of teachers' tone and manner toward children. It was present in the built-in hegemony that creates a "goodness of fit" (Keogh, 2000) between a school and some of its students, but not others. It was present in some teachers' discomfort with, even fear of, the behavioral styles of their students and in the low expectations that accompanied this discomfort. We suspect that the more vulnerable children were affected by these biases in ways that our research was not able to substantiate. In contrast, bias was countered by professionals whose authenticity allowed them to develop the skills of a border-crosser (Giroux & McLaren, 1994).

While teacher bias can most often only be inferred, teachers' behaviors are readily evident. In the following chapter we will paint a broad picture of the types of instruction and behavior management we observed across the 12 schools. We argue that the institutional bias against schools serving the poorest, Black populations resulted in an imbalance of teacher quality that limited these students' opportunity to learn. This placed the most vulnerable students at increased risk of school failure and special education placement.

CHAPTER 5

In the Classroom
Opportunity to Learn

We ask whether the school experience itself contributes to racial
disproportion in academic outcomes and behavioral problems that lead
to placement in special and gifted education . . . our answer is "yes."

—M. Suzanne Donovan & Christopher T. Cross,
Minority Students in Special and Gifted Education (2002)

Six hundred and seventy-nine observations over 3 years revealed a clear trend in which the weakest classrooms were in schools serving the lowest-income Black populations. This reflected the pattern noted earlier of a discrepancy in teacher qualifications according to the economic level of the student body. In these schools, the quality of teacher instruction and classroom management was extremely variable, ranging from excellent to absolutely unacceptable. In most other schools, teacher quality was much more even, with no teachers exhibiting the extremely weak skills observed in the low-income, predominantly Black schools.

What do we mean by "extremely weak" teaching? We mean classrooms in which teachers were often distraught or angry; where rough reprimands, idle threats, and personal insults were common; and where teachers' attempts to curb out-of-seat and off-task behavior were either sporadic and ineffective or unduly harsh. In these classrooms, instruction was frequently offered with no context, no attempt to connect to children's previous learning or personal experience. Here, rote instruction took the place of meaningful explanation and dialogue. Often, poorly planned lessons were at the heart of the problem.

In the previous chapter, we offered an example of an excellent Anglo American teacher, in a predominantly Haitian school, who effectively crossed "the bias barriers" in her instruction. This teacher was one of a handful of excellent teachers in the school. In a classroom just below hers, a 2nd-grade teacher, trying to use group work, had not thought through the details or timing of the tasks. When the children became inattentive or disruptive, the teacher would give up on the activity and introduce another poorly structured task. Another very weak 2nd-grade teacher tried to recapture children's attention by suddenly requiring them all to raise their hands or put their hands on their heads for a few moments. Across the hallway, a 3rd-grade teacher continually threatened punishments that he never implemented and finally resorted to a threat to keep the children from going to lunch, which, of course, he could not do. Upstairs, another 3rd-grade teacher would repeatedly insult and physically threaten children.

We contend that this discrepant teacher quality limited poor Black children's opportunity to learn. While not the only factor, this was a key feature that pushed vulnerable children toward the failing end of the continuum. We present examples from two contrasting schools: In the first, there were only a few teachers whom we rated as highly effective, and in the second, there were only a few we considered weak.

CONTRASTING SCHOOLS: INEQUITY IN OPPORTUNITIES TO LEARN

Creekside Elementary: Few Effective Teachers

We conducted 33 observations across 18 general education K–3 classrooms at this predominantly Black school, where 97% of the students were on free or reduced-price lunch. Our overall evaluation was that three teachers were very effective, seven were average, and eight were weak. As in many of the schools serving low-income, predominantly Black students, we witnessed a great deal of yelling and many teachers who really seemed frazzled, frustrated, and uncertain about how to manage their students. In many classrooms, students seemed out of control, with very little teaching or learning taking place. When we did see instruction, much of it was uninspired, to say the least (for example, of the rote or "do the exercises in the book" variety), as in our first example below.

The following brief excerpt is from our field notes of an observation in a 3rd-grade classroom, taught by an Anglo American teacher with several years' experience. We considered this teacher to have adequate control of the class, but to be weak in instruction. This teacher's failure to engage students in meaningful learning activities was typical of the instruction we saw in many classrooms in inner-city schools and is of great concern because it compromises students' opportunity to learn. The excerpt focuses on the lack of context for the lesson as well as on the teachers' low expectations for students' performance:

> It's time for social studies. The teacher hastily explains that students are to copy a sentence from the board: "There are seven continents: . . ." She emphasizes, "To get an A, you must write neatly on the lines and include your name and the date."
>
> [Observer's Comments: There was no look at a map, or identification of the continents, or linking with prior knowledge, or questioning, or checking for understanding. The teacher read the

sentence to the students very quickly and told them to copy it. That was it. What struck me most was the low level of the work—no thinking involved whatsoever that I could tell. And I doubt much learning took place, either, except that Ms. A really likes for writing to be on the lines. And this is a third-grade class!]

The next example is from a lesson on the five senses that was so poorly con-ceptualized as to make little sense to 1st-graders in a self-contained ESOL class for students at a beginning level of English proficiency. The teacher, who was Anglo American, and relatively new, was very verbal and rarely used the visual cues and other ESOL strategies that might have facilitated both her work and her students' learning. The example demonstrates ineffective ESOL instruction as well as poor classroom management:

The class was learning about the five senses. . . . The teacher said, "The last sense is the sense of touch. That means you feel." The teacher directed students to feel the floor with their elbows. "Can you feel it?"
   [Observer's Comments: I noted that kids couldn't follow this, didn't understand what to do.]
   The teacher yelled, "Some of you are being extremely rude. You are moving all around." Then she asked more calmly, "So you did feel the floor with your elbows, but do you normally feel with your elbow?" A few students responded, "No." The teacher asked, "What am I using to pick this up?" Next she yelled again, "You just finished telling me you were listening, Ezekiel. Were you lying to me? I'm only going to call on the people who are listening." Then she asked, "What am I using?" A girl said that she was using her hands and the teacher responded, "Excellent." Then she said, "Jefferson, touch my leg." "Go ahead. . . . what are you going to use to touch my leg?" Jefferson responded, "I use my hand." The teacher next snapped her fingers. . . . She turned to a boy standing in the corner (being disciplined): "I'm very unhappy with you. Turn around." To everyone else, she asked, "If I wanted to eat cake, what sense would I use?" . . . The teacher said, "My point is that you use your sense of taste to decide if you like it." She yelled, "Pay attention to me, not his shoes! His shoes aren't going to give you a grade. I will." "If one more person touches shoes, I'm going to throw it in the garbage. It's important to make sure your shoes are tied, but not while I'm teaching."
   [Observer's Comments: The students weren't really following this, or "getting it." There are so many ways to teach the senses! I'm not sure how much they understood, but these are ESOL 1s and 2s and she did not use visuals or other ESOL techniques—she just talked.]

We observed in this class seven times and found that the preceding example was typical. Although this was a school where the child study team (CST) process was underused and very few referrals were made, this teacher referred seven of her students, including Ezekiel. She was very verbal, yelled a lot, and rarely used visual cues and other ESOL strategies. Yet at a CST meeting for Ezekiel, the teacher told the committee that she frequently used "visuals, manipulatives," and other ESOL techniques, "but he doesn't retain it. He can't transfer it to do it on his own." Our observations suggest, however, that Ezekiel and his classmates did not retain what was being taught because information had not been presented in comprehensible ways in the first place. This and the previous example illustrate a lack of planning and preparation for what potentially could have been rich topics of instruction. The standard of instruction in this and other, similar schools was clearly lower than that observed in schools in higher-income neighborhoods.

The following example is from a different 1st-grade class, from an observation of a science lesson taught by a Hispanic teacher who, like the previous teacher, was in her first few years of teaching. It is similar to the preceding example in that it also illustrates weak classroom management and instruction, as well as a lack of planning.

> While asking about plants and animals, she is passing around Unifix cubes for the math lesson that will follow. Jamal throws his at his neighbor. The teachers tells him, "Jamal, go to time-out for a couple of minutes." She then continues with the lesson: "Trendon is going to tell us one of the differences between plants and animals." A student says, "Plants can't walk." The teacher interrupts, "Jamal, would you please put your shoes on and turn around and put your nose in the corner." Kids are playing with their Unifix cubes. . . .
>
> More and more students are playing with their cubes. The teacher's voice rises. "If I hear another block rolling across the table, I'm going to take them away from you." She says something else about plants and animals and how animals can communicate, but then yells, "Leave them still [the blocks]! Didn't I say not to use them yet? I don't want to see you pulling them apart." Students are still playing with blocks. (She previously had said that she would take them away, but doesn't.) Now a student holds up his cubes with his pencil stuck on top. The teacher says sternly, "Darian, take your pencil off of there." "Michael, don't sit on your desk. You can only sit on a desk when you've finished college."

If only the teacher had waited to pass around the Unifix cubes! This teacher's good intention of using manipulatives for the teaching of math concepts was defeated by the critical mistake of distributing the cubes before the appropriate time. Having introduced this inevitable distraction, the teacher followed her mistake with empty threats that continually undermined her attempts to conduct the science lesson. It seems that the natural result of such a tactical error would be evident to any adult, yet such errors were frequent in classrooms such as this. Principals in inner-city schools lamented that they were stuck with "the bottom of the barrel" when selecting new hires. As illustrated by this example, however, we often had the impression that we were watching well-meaning teachers who were not adequately prepared for their assignments. It was clear that these teachers needed extensive professional development and support, yet we saw very little of this provided.

The next example is from a 3rd-grade class taught by an experienced Black teacher who was known for being an advocate for her students. Eight students were sitting at computers working on math. Their computer screens showed pictures of ones, tens, and hundreds blocks. The teacher was instructing the rest of the class.

> The teacher is at the front of the room. She asks students to take out their math books. Most students do so. The teacher says, "Johnson, you need to get out your math book. We are on page 149." A boy by me at the computers is shouting something in a loud voice, in Haitian Creole. The teacher adds, "Get out a piece of paper." Mike and Zachary are talking loudly, fooling around and laughing. Zachary now takes out a piece of paper and writes his name. Mike does not.
>
> The boy at the computers is still talking. I hear, "Dr. Poo Poo." Another boy at the computers says, apparently to me, "Dr., he's cursing." Then to the teacher he says, "Ms. _____, he's talking about her mama [apparently mine]." The teacher says to the boy in question, "Why are you acting like this?" Another boy at the computers says to his neighbor, "Did you hear him talking about her mama?" The boy who had been shouting now calls out, "I didn't say her mama's stupid!" The teacher says, "Edgar, get off [the computer]." He does not.
>
> Now the teacher turns her attention to the class. She says, "Take out a sheet of paper. We are going to do math." In a sarcastic tone, she adds "I love the way you waste your time." "You are going to look at problems and tell me what the thermometer says. I'm going to put the problems on the board and you are going to tell me if it's cold, warm, or hot." Perhaps three students are paying attention, while the others are watching the kids who are fooling around at the computers or at their seats, talking with their neighbors. One is playing with pencils in his pencil box.

This vignette illustrates how challenging it was for teachers to try to conduct a lesson while simultaneously managing students on computers. This difficulty was evident in many of the classrooms in the inner-city schools in which this computer program had been adopted. It was certainly typical in this classroom. Further, the teacher seemed at a loss to know how to respond to some of the boys' impolite behavior and really had no control over the flow of interactions among her students. Yet, in one notable exception, we learned that these same students were capable of focused, productive engagement in a well-structured and motivating task: We observed them taking a practice test in preparation for the upcoming mandatory statewide testing, and we were struck by how engaged they were, both while taking the test and while going over the answers, enthusiastically exclaiming, "Yes!" when an answer was correct. In contrast to other "lessons," this clearly was a meaningful activity for them, in that everyone was focused on the same activity and there were no interruptions. This contrast revealed that it was not the students who were lacking, but their teacher. Their motivation to do well on the test underscores the sad conclusion that excellent minds were being wasted in this school.

Some children, of course, were fortunate to be in the classrooms of the three strong general-education teachers we observed. These teachers, two African Americans and one Hispanic, had succeeded in establishing a positive rapport with their students and were effective at management and instruction. Lessons were appropriate, engaging, and well-paced and students seemed excited about learning. High expectations were evident.

Bay Vista Elementary: Few Weak Teachers

Bay Vista was the antithesis of Creekside. At this predominantly Hispanic school, in which 68% of the students were on free or reduced-price lunch, we observed 34 K–3 general education teachers. We considered 24 of these teachers to be strong, nine to be adequate, and one to be weak. Overall, teachers seemed enthusiastic, well prepared for lessons, skilled in presentation and engagement, and "connected" with their students. We noted many examples of stimulating instruction and effective classroom management. The coordination across classrooms and within grade levels was impressive. The positive thinking among teachers, their belief that they were "doing it right" and truly helping their students seemed palpable, a feature lacking in schools such as Creekside. As we walked into classrooms, we were struck with the impression that teachers really were *teaching*, not just sitting at their desks or giving assignments.

The two examples that follow indicate the rapport that was evident between teachers and their students as well as highlight effective instruction. Teachers used praise frequently and criticism rarely. This first example, from a bilingual 1st-grade class, represents the imaginative nature of many lessons as well as context and relevance:

> The teacher was walking around the room with a plastic board that had green glitter on it. She asked the students to place their hands on the glitter and then shake hands with the student next to them. When she had finished asking all the students to do this, she explained that, like the glitter, germs are easily transferred from one person to another. She explained that the germs could not be seen like the glitter could be, and that germs could only be removed with soap and water. The teacher explained that this is why it is important to take showers and wash our hands. She asked the students what they could do to stay

healthy. Students raised their hands and waited to be called on before responding. Next the teacher explained the assignment. She told them they were to write two ways of staying healthy. She wrote the following on the board: "*Para ser saludable debo* _____. *También debo* _____." (To stay healthy I should _____. I should also _____.) The teacher handed out white notebook paper to the students. She asked them if they had any questions. No students raised their hands. The students began to work on their assignment. They were quiet, focused, and on task.

This next is from a bilingual kindergarten class:

The teacher told them that now they were going to do something special, that she had a magic word. She said, with great suspense, "*Científicos*." (Scientists.) She asked what it meant. A student said, "*Locos*." (Crazy.) The teacher shook her head and said no. Another student asked, "*Mágicos?*" (Magicians?) "No." Other students guessed, but their guesses weren't close. The teacher said that she was going to tell them. "*Son personas importantes que hacen experimentos.*" (They are important people who do experiments.) She said the last word with emphasis, and then, after a slight pause, building suspense, went on, "like discovering medicine." "They were the ones who observed that plants need water and sun to grow." The students were listening, enraptured. The teacher told them they were going to become scientists. She had them put on their thinking caps, special glasses, special gloves, and lab coats (all in pantomime). A student said, "*Y los pantolones!*" (And pants!) The teacher said that they didn't need pants because they had their lab coats. Now they were going to say the magic words and they would become scientists, "*Uno, dos, tres, cachachumbre.*" She shook all over while saying this. Then she said, "There are many intelligent and special scientists in this class." She put two glasses on each table. A student said (while she was doing this), "*Yo quiero mi mamá.*" ("I want/ love my mother.") The teacher responded, "*Yo también.*" (Me, too.) The students laughed. The teacher told them not to touch the glasses or they would get contaminated. She asked if they knew what that meant, and explained it meant "dirty." Then she let some students bring one of the cups from their table and go with her to get water.

These examples contrast noticeably with those from Creekside. Lessons were carefully planned and well prepared, and appropriate props were used. Instruction was motivating and exciting, at an appropriate level for students, with support so that they could be successful. Notably, these examples were not rare exceptions but the norm. We were confident that, in contrast to students in some of our other schools, students at Bay Vista were receiving an adequate opportunity to learn.

CONTRASTING CLASSROOMS: STUDENTS' VARIABLE
BEHAVIOR ACROSS SETTINGS

Besides revealing the pattern of variability across schools, our observations led us to a second clear-cut conclusion: Children's classroom behavior could not be assessed without reference to the skills of the teacher. We saw the same children behave very differently with an effective teacher as compared to an ineffective teacher, and we saw two classrooms side by side that were like night and day despite the fact that the children were from the same neighborhood and had the same racial and socioeconomic characteristics. We must note that the excellent teachers we saw in these schools proved absolutely that most of the children were malleable and responsive to their school environments.

In the better schools, where teacher skills were more consistent, the range of children's behavior across settings was noticeable but not extreme. In schools with wide teacher variability, contrasting behavior across settings could be dramatic. Below, two examples of the behavior of a group of kindergartners in a school serving a low-income African American population illustrate how the variability in teachers' skills resulted in totally different child behavior.

AN EXEMPLAR: FROM "I AM SPECIAL" TO CHAOS

Ms. L was an African American kindergarten teacher who told us that she saw her 16 years of teaching in this neighborhood as an opportunity to "give something back." She explained that because many of her students come from homes where they are given a great deal of responsibility for taking care of themselves, they have to be explicitly taught to comply with the behaviors expected in school. She said that this takes no longer than the first half of the fall semester. Our first observation in her room was toward the end of the school year, and on that occasion we observed 22 kindergartners filing into their classrooms from lunch with their fingers on their lips to remind themselves to be quiet. Six children went directly to the computer and the others to their desks without having to be told where to go. In the subsequent fall, we had the opportunity to see the beginnings of Ms. L's program, as noted in the following excerpt from an observation in the last week of August—the second day of the new school year:

> Ms. L leads her children in very quietly and tells them it's story time
> so they should sit on the mat. The kids go quickly over to the mat and
> sit. There are about 15 kids, all Black, half boys and half girls. All the
> children are dressed very neatly, most in school uniforms but a couple
> of girls are in very pretty dresses. Most of the girls have their hair
> braided neatly, some with dozens of beads.
>   Ms. L stands in front of them, next to a small white board on
> which a few words are written. She begins by showing them the cover

of the book and reminding them that they started reading it yesterday. [The story is "I Am Special."] She has a pleasant expression on her face and smiles frequently, speaking in a soft voice. Soon after beginning, she says quietly to a child, "Leroy, I've had enough, I've spoken to you three times. Now come and stand by me and I'll help you control your body, since you can't." Leroy comes over to her and stands at her side. . . .

She begins questioning to elicit the title of the story. . . . She encourages tangential discussions about several points, such as Leo being a sloppy eater. She points to the white board, where three words are already written—*late, bloomer,* and *sloppy*. . . . Throughout the story the children are attentive and participate well. At the end of the story the children clap spontaneously. She smiles and says, "When we like something, we don't have to clap. Let's learn how to rate the stories by a sign." She demonstrates thumbs up, thumbs down, and a shake of the fingers for "so-so." She asks them to rate the story and most give a thumbs up; one or two indicate so-so.

She goes on, "What was a special thing that Leo learned? Think! When you have an answer, hands up." The children raise hands and one says, "He can skate." She looks at him quizzically and smiles, shaking her head "no." Several children are calling out excitedly and she pauses, telling them that all they need to do is raise their hands and that she won't call on those who are yelling, "Me, me." She says, "You have to follow the rules."

Then Ms. L leads them in Simon Says, but tricks them by doing something different from what she's telling them to do (puts her hands on head while saying, "Shoulders"). The children have a hard time following the spoken direction and most tend to imitate what they see her doing. She keeps at this, pointing out to them that she's "tricking" them and they need to listen to what she says no matter what she's doing. The children are all smiling, trying to beat her trick. She does body parts, and as she asks them to name the parts they shout excitedly. She tells them, "I like it when you talk soft." And she models a soft voice. The children begin to imitate her soft voice and their tone is much lower for the rest of the exercise.

Then she tells them it's time to go out to PE and says, "Yesterday when we did our tour, I showed you how to go to PE." . . . As she's reminding them, a girl standing in front of her is trying to scratch her back and Ms. L reaches over gently and scratches it for her without stopping what she's saying. She then tells the "young ladies" to walk to the door, then the "young men." The children follow her instructions quietly and form a line at the door.

After several such observations, our researcher was shocked one day, some months later, as she followed Ms. L's students from their homeroom to the music class. This teacher was one who, in our discussion of teacher styles, exemplified the profile of what we called the "passive" teacher. The excerpt is an abridged version of two full pages of field notes:

> The students walk quietly, then line up against the wall outside the music room. The teacher opens the door. . . . She is an older White woman in her forties or fifties. She appears to be soft-spoken and easygoing. The students run into the classroom. . . . Some are crawling on the floor . . . most have taken off their shoes. . . . Matthew does flips across the classroom. He stands on a stack of books. He and Tom chase each other around the room. It is total chaos. The children are sliding across the floor in their socks . . . the teacher turns to the class and counts for quiet: "One, two, three." They quiet down but continue to run and play. Quintana is crying because she fell while running and the other children laughed at her. . . . The teacher says, "I don't think that's nice." She is holding on to Brenda. All but two boys are running and sliding. The teacher says, "Can we sing a nice song?" Brenda yells, "No!" The boys are play fighting and Brenda joins in. . . .
>
> The teacher has absolutely no control of the class. . . . Some students are sitting on the guitar and other instruments. . . . Tom is on top of the piano. . . . Dequon is hitting Leroy. Now Leroy is crying like a baby, and so is Ben. All the other boys join in. . . . The boys are scattered across the classroom, on the floor, throwing fits and crying like babies. . . . The girls are running and sliding. Quintana falls again and begins to cry. The teacher is trying to get the boys to stop. The more she pleads, the louder they get. . . . Finally, the teacher mentions treats. The students quiet down immediately. They straighten up long enough to get a treat. . . .
>
> [At the end of the period] the homeroom teacher arrives to pick up the children. As I leave, the music teacher says to me: "This is exactly the same thing that follows them [these students] through the grades. If you can find some way to change it, God bless you!"
>
> The students line up for their homeroom teacher. She says, "How do we carry books?" because the children were dragging their books. The children hold their books in front of them. They follow their teacher quietly to the homeroom.

The music teacher's comment at the end was typical of the comments we heard from the weakest teachers, who usually showed no awareness of their role in children's behavior. This classroom was an extreme example but was not the only chaotic room we observed. It contrasts sharply with the careful, caring, effective instruction we saw in the students' homeroom.

We believe that the differences between these teachers reflect both teacher skill and teacher expectations. Clearly, Ms. L had a repertoire of skillful instructional techniques, while the music teacher did not. More important,

Ms. L understood that the children possessed skills that were helpful to them in their homes and communities; she understood also that their success in school would be contingent on their learning the behaviors and skills valued in this new setting. She was confident that her students would learn what she taught them, and her confidence in them and in herself was evident to the children. Further, she treated them with respect and expected no less in return. *She was teaching them "the culture of power," and they learned it willingly.*

We found it troubling that, despite this obvious variability in classroom contexts, the environment of the regular class was seldom taken into account when children were referred to a CST, so the question of how these children might have performed in more effective classrooms was never raised. In the exception that proves the rule, we note that there was only one school CST in which we sometimes saw a recommendation that the child be changed to another class as an "alternative strategy," to see if a different teacher could better meet the child's needs.

CONCLUSIONS

In describing teacher influences on student achievement, Brophy (1986) noted, "The most consistently replicated findings link student achievement to their *opportunity to learn* the material, in particular to the degree to which teachers carry the content to them personally through active instruction and move them through the curriculum at a brisk pace" (p. 1069; emphasis added). Similarly, Lee (1982) conducted classroom observations and interviews in 55 schools serving low-income, culturally and linguistically diverse students and found that more time on instruction, greater correspondence between tests and curriculum material covered in class, and increased on-task behavior raised student achievement. Others have viewed opportunity to learn as an equity issue. Murphy (1988) discusses educational equity in terms of access to learning, to resources, and to school, especially among students who are tracked in low-ability groups.

This concept of adequate opportunity to learn is also a fundamental aspect of the definition of learning disabilities as part of its exclusionary clause—when a child has not had sufficient opportunity to learn, the determination cannot be made that she has a learning disability. Unfortunately, the classroom context is seldom taken into account as a source of children's learning and behavioral difficulties (Keogh & Speece, 1996) and is readily forgotten as soon as the search for intrinsic disability begins. As we consider why students from certain ethnic groups are overrepresented in high-incidence special education programs, this is a critical issue.

Our observations left no doubt that, overall, the schools serving the poorest Black neighborhoods had the most extremes in quality of instruction and classroom management. Although we saw some pockets of excellence in all schools, we emphasize that extremely unacceptable quality was seen only in those schools. In one sense, socioeconomic status (SES) seemed to be very important, since it seemed to make the difference between fairly even and very uneven teacher quality. Thus, in the one higher-SES Black school, the overall level of instruction was far more even than in the poorer schools, and we saw nothing there to compare with the worst classrooms in the poorest schools. Based on this comparison, it would be tempting to conclude that SES was the determining factor regarding teacher quality.

Race/ethnicity, however, seemed to be a key factor within the low-income populations, with the highest-poverty Black schools tending to be worse off than the highest-poverty Hispanic schools. When this observation was broached in our interviews with school personnel, a common reaction was to blame the children, with the statement that the Hispanic children are more compliant and more focused on school than are Black children. Some personnel distinguished between African American and Haitian children, saying that the latter are generally very compliant, while the former are hard to handle. These features were attributed to more positive parental attitudes and child-rearing practices among the Hispanic and Haitian populations, although school personnel also commented that immigrant parents' support of education was limited by their demanding work schedules and low educational levels. Interviewees who made these comments tended to see African American parents in the low-income areas as simply not caring about their children's schooling.

In light of our evidence of successful instruction and classroom management by teachers such as Ms. L, who easily taught her African American kindergartners the behaviors and social interaction styles that are valued in school, we find it impossible to blame the children and their families for disorderly schools and classrooms. Throughout this book, we argue that school practices, such as limited opportunity to learn, present a powerful explanation for many children's educational outcomes. This explanation competes with, and easily trumps, the assumption of intrinsic or school-induced cognitive deficits. Students in predominantly Black schools were more likely to experience ineffective teachers than were the children in schools that were of higher SES or not predominantly Black. When added to our previous arguments regarding ineffective administrative practices and pervasive, though often covert, racism, evidence of diminished opportunity to learn is but one more factor contributing to the pattern of institutional discrimination that works against children in the poorest, Black neighborhoods of this school district. When applied to the question of special education placement, the variable quality of instruction and the evidence of diminished opportunity to learn indicate that we have no way of knowing how referred children would have fared in more appropriate educational settings.

The variability in school contexts described in this chapter provided the most vulnerable children with considerable "school risk" (Keogh, 2000), which Shores et al. (2020) describe as "cumulative categorical inequalities" (p. 2111), such as retention, suspension, or further exclusion from opportunities for gifted or advanced placements. In the following chapter, we address an aspect of risk that seemed self-evident to school personnel—the family and community contexts from which children came. It was ironic that school personnel indicated great concern for family contexts but showed little awareness of the role of context in school-based risk.

The Construction of Family Identity
Stereotypes and Cultural Capital

> Imagine that you are a parent and I say to you, talk to me a little bit about
> Kaura. Who kept Kaura before she started at school? . . . I am sure you will tell
> me it was one of your relatives, it was your church nursery . . . somewhere that
> you were comfortable with because you believed in those people. So we [the
> school] didn't touch Kaura until she was already 4, 5, 6 years old and these
> beliefs were already in her. . . . So you can't come in here and say that if Kaura
> is not reading and writing and can't pay attention and always wants to play,
> it's because the White teacher did it, or the Black teacher did it, or that
> Hispanic teacher did it. There are some things that happened long before
> Kaura began school. . . .
>
> But now that Kaura is in school, we need to work together. Now what are
> we going to do to make a difference in Kaura's life? But all too often, what
> happens is that when that child hits school and they hit one of these teachers
> who are not really teachers, they want you to take Kaura home and send them
> a better Kaura! Send them a Kaurine! These are people who do not accept that
> the parents are sending us their best kid every day. They do not have another
> one at home that they can send us. But we have people that have not accepted
> that fact—that this is the product and we have to work with this product.
>
> —African American principal

The foregoing statement by an African American principal at an inner-city
school illustrates the complementary influences of the two contexts that exert
the greatest influence on children in their formative years: home and school.
This insight can be framed in the terminology of risk: Either family risk or
school risk, or both, may influence children's educational outcomes (Keogh,
2000). A third factor in the mix is individual risk, the possibility that the
source of children's difficulties may lie beyond either home or school, in children's own biological makeup—that some children simply "have" intrinsic
deficits, regardless of their circumstances. We contend that inappropriate at-
tribution of learning difficulties to individual or family risk is itself an element of school risk, and that it arises from a failure to carefully consider the
individual/family/school interface.

So far, this book has focused on some of the risks in schooling. The majority of the school personnel in our study did not acknowledge this element of risk. Rather, they focused on family and community roles in the "nature/nurture" argument. While many expressed a strong belief that school-identified disabilities represented genuine intrinsic deficits, the majority added the nuance that there is a "fine line" between intrinsic and environmentally induced deficits. While many school personnel spoke of poverty as the key factor, many seemed to assume that poverty was synonymous with poor parenting and lack of interest in children's education. Overall, the most powerful message from practitioners was "It [disability] comes from the home."

In this chapter, we focus on school personnel's views of family contexts in children's education and on the impact of those views on children's educational careers. We present examples of these views, juxtaposed with portraits of those families that we were able to interview, visit, or both. In some cases, the information we were able to glean did corroborate school personnel's beliefs about the families. In most cases, our information provided a very different picture. Overall, four concerns are most striking in these stories: First, stereotypical images of families were usually based on a single piece of information that was enough to damn the family in the eyes of school personnel. Second, school personnel made no effort to counter negative beliefs with information on family strengths. Third, the families lacked the social and cultural capital to effectively challenge these stereotypes. Fourth, the accumulation of negativity around a family actually affected the outcomes for some children.

SCHOOL VOICES: "IT COMES FROM THE HOME"

School personnel's descriptions of the role of family contexts in children's school failure centered on four aspects: The "fine line" between nature and nurture, the impact of poor parenting, children's limited cultural and social experience, and caregivers' lack of support and monitoring of their children's schooling. Although we will not detail it here, there was a common sentiment among Hispanic and Anglo American school personnel that African American family and community environments tended to be more detrimental to children than those of immigrant families.

Nature/Nurture? "A Fine Line"

The delicate balance between detrimental circumstances, school failure, and special education placement was illustrated by the words of an Anglo American teacher at a predominantly Haitian school in a low-income neighborhood:

> They [the parents] really don't understand [what the school is expecting]. They can't help their children. They're not home. These children are very much latchkey kids. They fall behind. So, yes, they

end up in a special education program because there's nobody there and the longer that goes on the further behind you get, and I think our hope is . . . when you get into special ed and you're working in a smaller group at your level and you get brought up to where you should be, then you get out. . . . If you continue to stay in a class with 35–40 kids, you're never gonna get what you need.

Despite this description of the interconnectedness between minimal home support, academic failure, and subsequent special education placement, the same teacher went on to say:

I don't think you can just manufacture these deficits. You know, they're either there or they're not there. . . . These problems are really . . . they're real. . . . Whether it's from outside or within. And if it's something extrinsic that can be fixed then they get out of the program. . . . This is not a placement for life.

The belief in intrinsic deficits came through clearly in many interviews, as typified by the following statements:

Basically . . . there are minority children who do have these problems. They're not social, and they're not administrative, and they're not due to any devious behavior. Don't misunderstand, there are children who belong in these classes because they do have problems that're intrinsic to the child.

In the simplest words:

Some children, you know, are just born with it. . . . You know, like some children have blue eyes.

Some teachers also expressed the opinion that minority children were actually underreferred, many needing special education services and not getting them. We particularly heard this at one of our predominantly Haitian schools. For example:

People say that there is disproportionate representation, but I don't see it, not here anyway. They are underrepresented. I think the process is too slow, takes too long, and by the time they are finally placed, it's too late. There are many reasons for this, associated with poverty, malnutrition, low-birth-weight babies.

"The Parents Are the Problem!"

While many emphasized the interplay between nature and nurture, most school personnel were inclined to blame nurture, with a focus on both family dynamics and broader societal contexts, including historical influences, economic circumstances, personal crises, cultural/social experience, and immigration status. Some school personnel spoke of families' problems in a tone of negative judgment, but others spoke with a sympathetic understanding of the impact of many negative influences on family adjustment.

The comments below, all made by personnel at schools serving low-income predominantly Black or mixed Black and Hispanic populations, placed the blame squarely on family life factors:

> The parents are the problem! They [the children] have absolutely no social skills, such as not knowing how to walk, sit in a chair. . . . It's cultural. Because most of these children have been to preschool and they're still so delayed. Their physical needs are not attended to. They're often dirty, head lice among the Hispanic children, poor hygiene and clothing . . . hungry, cold. . . . The big problem is poverty. I spend 50% of my time taking care of them other than teaching, and this includes downtime because of behaviors such as fistfights, tantrums, aggression.
>
> This woman asked her class: "How many kids have been exposed to guns?" And everyone except four kids in her classroom had either seen a gun, held a gun, or something.
>
> This child has severe behavior problems. His mother was a crack addict and gave him up at birth. The foster mother adopted him several years ago . . . and her husband, who was like the child's father, was shot and killed.

While there were, no doubt, factual bases for many of these statements, it was disturbing to note that, for many school personnel, labeling parents with derogatory terms seemed to be an acceptable part of school culture. One teacher, on the way from two child study team (CST) conferences, rolled her eyes and exclaimed to the researcher: "The first mother is retarded; the second one is crazy!"

"A Lot of Them Think the World Stops Right There at 14th Street"

Another aspect of detrimental family circumstances reported by school personnel was what we came to refer to as "cultural-knowledge set." This view tended to place the blame on culture and experience rather than on parents' own actions. The following statement by an African American professional at a predominantly African American school in one of the poorest neighborhoods typified this perspective:

> Most of the kids think the world stops at 14th Street. . . . I would give children a ride home in my car and they really didn't know how to get in the car, sit down, and close the door. It was hard for the child to open the door. I remember once we went on a field trip to the zoo and these kids were on the bus on the highway and they, I mean it was like the

best experience they ever had to be on the bus, riding on 836 way up there and they saw all the houses and the trees and the buildings. And were like, "Wow! What's this?" A lot of them think the world stops right there at 14th Street so they don't dream.

Other versions of this theme focused on immigrant children:

Many students come from Central or South America and they come and develop little countries or little cities within this country and most of . . . their parents are illiterate, you know, they can't read or write so they don't get the help at home. So, I feel that comes into play, not that I would place a child like that in special ed, but that comes into play where teachers lack the efficiency and want to place them because of that sometimes.

"With Parental Participation, They Will Not Be in Special Education"

The majority of teachers identified poor parental participation as a key factor in special education placement. These comments focused mostly on parents' failure to monitor homework and respond to school recommendations or requests for conferences. For example:

I don't have a lot [of caregiver involvement] and I don't know if they understand what they're supposed to do. A lot of times they'll come to me and say, "I haven't seen any homework," or they'll say, "They don't have homework." And then they say, "I have to look in their book bag." And I'm just wondering, shouldn't you be looking in the book bag as a parent, you know, why are you taking a 6-year-old's word for it that they don't have homework? Look in their book bag!

In Sunnybrook, the school to which African American students from a low-income area were bused into a predominantly affluent Anglo American student body, school personnel described a dramatic difference in students' preparation for schooling according to community background. The implications for parental input were implicit in the following speaker's meaning:

This is a unique community in that these children come into our school well prepared academically, and so there is a blatant, blatant disparity when you look at a child who is coming from the community and one who is coming from [the African American area].

Moreover, some personnel saw the effects of parent participation on student educational outcomes as very direct:

With parent participation, they will not be in [special education] programs. Typically, the children who are being placed do not have any parent participation at all from caretakers.

As our case studies in later chapters will show, we did not find this last statement to be true. Moreover, despite this strong trend of complaint about lack
of parental involvement, we noted that high levels of involvement in school-
based conferences did occur in schools or even classrooms where school personnel made consistent efforts to "get parents in" and to develop respectful
relationships with parents. We found that school personnel's efforts were
far more predictive of parental response than were the parents' socioeconomic status (SES) or ethnicity. For example, the success of intensive efforts
to include parents was powerfully demonstrated in one school with a mixed
Haitian and African American population. The counselor reported that parental turnout was "remarkably good, though not yet 100%." When asked
what accounted for this, she replied, "We make a pest of ourselves!" Our
observations corroborated this: Efforts to encourage parents' attendance included letters, phone calls, visits by the community involvement specialist
(CIS, paid for by Title I funds), who was Haitian, and even the giving of
rewards to children for taking home letters to parents about conferences. In
our observations of 12 CST or placement conferences, there were only two
for which the parent did not come in.

    The job of the CIS was to act as a liaison with families. These personnel
were usually of the same ethnicity as the predominant group of students, and
some were very effective in assuring high parent turnout at CST and staffing
conferences. In these Title I schools, it was the CIS and the counselors who
worked most closely with the parents, and they tended to speak of families in
much more understanding tones than did the teachers. For example, in one
predominantly African American school, a Hispanic teacher said, "There's
virtually no parent participation. Only a few cooperate," while the African
American counselor estimated that 70% of the parents cooperated with
school requests, despite the presence of what several personnel described as a
general sense of despair in the neighborhood. This counselor explained that,
for many parents who did not cooperate, "a lot of the problem is that they
don't know." The CIS spoke in the same vein regarding parental participation
through assistance and attendance at conferences:

> The parents are not more involved because they are not educated. . . .
> They didn't like the school when they were here. They didn't finish
> school. And it's kind of hard to be excited about something you didn't
> like, to pass it on to your children. . . . I have one parent who tells
> me she only got as far as second or third grade herself. . . . They are
> embarrassed to even let their children know. . . . It is easier to push a
> child away or talk down to them to keep them from being aware of the
> real situation. . . . A lot don't volunteer at the school because they'd
> have to watch a child read. And they don't want to do that because they
> can't read the book [themselves] . . . . I've heard [teachers say], "These
> people just want money. They don't care." The parents do care about
> their children, they just don't know how to deal with it or respond to it
> like you would.

Overall, negative indictments of families constituted the most pervasive view in the entire set of perspectives offered by school personnel in our study. Fortunately, we were able to use observations of school-based parent-professional interactions, as well as home visits and interviews, to gain some balance to these views. We were particularly interested in more close-up information on African American families, in view of the extreme negativity regarding this group. We learned that school personnel often did not attempt to gain the information needed to arrive at a true picture of family situations. Rather, they seemed to rely on stereotypical images for their constructions of family identity. We focus here on what we learned about family environments, and we refer readers to a further discussion of attempts at parent advocacy in Harry et al. (2005).

HOME VOICES: "DOING THE BEST I CAN"

Our views of parents' perspectives came from two sources: school-based conferences and home visits. In this chapter, we will refer to the former source only as a background to the more in-depth, personalized information we garnered from the latter. Thus, after a brief overview, we will focus on two case studies whose details illustrate the disservice that can be done to families by deficit assumptions and stereotypical thinking.

Fleeting Views

We observed many school-based conferences with parents who were obviously in dire need of help. We saw one young woman whose demeanor, dress, and apparently nonchalant attitude during the conference would readily lead school personnel to assume that motherhood was low on her priority list. We saw another who seemed desperate in her denial of her child's need for help. In the low-income, predominantly African American schools, we observed several conferences for children whose families seemed to fit the profiles described as detrimental. For example, in one school all four children whose conferences we observed had close relatives who abused drugs and who were in trouble with the law. In one conference, a grandmother, distraught by her daughter's drug abuse and incarceration, and the murder of her grandson's father, burst into tears under the school personnel's questioning.

One parent whom we came to learn a lot about, but whose home we did not visit, was Ms. Brown, an alcoholic whose efforts to participate in her children's schooling made her the butt of much amusement and criticism. In this inner-city school, an open-door policy encouraged parents to drop into classrooms and Ms. Brown frequently appeared in the classroom obviously inebriated, much to her son Jimmy's chagrin. After two CST conferences, both attended by Ms. Brown, the decision was made not to refer Jimmy for evaluation because the multidisciplinary team felt that he was progressing as well as he could under the circumstances. A year later, Jimmy and his sister were removed from the home by the state's child welfare department because of extremely detrimental physical surroundings, and a teacher who visited Jimmy in his foster home reported that he seemed much happier. What was surprising in this case was that although school personnel had visible evidence of the mother's alcoholism, it was at least 2 years before the case was reported to the relevant state agency.

Taddeus was another child whose home was reputed to be detrimental, in this case because of a history of involvement in drugs and violence. Taddeus, a handsome, nattily dressed 2nd-grader with a wide, shy smile, was described by his teacher as "knowing nothing" and being "on the moon." Having been tested in his 1st-grade year and found not to qualify for special education services, he had been retained in the 2nd grade. The teacher said that she heard that there were gangs at his home and that his cousin was killed recently, and she could not figure out why Taddeus had not qualified for special education. In our only visit to this home, the mother confirmed that a sibling and a relative had been seriously injured as a result of being "caught in crossfire." The mother's description of Taddeus was very different from the teacher's, emphasizing that, although he was not doing well at school, "he's great with his hands and can fix anything." Pointing to a child's bike in the corner, she explained that people in the neighborhood pay Taddeus "to fix bikes and things."

Miles was another child whose family we visited only once. An African American kindergartner in a low-income neighborhood, Miles was found eligible for LD services and was retained in kindergarten. On our visit to Miles's home, his mother apologized that she had no living room to invite the researcher into. Her half of the house consisted of a series of three rooms off a hallway, so the interview was conducted in her bedroom. When the researcher commented on her son's excellent vocabulary (his suggestions for zoo animals included *sea lion* and *otter*), the mother said that Miles had never been to the zoo, but learned a lot of vocabulary from the Disney Channel, which the family watched together once a week. Showing great interest in the meaning of the "learning disability" label that was being applied to her son, Miles's mother exclaimed, "Well, you see, I'm doing the best I can!"

Another parent we came to know beyond the school walls was Janey, mother of Anita, a 1st-grader placed in special education. Janey described herself as a "hillbilly," and her daughter's father as a "wetback" (a Mexican migrant). This mother was a regular volunteer in her daughter's classroom, but was described by school personnel as "retarded." Our interviews with her revealed that she had been in a special education program herself, but her keen understanding of the special education system belied the belief that she was retarded. While acknowledging that she did keep her daughter home too often, Janey argued that the school was not doing its job. Indeed, when her daughter was placed in the LD program, Janey accurately described to us the poor instruction the child was receiving and the lack of adherence to her individual education plan (IEP), which we also observed.

These brief vignettes point to the range of challenges faced by families of whose lives we were able to gain only a fleeting glimpse. In search of in-depth understanding of family situations, we relied on information from the 12 case study children as well as three others whose families agreed to participate in interviews, home visits, or both. These 15 cases were as diverse as the entire cohort of participants in the study, but most of them did have problematic family circumstances that typified the kinds of complaints school personnel expressed about families.

Close-Up Views

Although school personnel often used terms such as "single parent" or "intact" to describe families, these classifications were meaningless in light of the array of family configurations to which we were introduced. Contrary to the mainstream notion of a "single parent" family, we found that all the families we met had more than one adult in the home—whether a stepparent or members of the extended family. All had other children—whether siblings or cousins—living in the home.

The configurations of the 12 families of case study children were as follows: One Haitian family appeared to be headed by two biological parents. Two other families, one African American and one Haitian, were headed by fathers as the primary caregivers; one mother was hospitalized with a psychiatric illness and the other lived in Haiti. Another African American child lived with her paternal grandmother and an aunt, since her mother was in jail; her father was a frequent visitor to the home and participated in school-based conferences. Five children (two African American and three Hispanic) lived with their mothers; in one case the mother had a psychiatric illness and was the child's legal guardian, while the father also was involved in child care; in another case, the father was in Puerto Rico and the child lived with her mother, siblings, and an infant nephew. Two other children—one Haitian and one African American—lived with their mother and a stepfather. The 12th child lived with an adult relative and had experienced the deaths of adult family members, including his father; the caregiver he lived with was himself quite ill and passed away toward the end of our study.

Many of these configurations represent what school personnel tended to describe as "dysfunctional." However, when we stepped inside children's homes, we saw another side of the picture—a side that spoke of families' caring for and pride in their children. Their ways of caring and the sources of their pride were not always consonant with what school personnel would count as important, but it was evident to us that the parents were making an effort to fulfill what they perceived to be the important responsibilities of parenthood—providing nurturance and love.

We will focus here on the family environments of two case study children whom we were able to follow extensively. Details of how the children came to be designated as having disabilities will be given in Chapter 11, where we address the social construction of the EBD category. We visited these homes six times each, and we emphasize that, although we do not know the families well, our visits were enough to dispel the cloud of suspicion that had been cast over them. Certainly, their difficulties were readily evident, but so were their strengths.

Jacintha: "Bring Momma's pen, baby." Robert was an African American 2nd-grader in one of the most denigrated neighborhoods of the city. His was the school previously reported to have suspended 102 children out of a total of 603 in one year, based on a "zero-tolerance" policy by which kindergartners through 5th-graders were placed on 3-day, out-of-school suspension for fighting. The stereotype that influenced school personnel's response to Robert's mother was that of a drug-abusing mother who had more children than she could handle.

We visited Robert's home six times throughout the period of our research. At first, finding the house was a challenge. Located in the heart of the city, this two-story block of eight apartments was about 100 yards away from a bridge under which homeless persons frequently built their temporary shelters. The apartment was on the ground floor, with a narrow, lopsided porch that served this and the apartment next door. The entrance to the apartment was a swinging door with broken slats that, over the course of the 3 years in which we visited, eventually disappeared entirely, leaving open spaces through which one could peer into a living room that was about 10 feet square. The living room contained a sofa for two, a chest of drawers and mirror, and a playpen in which the 2-year-old slept. This room merged into a passageway that led, on one side, to a tiny kitchen and, on the other, to a bathroom and two bedrooms. Four siblings slept on two bunk beds against one wall of their room. Against the other wall was a long shelving unit covered with colorful cloth that matched the curtains. Behind the shelf covering was a collection of probably 100 children's books.

Robert's mother, Jacintha, was a petite woman whose speech and deferential manners reflected her Southern origins. Warm and enthusiastic in her manner, she welcomed our research team and spoke openly of her family life and the challenges she faced. The most dramatic impression of this family was of the loving and demonstrative relationship between this mother and her children. The family interactions supported Jacintha's explanation that she had nine children because she "just loves having children." The four eldest lived in another state with their grandparents. The five who lived with Jacintha were very physically affectionate with her, as illustrated by 8-year-old Robert's lying across her lap and looking up at her as she talked with the researcher.

Three small but very telling interactions further demonstrated the competence and caring of this mother who lived in such limited circumstances. First, Jacintha's ability to organize her household was evident in a quick moment: When asked for a pen to sign the research consent forms, the mother said to her 4-year-old, "Bring Momma's pen, baby." The child went directly to a drawer in the small desk and pulled out his mother's pen. Later, as Jacintha was describing to the researcher how she loves to read to her children, one of the children ran to a cupboard against the wall and opened it, and dozens of children's books came tumbling out. On the same occasion, as the mother talked about the family, one of the children brought out a collection of small photo albums to show the researcher. Each album was filled with photos of an individual child, and in the front of each album was inscribed, "To: [child's name] from Mom and Dad with love, Christmas 19____."

This mother was often described in very derogatory terms by some school personnel. While some acknowledged that she was polite and well spoken, others focused on their knowledge that she had a history of drug addiction, or on the fact that she had nine children in all, by more than one union. The last two facts led school personnel to preconceived beliefs about Jacintha that are evident in the following two episodes. On one occasion an administrator commented that the mother had "five children here and four farmed out somewhere else." The fact that the four older children lived in another state with their paternal grandparents was verified by the researcher, who met these children one summer when they came to stay with their mother. The children's traditional Southern manners ("yes, ma'am; no, ma'am,") put their city siblings to shame and contradicted the connotation of irresponsible child-rearing inherent in the notion that they had been "farmed out somewhere."

In conversations with the researcher, Jacintha spoke openly of her history of drug abuse. By her account, she had been "clean" for several years. Nevertheless, when she lost about 15 pounds over a summer, a faculty member commented that "you can always tell when she's back on drugs because she loses weight!" Our interpretation was rather different: Just a week earlier, the researcher visiting Jacintha expressed surprise at her weight loss over the summer. Turning to show off her trim figure, Jacintha exclaimed: "Slim-Fast, girl! It's fabulous! You wait right here and I'm 'a get you a tin. You'll see how good it works!"

School personnel's persistence in negative and poorly based beliefs about Jacintha was puzzling and troubling because this mother consistently showed herself to be a caring and responsible parent. She attended every CST or placement conference for her child and participated in a polite, deferential, yet firm manner. For example, when her son was eventually placed in an EBD program and the multidisciplinary team had to ask her to sign for permission regarding the possibility of physical restraint, she showed great concern and asked for examples of exactly what that would mean. She could always report exactly what medication her son was on and how he was responding to it. Nevertheless, some school personnel were consistently rude to her, as the following excerpt from a field observation indicates. The committee chair asked whether Robert was receiving his medication at school:

A team member replies: "He does not get it here." Everyone looks puzzled again and the speaker, who is sitting behind the mother, mouths

the word "*she*" and, pointing to the mother, makes a gesture of cutting
across the throat. She is saying that the mother stopped the medication
being given at school. Her facial expression as she does this appears
angry and annoyed, as she scowls and points at the mother with an
accusing gesture. The mother is not intended to see this, and does not.
A second later, the speaker seems to realize that her lack of voice came
across as a silence in the room and that everyone, except the mother,
is looking at her. She mumbles something like, "It [the medication]
was stopped." At this point, I do not look at the expressions of others
but can feel the discomfort in the room. Everyone has seen the team
member's gesture except the mother, whose back is directly to her.

The faculty member's negativity on this occasion was but another example
of her vindictive attitude to Jacintha and the advantage that was taken of
this mother's deferential attitude to school personnel. In the previous year,
Robert had been placed on half-day suspension, and the same faculty member told the researcher that this action was taken to show the mother that
she had to be responsible for Robert's troublesome behavior. Jacintha, meanwhile, had easily understood this message, explaining to the researcher that
Robert was put on half-day suspension to "punish me." This "punishment"
involved Jacintha being required to come for Robert at 11:00 A.M. every day,
which she did for 5 months, walking approximately 10 blocks with her two
younger children in tow. The half-day placement meant that Robert had to
miss school sometimes when his mother had a medical or other appointment
for herself or the other children, because she could not be back at school by
11:00 A.M. When it was suggested that she should go to the school district
to complain about this action, Jacintha replied that she would "just leave it
to God."

The principal of the school was the same African American woman
whose insightful comments about a hypothetical "Kaurine" were cited as
the introduction to this chapter. Yet it was the principal herself who ordered
Robert's half-day attendance in school, arguing that because of his behavior
he was, at that time, "not capable of benefiting from a full day of school."
This arrangement remained in place from January until the end of May, despite the fact that, in January, Jacintha had signed permission for a psychological evaluation. In May, when Jacintha refused to come for Robert any
longer, he was reinstated in the full-day program and evaluated for special
education placement.

Grandma S: "There's nothing wrong with her. She just wants her momma."
Kanita was an African American 2nd-grader who was placed in an EBD program in an inner-city school. The stereotype that dominated school personnel's view of Kanita was that her mother was incarcerated and there were "a
bunch of people living in the home." On the basis of this information, school
personnel expressed the belief that the family was "dysfunctional."

Six visits to Kanita's home provided us with a very different picture. The attractively painted single-family dwelling had belonged to Kanita's paternal grandparents for more than 30 years. In this house, Mrs. Smith and her husband had raised her family of six children on the prized American principle of hard work. The family's small business had, for more than 20 years, been the location of weekend and vacation work for all the children, and Mrs. Smith told us that many a Christmas Eve would find the entire family over at the business working until midnight. Mrs. Smith's father had been the founding pastor of a nearby Baptist church, which she and some of the grandchildren still attended. Mrs. Smith's children had all moved on to establish their own families, and her living room shelves attested to the many grandchildren and three "great-grands" who now enriched her life.

At the time of the study, we learned that Kanita and one of Mrs. Smith's daughters and her child lived in this home. This family had considerable cultural capital in their community. In contrast to school personnel's view of this home as a place where a "bunch of people" lived, the strength of the extended family unit was evident in the home's function as a center for the grandchildren to come to after school until their parents could pick them up. Cousins, aunts, or uncles were frequent visitors during all of our six visits to the home.

Kanita had lived with her grandmother since she was a baby, when her mother was incarcerated. Her father, who lived elsewhere, was in close touch with his daughter and either he or one of his sisters would attend school conferences along with Mrs. Smith. At the placement conference, Kanita's grandmother and aunt both acknowledged that the child's behavior was troublesome, but when told that Kanita had qualified for an EBD program, the grandmother stated flatly: "There's nothing wrong with her. She just wants her momma."

It was evident that Kanita was treasured by this family. Her school awards, sports trophies, and photos were prominent among the family mementos in the living room. Mrs. Smith loved to bring out her album in which she kept Kanita's school records and awards all the way from Head Start to the time of our study. Report cards, classroom certificates, a certificate of Kanita's participation in a regional mathematics competition, notes from classroom peers and teachers, and Mother's Day cards from Kanita to her mother and grandmother were all carefully pressed into this album. Pride in Kanita's accomplishments was evident in the family: On one visit, an aunt, standing in the kitchen as the researchers talked with Mrs. Smith, called out to remind her mother to tell us about Kanita's excellent performance on the statewide testing. On the same day, her cousin, coming in after school and realizing our university affiliation, asked quickly: "Is Kanita going to college?"

Kanita's psychological evaluation offered a sobering picture of the power of negative stereotyping. Prior to the actual evaluation, the psychologist reported to us that this child was from a "dysfunctional family," the mother being in jail. The first 2 hours of evaluation were based on the Weschler

Intelligence Scale for Children (WISC)-III, on which Kanita cooperated fully and earned a composite score of 107 with a score of 118 on the "freedom from distractibility" subscale. When the psychologist began the projective testing by asking Kanita to draw a picture of her family, the child did so eagerly, with a big smile. As the questioning on these tests focused increasingly on personal family information, however, Kanita became more withdrawn. For example, when the psychologist asked Kanita to name one of the figures, the child did so in a soft voice. The psychologist repeated, "Who is it?" Kanita replied, "My cousin." The psychologist asked, "How old is he?" Kanita's replies were too soft for the researchers to hear, but we saw her shrug several times. The psychologist asked if this cousin lived in the house and if he slept in Kanita's bedroom. As the subsequent series of questions focused on details of Kanita's bedroom, the child answered softly, gradually becoming more restless, fiddling with the tabletop and moving around in her chair.

The psychologist then turned to a series of questions about Kanita's mother, including why she was incarcerated and whether she had been on drugs. The family questions finally ended with the psychologist asking Kanita to tell her "everybody that lives in the house," to which Kanita listed about nine names. The psychologist asked Kanita if it was a big house and Kanita said yes. From these tests the psychologist went on to the sentence-completion test and the Roberts Apperception Test. By the end of the session, Kanita had slid almost halfway under her desk and was giving virtually no answers.

After the evaluation, the psychologist offered the researchers the interpretation that Kanita's growing recalcitrance was a sign of "denial of her feelings" in the context of a "dysfunctional" family. The psychologist rejected the suggestion that Kanita's withdrawal may have been indicative of embarrassment or distress, arguing that children in this neighborhood were so accustomed to having family members who were on drugs or incarcerated that they were generally quite "blasé" and would speak openly of these matters. Thus, the psychologist concluded that Kanita's resistance to the topic was not normal for a child in this social environment. Nor did the psychologist entertain the possibility that the child, like many children in inner-city neighborhoods, had likely been taught not to reveal family information to strangers, especially White strangers. Finally, it was evident that the psychologist's line of questioning regarding the sleeping arrangements for Kanita's cousin represented poorly veiled hints at the possibility of improper relationships within the family. We feel certain that Kanita's sensitivity to this insinuation contributed to her increasing reluctance to participate in the projective testing.

The outcome of the evaluation was that Kanita qualified for a placement in a self-contained EBD class at a different school. Kanita's placement in this program turned out to be a "double-edged sword," since, in the hands of an effective teacher, she did very well both academically and behaviorally and was soon partially mainstreamed. However, she was so stigmatized by the EBD label that her behavior in the general education settings, though no different from that of many of her peers, was frequently interpreted as problematic. By the 4th grade, Kanita was placed, part-time, in a gifted pro-gram, where the teacher asked us if her status as a child with EBD was "a mistake."

STEREOTYPES, CULTURAL CAPITAL, AND "RISK"

The two preceding cases point to the power of racial and socioeconomic ste-reotypes to exacerbate the difficulties of children whose families lack the cul-tural capital valued by schools. In both cases, school personnel constructed their images of children's families on the basis of uninformed and untested negative assumptions. In the face of the families' lack of cultural capital, school personnel used their unchallenged power to make decisions that were not in the children's best interest. These stories illustrate a statement by Skiba and Peterson (2000) that "information about inadequate family resources or family instability is used to affix blame, creating an adversarial climate between home and school" (p. 341).

"Risk" in Family Configurations

The NAS report on minority overrepresentation in special education (Donovan & Cross, 2002) emphasized the impact of detrimental social and biological influences on children living in poverty. The authors devoted a chapter to a detailed summary of findings regarding the detrimental effects of such factors as lead-based toxins, alcohol, iron deficiency, and maternal depression on the cognitive and behavioral development of minority children living in poverty. The history of American racial politics prompted some scholars to express concern that the NAS's highlighting of these issues was another version of "blaming the victim," suggesting that poor, in particular, African American, families were at fault for raising their children in detrimental circumstances. We believe that what was missing from the NAS's analysis was insight into the responsibility of public policy for many of these circumstances. Indeed, around the same time, the NAS (2002) also published a report, which de-tailed the extensive discrimination against minority groups in the health care system.

Another line of research on family "risk" factors is found in Nichols and Chen's (1981) family profiles, which focused on poverty; unsafe neigh-borhoods; large family size; residential instability; and parental characteris-tics, including absence, poor mental health, criminality, and substance abuse. Sameroff and colleagues (1993) developed similar profiles but stressed that it is the combination of several such features, rather than any single feature, that indicates risk. Blair and Scott (2000) applied the question of demographics directly to special education placement and found high correlations between key demographic indicators and special education placement, which, they argued, proves the lasting influence of early environments and experiences.

Shifrer et al. (2010) in analyzing data on disproportionality argued that low SES was the predominant contributor.

While we do not doubt the importance of the formative childhood years, we contend that demographics do not tell the whole story. As researchers have demonstrated (e.g., Clark, 1983), dynamics within families can provide protective factors that result in considerable resilience. Moreover, research on culturally responsive pedagogy shows that schools *can* make a difference (Hilliard, 1997). If children who have started life with detrimental influences are further exposed to detrimental schooling, we cannot place all, or even most, of the blame on the preschool years.

Kanita's family did not fit the profile developed by Sameroff et al. (1993). To the contrary, it was based on a strong extended family unit, supported by the flexible extended systems known to be typical of traditional Black family structures (e.g., Hill, 1971). These include grandparent involvement, adult sharing of financial and practical responsibility, and sibling responsibility. Information on Robert's family suggested that this family was indeed particularly vulnerable by virtue of several "risk factors." Nevertheless, two aspects of the story are particularly disturbing: First, school personnel made no attempt to ascertain the family strengths that did exist, and, second, decisions made about Robert suggested an attempt to undermine rather than to assist this vulnerable family.

Social and Cultural Capital

The concepts of cultural and social capital are very helpful in interpreting the interactions between school personnel and the parents in these stories. Lareau's (1989) comparison of the home-school interactions of working class versus professional parents showed how social connections and the cultural styles of parents accounted for differential reception by school personnel. Proposing an analysis of what constitutes parental cultural capital in school contexts, Lareau and Horvat (1999) offered a list of characteristics that included "parents' large vocabularies, sense of entitlement to interact with teachers as equals, time, transportation, and child care arrangements to attend school events during the school day" (p. 42). These researchers argued also that school personnel approved only those "socioemotional styles" that reflected trust in school personnel and acceptance of their recommendations.

Meeting these expectations can be difficult to achieve. As Bowers (1984) argued, because social interaction is premised on unspoken, "taken-for-granted" beliefs, parents' mastery of the "communicative competence" needed for home-school interactions requires an "explicit and rational knowledge of the culture that is being renegotiated" (p. 29). Studies by Harry and colleagues (Harry, 1992; Harry et al., 1995, 1999) illustrated how difficult this challenge was for Puerto Rican, African American, and other culturally or linguistically diverse families from low-SES backgrounds.

What does cultural capital look like when low income, minimal formal schooling, and linguistic difference intertwine with race in a racialized society such as the United States? Lareau and Horvat's (1999) study of contrasting interaction styles of White and Black parents indicated that cultural capital and race are often inextricable in the context of the U.S. history of racism. While traditional conceptions of cultural capital, as outlined by Bourdieu (1986), tended to focus on material and symbolic indicators of cultural capital, Lareau and Horvat (1999) attended to something far more intangible— the psychological impact of historical racism on parents' access to cultural capital and the means needed to activate that capital. Thus, they found that Black parents' knowledge of the school district's history of racial discrimination resulted in their inability to approach school personnel from a posture of trust. In contrast, White parents, not wounded by this history, generally did trust the school and interpreted any inappropriate actions of school personnel on an individual basis. Lareau and Horvat (1999) argued that in this context, being White became "a type of cultural capital" (p. 42), "a largely hidden cultural resource that facilitates White parents' compliance with the standard of deferential and positive parental involvement in school" (p. 69). These researchers did not present this as a fixed characteristic, however. Rather, their study showed that middle-class Black parents, while also suspicious of the school, mastered the interaction style that was valued by school personnel and succeeded in "customizing" their children's education without ever revealing to school personnel that they harbored misgivings based on race.

Lareau and Horvat's (1999) findings were relatively clear cut in the context of a school in which Black students were in the minority as compared with their White peers and, more important, in which the majority of school personnel were White. In our study, however, the schools that had large proportions of Black students usually also had significant proportions of Black faculty and often Black administrators. What is the role of race in such contexts?

Cultural Capital in a Racialized Society

The neighborhoods where Kanita and Robert lived reflected three commonly held criteria for stereotyping: Black, poor, and dangerous. While the school that Robert attended had a growing population of Hispanics (19%), the neighborhood had a long history of being predominantly African American. Moreover, Robert's school itself was the alma mater of many African Americans who were of considerable status in the city and who were reported to be quite involved in supporting the school's needs. However, over the years, city restructuring and funding patterns contributed to the neighborhood becoming one of the most denigrated in the city. Kanita's neighborhood was seen as more "working poor" than Robert's, but would also be considered "inner-city," in the common use of that term to indicate low-income Black residents.

To what extent did race contribute to the stereotyping of these families? At face value, race does not appear to be an essential ingredient. In Kanita's case, the three key school personnel involved were all White (Anglo American ethnicity)—a referring teacher with very poor classroom-management skills, the administrator who handled the referral-team process, and the psychologist. However, in Robert's case, with the exception of the psychologist, the key personnel involved were African American—the team member who gestured rudely behind Jacintha's back; the administrator who made the decision to place Robert on half-day attendance; and the referring teacher, whose negativity and poor classroom management made it impossible to know what Robert's potential was.

If we understand racism as an insidious ideology rather than as a simple matter of prejudice between individuals of different races, it is easy to see how members of a racialized society are predisposed to make intuitive negative associations based on race, even within their own group (Bonilla-Silva, 2006; Delgado & Stefancic, 2000; Ladson-Billings, 2021). This type of ingrained racism seems a likely part of the negativity we noted, operating like a lens that colors, even distorts, one's view. Through this lens, the image of these neighborhoods as beset by guns, violence, drugs, and family dysfunction condemned all who lived in them.

We do not dispute that many detrimental influences did affect the quality of life of many children in these schools. We do contend, however, that in the family stories told above, generalized knowledge of the neighborhoods combined with minimal and superficial knowledge of these families to produce a mindset that was detrimental to the children. Looking at each family as an individual unit, we argue that these stereotypes did a great injustice to these families and children.

CONCLUSIONS

The contrast between our findings and school personnel's views of families illustrates the terrible power of stereotypes. Certainly, our observations showed the tremendous challenges of poverty, personal loss, and limited education faced by these families. We acknowledge also that there is a strong likelihood of volunteer bias, in that those families who agreed to participate were those who knew they had nothing to hide; who knew that they were, as one mother put it, "doing the best they could." So our discussion here is not intended to put forth the case that there were no families whose lifestyles and challenges contributed to their children's difficulties in school. Indeed, it seems reasonable to assume that even the strong families we met were struggling against odds so powerful as to place children at increased risk for school failure or even special education placement.

Nevertheless, we believe that our portraits of family strengths are also irrefutable and that tapping into these strengths could have made an important difference. No one knew that Miles's surprising vocabulary reflected his mother's use of the Disney Channel as a source of educational activity and family solidarity; that Robert's mother's tiny apartment, in a building for which no landlord was held accountable, housed a large collection of children's books from which she taught the toddlers "their ABCs"; that Taddeus's mother, against a background of family tragedy, took great pride in her son's mechanical abilities; or that Kanita's grandmother, cherishing and nurturing the talents of a gifted child whose mother had "chosen the wrong way," had carefully preserved all of her granddaughter's school reports and awards from Head Start until the 5th grade. Although all these caregivers came to CST conferences and participated to the best of their ability, the image of the ineffective, minimally involved parent persisted, because most of these efforts and activities did not meet the criteria school personnel had in mind when they spoke of "parental involvement."

The saddest part of these stories is that the family strengths we were able to discover in just a few visits and conversations went unnoticed by school personnel, whose views and decisions were central to these children's educational careers. This lack of recognition, a recognition supplanted by disdain and disinterest, contributed directly to decisions that were not in the children's interest and that were not challenged by any of the parents, although the parents disagreed with some of them. These parents had neither the social capital, in the form of social connections, nor the cultural capital, in the form of knowledge of rights, logistical supports, or faith in their own voice, to challenge such decisions.

In the preceding few chapters we have addressed systemic as well as personal biases that affected outcomes for children. Overall, we believe that a powerful combination of biases interwove race with poverty and marginalized family structures or lifestyles. Explicit negative biases were most evident when these factors were thought to coexist with African American ethnicity. The implications of this legacy of historical racism are enormous and should be directly addressed in teacher-preparation programs with a focus on preparing teachers to be activists in the service of social justice (Milner, 2008; Sleeter, 2017). Our findings echo Delpit's (1995):

> Teacher education usually focuses on research that links failure and socioeconomic status, failure and cultural difference, and failure and single-parent households. . . . When teachers receive that kind of education, there is a tendency to assume deficits in students rather than to locate and teach to strengths. To counter this tendency, educators must have knowledge of their children's lives outside of school so as to recognize their strengths. (p. 172)

CHAPTER 7

At the Conference Table

The Discourse of Identity Construction

> I test; I write my report; I write my recommendations and I give it to the placement specialist. . . . We discuss it and we come to a decision. And we discuss it prior to the meeting just to make sure we are providing the best for the child. And once we have a unified front for the parents, we can bring them in just so they know what is going on.
>
> —School psychologist

The statement above typifies the argument of Mehan et al. (1986)—namely, that the special education placement conference is essentially a "ratification of actions taken earlier" (p. 164). Mehan and his colleagues emphasize that this process should not be interpreted as a "conspiracy," but as a "culmination, a formalization, of a lengthy process that originates in the classroom . . . when the teacher makes the first referral" (p. 165). They continue:

> We should not disparage this process of everyday decision-making by comparing it with rational models, formal reasoning, or scientific thinking. . . . Instead, it seems more appropriate to call into question the efficacy of scientific reasoning as a model of everyday reasoning. There are good organizational reasons why decision-making occurs as it does. The decision-making circumstances assumed to exist by the rational model are not available to problem solvers in formal organizations like schools. . . . Furthermore, the rational model assumes that all the factors being considered in the decision-making calculus have equal weight. . . . But, as we have seen, a single factor, such as the space available in the program, may outweigh all others in its consequences for decision makers. (p. 166)

Certainly, the reasoning we observed in the decision-making process was far from scientific or rational, if we understand these terms to mean a process that moves logically from a particular premise or set of premises, with the intention of accomplishing a specific goal or set of goals. However, if we bear in mind that, as Mehan et al. (1986) suggest, decisions must take into account multiple individual perspectives as well as numerous organizational factors, some of which may never have been included in the original premises, then the rationale for decisions becomes easier to understand. We found that the school district we studied had, indeed, a very rational plan for decision-making, but that the actual process was often driven by agendas and perspectives that could not be found anywhere in the official plan.

While our purpose is not to disparage, we believe that it is important to understand and make explicit the many forces that push decision-making in one direction or another. This is critical because it shows that the overrepresentation of minority groups in special education should not be understood to mean that these children *have* more disabilities than others. Rather, we believe that institutional and personal biases and beliefs combine with political pressures to produce a pattern of minority overrepresentation.

The main premise on which high-incidence disability placement is based is that the failure of some children to succeed in school is the result of disabilities. This premise gives rise to a mindset that seeks the problem within the child. It is the responsibility of school personnel to identify those children and provide them with appropriate, individualized services in the least restrictive environment. The main goal is to remediate the children's difficulties as far as possible so as to allow them to be successful. Based on these premises and goals, the school district developed the model of "collaborative consultation," described in what follows, which would lead, when necessary, to appropriate special education placement. We remind the reader that this study took place before the introduction of the RTI process.

THE RATIONAL MODEL

The school district required at least two conferences, and preferably three, for each child being considered for special education placement. At the first conference, the child study team (CST) would respond to a referral; at the second meeting of the CST, the decision would be made to refer a student for a psychological evaluation; at the placement conference, the findings of the psychologist's evaluation would be reported and a decision made about placement. Certain key school personnel were required to attend all conferences, and parents or guardians had to be invited. All personnel involved in the referral process could describe it readily, as in the following statement by a special education teacher:

> The classroom teacher will usually come to the assistant principal and say, so and so is really having problems with their schoolwork. Then we usually will meet, but the person has to have documentation that they have spoken to the parents and that they have tried a few different strategies. This makes the parent aware of it and we see what the parents have to say. And then if there really is no change, then we meet in a group, we invite the parents and we talk about what the child is doing in class and we come up with some strategies to see if we could

help the child before we do anything further. Then after 2 or 3 months, we meet again to see if there has been any change, either positive or negative. And then if there really is no substantial change, if the parent is agreeable, we decide to see if there is a processing deficit of any kind that would qualify [the child] for a learning disability. We also give them a hearing test and a vision test. We want to try and rule out all kinds of things before we go that way. Then we put all of the pieces together, of course there is some intelligence testing, too, and then we see if there is a need for placement.

We rarely saw the process carried out in quite this idealized way. A few inner-city schools that had full-service programs seemed particularly effective at trying alternative strategies before referring a child. For example, in one school that served a mixture of low-income African American and Hispanic students, there were several supportive structures and approaches that fed into the CST process. At the first signs of trouble, a screening committee used a flow chart to guide the steps required to obtain assistance from outside agencies. If the problem persisted, then the case would go to the CST. This school also had informal supports that allowed counselors to respond to teacher referrals in formats such as a daily lunchtime group-therapy session.

Regardless of variations, most conferences we observed resembled the official process in terms of the chronology of steps taken, the paperwork submitted, and the personnel participating. In all cases, however, the details of interpersonal dynamics, personal and professional beliefs, and official and unofficial agendas affected both the process and the outcomes of these conferences.

PLACEMENT PATTERNS ACROSS SCHOOLS

We have noted before that the overall placement rates in the 12 schools offered no clear-cut pattern of relationships between overrepresentation and socioeconomic status (SES) or ethnicity. Although we can see that poverty and ethnicity combined to work against children's success in a number of ways, we argue in this chapter that school cultures and the actions of key individuals were more important than were any objective features of children or school contexts.

We refer the reader once more to Table 2.4, at the end of Chapter 2, which shows that similarities in SES did not predict similar special education placement rates across schools. The four highest-income neighborhoods are placed at the top portion of the table. These schools served a range of ethnicities. In the eight schools in the lower portion of the table, Black and Hispanic students represented a range from 82% to 99% of the population, and 88% to 99% of children were on free and reduced-price lunch (FRL). In these settings, with the sole exception of one excellent school, Green Acres, several administrative issues tended to combine with poor instruction to exacerbate children's problems. Yet placement rates across these schools varied widely—from 3.5% to 9.8%.

In three schools that served higher-income populations, Bay Vista, Clearwater, and Blue Heron, the range of children on FRL was from 65.6% to 70.1%, which can be considered mid-SES, relative to the generally low income levels in this school district. In this group of schools, we rated instruction as generally very good, and achievement levels were better than at the schools with higher poverty levels. However, this did not mean that children were less likely to be referred to special education. Table 2.4 shows that Blue Heron, serving a predominantly Hispanic population, was the highest-referring school, with a placement rate of 12.5% in LD, although its rate of 65.6% FRL was the lowest in the entire group of 12 schools. Bay Vista's demographics were very similar, with an FRL rate of 68.7% and a predominance of Hispanic students, yet its placement rate of 6.6% in LD was approximately half that of Blue Heron. Clearwater, whose population was predominantly Black (mixed African American and English-speaking Caribbean ethnicities), had the lowest rate of LD placement (4.1%).

Ethnicity was as complicated a factor to interpret as was SES. For example, comparing Creekside and Palm Grove, which had a predominance of Haitian students of the same SES level (more than 97% of the students on FRL), we see that Palm Grove placed almost twice as many students in LD as did Creekside (6.8% versus 3.5%). We rated classroom instruction in both schools as very variable. The four schools with mixed ethnic populations served a much smaller range in LD—from 4.1% to 5.8%.

Only one school, Sunnybrook, presented a clear picture of a combination of ethnicity and low SES at work. As the only school in the sample serving a high-SES neighborhood, 55% of the student population was White (Anglo American), 23% Hispanic, and 17% African American, the last being bused in from a low-income neighborhood. The percentage of students on FRL was only 18.5%, which was accounted for by the African American population. In this school, we did see a clear pattern of combined low SES and ethnicity as an obvious correlate of high special education placement: Although the overall LD placement rate was low (4.1%), the rate of placement of African Americans resembled the nationwide disproportionality pattern. That is, Black students were represented in special education at twice the rate of their presence in the school population (35% in LD; 17% in the school population). Further, since we could not obtain access to the necessary records, we were unable to ascertain what percentage of students were identified as ID or EH and transferred to schools that offered these more restrictive programs.

To summarize, neither SES, ethnicity, nor general school quality could be relied on to explain placement rates in any given school. While it is clear that these factors played a role, it was also evident that each school seemed to have its own culture of referral, one that reflected the beliefs of individual teachers, administrators, and psychologists as well as pressures from the school district.

THE CULTURE OF REFERRAL

By "culture of referral," we mean the attitude toward and beliefs about children who were not doing well in the general education program, as well as beliefs about special education. Important beliefs included how quickly teachers and administrators assumed that low performance or behavioral difficulties were indicators of "something else" at work, whether these children were seen as "belonging" in general education, whether special education was seen as the solution either to the children's difficulties or the classroom teacher's frustrations, and whether special education placement was considered an appropriate response to external pressures resulting from high-stakes testing.

Although in all schools there were individual teachers whose referral patterns were either much higher or much lower than the average among their colleagues, each school faculty tended to show its own pattern of referral rates. Our observations and interviews revealed that administrators' beliefs and policies were greater determinants of these patterns than were the characteristics of the children themselves. This was underscored by very different rates at schools serving very similar student populations.

GUIDELINES FOR REFERRALS

The decision to refer must be demonstrably within the "disability" belief system, in that the referring teacher must feel reasonably confident that the child will "meet criteria" for one of the disabilities. For LD, this means the presence of a discrepancy between measured IQ and academic achievement. For ID, this means an overall "flat profile," falling well below age norms. For EBD, this means that academic achievement must be affected by evident emotional disturbance.

Beyond these general requirements, some schools and some administrative regions had specific guidelines. A common theme was to make the CST process "more selective." In one region, this took the form of an explicit expectation that the "success rate" should be high, that is, that a high percentage of those referred should be found eligible for special education. At another school, which had a relatively high rate of placement in LD (6.6%), the process appeared to be very careful. Administrators told us that great attention was paid to details of the "referral packet," such as considering the child's social and academic history, attendance patterns, and language, before bringing the packet to a CST conference. The assumption here was that there would almost always be two CST conferences before a child would be referred for evaluation. All members but the psychologist would attend both conferences. The psychologist would attend only the second. Personnel described this process as having "a lot of checks." Nevertheless, school personnel estimated that 70% to 75% of the children did go on to a second CST.

In line with the definitions of the high-incidence disabilities, there was a common guideline that referrals must reflect an academic rather than behavioral focus. We noted that most referrals were for primarily academic concerns, and some principals stated that they discouraged referrals that were basically a matter of "your classroom management," in order to encourage teachers to distinguish between their problems and those of the children. However, an outcome of this in one such school seemed to be that the teachers who were the weakest classroom managers seldom referred and simply kept jogging along with their disorderly classrooms. We also noted cases where students were originally referred for academic concerns, but the focus of the referral system soon shifted to behavioral issues (such as with Matthew).

There were other requirements that varied from school to school. At one school a kindergarten teacher informed us, "We are not allowed to refer in kindergarten." A 1st-grade teacher reported that "it is the ones who have made no progress in reading." At another school, teachers were asked to refer everyone who scored below a certain cutoff on Success for All reading tests. In the vast majority of schools, guidelines resulting from the pressure of high-stakes testing were particularly powerful and will be discussed later. Despite these guidelines, as early as the first week of the school year, many teachers could point out children who might be likely referrals. The children who "did not fit" were readily apparent.

THE TEACHER AS INITIATOR; HIGH AND LOW REFERRERS

Some of these children do not deserve to be in EH, but they have already gone through the process and the psychologist makes the recommendation. I don't know if something is wrong with the assessment procedures, but I think it is much more than the evaluation itself. I think it begins with the referrals. It needs to be questioned, what has been tried to help the child? What has the teacher done? Was the parent informed?

—Behavior management specialist

Regardless of the culture of a school, the classroom teacher is normally the initiator of the referral process. The literature on the topic of teacher referral indicates that approximately 90% of students referred by classroom teachers will be formally tested and of those tested, 73% to 90% will be found eligible for services in special education (Algozzine et al., 1982; Gerber & Semmel, 1984; Gottlieb et al., 1985; Ysseldyke, 2001). Simply put, if teachers do not refer, children will not be placed, and if teachers refer, the vast majority of the children referred will be placed in special education. Thus, to the extent possible, in selecting classrooms for intensive observations, we tried to select a high- and a low-referring teacher in the same school.

Patterns of teacher referral were as variable as was everything else in this study, with the exception of one common thread: The highest referrers were White, Hispanic, or both, while Black teachers tended to refer less often. It was not clear what was behind these differential rates. In Chapter 4, in our discussion of school contexts, we referred to a school in which there was a clear pattern of higher referrals by White teachers. Here, the White AP suggested that the African American teachers "don't believe in special education and don't trust the process for Black kids." The African American placement specialist offered an alternative explanation:

> Well, I think [it's because] the Black teachers can handle the Black kids better. They don't need to refer as much. . . . Because, you know, the Black kid is . . . hollering louder than anyone . . . so when they [the children] cut an attitude, you [Black teacher] know how to really go with it. But . . . an Anglo teacher would be offended or afraid of it, wouldn't even try to resolve it because she feels threatened by it. . . . The children only respect you if they see that you're there and you're consistent. If not, and they see your fear . . .

In contrast, one White administrator expressed the opinion that some Black teachers' style of discipline was too harsh. An African American administrator at another school believed that some Anglo American teachers just did not understand the children's situations and rushed to the notion of disability, displaying "referral fever." The most common theory was that it was mainly the strong teachers who referred a lot, the teachers who "cared." One school counselor typified this view, saying that referring teachers "have taken time out of their schedules to do a seven-page referral, and care desperately enough for children that need help."

As noted earlier, we did not detect systematic evidence of a simplistic ethnic bias in referrals. In the schools with predominantly Black or Hispanic students, there was little mixture in the classrooms, so there was no "other" group with whose referral rates we could compare. In these schools, there were some teachers who consistently referred high numbers of children, while others, teaching similar students, referred very few. Moreover, where there were Black and Hispanic groups together in a classroom, we usually noted no pattern of ethnic bias in referrals. In the only school in which African Americans represented an ethnic and low-SES minority group pitted against high-achieving, wealthy White students, there was a clear pattern in which referrals of African Americans were double those of White students. In this school it was evident that high standards were affecting referral rates. These variable patterns led us to develop an impressionistic typology of teachers that seemed to reflect teachers' philosophies, personalities, and/or implicit racial preferences.

Strong, High-Referring Teachers

Some of the strongest teachers we observed were high referrers. Others were not. In one inner-city school serving a predominantly Haitian population, we selected a very strong 3rd-grade teacher who was Anglo American and a veteran teacher of more than 20 years. In that year, she referred 15 children from her classroom or her SFA reading group, in all, more than a third of her students. These were all referrals for low academics, since this teacher's excellent instruction and classroom management seldom allowed for behavior problems to occur, even with the inclusion of one child who made himself a pest to the rest of the school. These referrals had very mixed results. At the end of the year, six had qualified, two parents had not signed permission for evaluation, one child was placed in an alternative-education class, two moved to other teachers, one left the school, and three were to be tested in the subsequent year. In the following year, the school cut class sizes in half for the early grades and this teacher then had approximately 19 children. Despite the smaller class size, by October she had already referred seven or eight children, more than one-third of this class. That year, she seemed to have a better "success rate"—five were tested and did qualify for special education. Several faculty members believed that this teacher referred far too many children.

At another school, the teacher we formerly referred to as Ms. Q was exceedingly similar to the one described above, except that she was Hispanic and much younger. This teacher told us that one year she had made so many referrals that "they" called her "downtown" to explain why. Her explanation was simple. The children needed help "desperately." She reported that she referred approximately 10 children from her class every year and said she had a "high success rate" among those who were evaluated; most qualified for LD, but a few for ID. She felt that she had a good sense for who had real problems. She spoke scornfully of the many teachers who "can't be bothered" to refer because "it's too much paperwork." She believed that special education was an effective intervention and that many children do return to the mainstream.

As we reported in Chapter 4, despite Ms. Q's evident preference for Hispanic over Black students, her referrals were proportionate to the ethnic makeup of her class. Further, while we did not always agree that every child that she referred was really problematic, many were, and we were impressed that she used the CST in line with the school district's ideal of "consultative collaboration" with parents, in which alternative strategies were suggested and implemented. We observed conferences for six of her students, and in five cases she subsequently felt that the parent conference and the strategies had helped and these children were doing better.

Strong, Low-Referring Teachers

The tendency for African American teachers to be relatively low referrers was evident across the schools serving low-income populations. Some, but not all, of these were very strong teachers. In one such school, the African American counselor (who had been a classroom teacher for 11 years and had just become a counselor) exclaimed:

> I have never written a referral on a kid. *Never*. I always feel like I can work with them. Some probably should have been referred, but I found a way to get them to respond. So, I haven't, I have not referred any children.

Two excellent Black teachers in another school offered different, sometimes contradictory opinions on referrals. The kindergarten teacher said she mostly thought that unless it was an emergency, kindergarten was too early, and the children needed a chance to catch up. However, in the second year, when she became a member of the CST, this teacher referred three children. Two of these were for seriously low achievement and were later placed in ID, and the third was a child who had been absent 28 times for the year and was retained and placed in LD pullout. When interviewed, the teacher said that she didn't think that being on the CST had changed her attitude toward special education, but that these three children really needed help.

The other very strong Black teacher offered several comments on the CST process, mostly negative. While she said that children with problems should be referred "earlier," not left until 4th grade to be referred, she also felt that the 1st grade was a bit too early. However, she was critical of the quality of special education services—she said that in her 23 years as a teacher, she had known only two children to exit special education. She felt that this contributed to a high rate of dropout among Black kids, and so she herself did not like to refer because of the stigma and ridicule the children endure when placed in special education. She concluded by saying that special education is a "big-time failure setup scapegoat!"

Weak, High-Referring Teachers

School personnel seldom spoke of this group of teachers, but we observed several. These teachers demonstrated both poor instruction and poor classroom-management skills. Ms. E, the "passive" type of teacher whom we described in Chapter 3, reported that her steadily increasing referral rate was now at about half her class. She attributed her African American students' problems to their family lives, but her classroom was typical of those in several inner-city schools—disorganized and inconsistent in discipline. This was the type of classroom from which our EBD case study students, Kanita and Robert, were referred, with no acknowledgment at the CST conferences of the classroom situation that had allowed their behavior to escalate.

A White 1st-grade teacher, whose classroom practice we described earlier as an example of diminished opportunity to learn, also referred at a high rate. In her ESOL class in a predominantly Haitian school, she referred seven of her students. Noting that it takes two teachers to fill out the forms, and frustrated by the slow pace of the referral process, she explained that many of her referred students were still not placed by 2nd or 3rd grade. Like other teachers with high referral rates, she saw herself as an advocate for her students, believing that special education would benefit them. She also blamed the school's practice of "pushing to get the 4th grades tested and placed [before the high-stakes testing]" while neglecting the needs of younger students. She said, "It is a vicious cycle because they never catch up. Students don't get the help they need until 4th grade and by then they are really low. . . . For so many years they have been playing catch-up and it is just a self-filling prophecy."

Weak, Low-Referring Teachers

These teachers were all too common in the inner-city schools, including those with lower referral rates. In many of these classrooms, taught by teachers of all ethnicities, there seemed to be no concern about the quality of their work and no concern about whether children made progress. Indeed, these seemed to be the teachers whom one principal described as "just coming in for the paycheck."

However, in other cases, low-referring weak teachers *were* conscientious and caring. For example, Ms. S, a Black 3rd-grade teacher at a predominantly Haitian school, saw special education as something to protect students from, not push them toward. She explained: "I don't refer kids for behavior. I only refer them if they are really low, when they need one-on-one." Although by all accounts she had a very "low" class, she did not make any referrals that year. She had five students who had already been retained and three more who would be retained that year. Although she herself had not referred any of her students, other teachers (that is, SFA) had referred two. In fact, 16 of her students were on the school's active Retention/Request for Evaluation Status Report because they had been referred by others or in previous years. At least five of these had been referred for a CST meeting the previous year (or earlier) but because their current teacher had not also referred them, their cases were still on hold. When questioned about this, she said that she was not aware that most of these students had been referred by a previous teacher. Like high-referring teachers, she saw herself as an advocate for her students. Yet her advocacy played out in different ways and she made tremendous efforts on her students' behalf. In the case of one boy, for example, rather than going to the CST committee, she tried to solve his problems herself by gaining parental permission to tutor him after school twice a week. Another student who was obviously quite intelligent despite his acting-out behavior had been referred to the CST for emotional and behavioral problems by a previous teacher. Ms. S did not follow through on the referral, instead pushing to have the boy placed in an honors class. She noted emphatically:

> And they can't kick him out. . . . He can do the work . . . they want him to sit quietly, but he can't. I don't care, as long as he does the work. If

he has any problems in the class, I tell him to come here. He lies on the floor by my desk and does his work. I tell him, "When you feel like you want to throw chairs, come to me." I talked with the teachers about his problems. I pleaded, "Don't kick him out! When he gets on your nerves, send him here."

To summarize, the referral process relied more on teachers' and administrators' personal beliefs about special education than on children's performance. Good intentions notwithstanding, the lesson learned was that we could not assume that referral rates or patterns reflected a systematic process.

ALTERNATIVE STRATEGIES

In addition to initiating a referral, teachers were responsible for following the referral or the first CST conference with the implementation of specified "alternative strategies," designed to address the child's needs, rather than going on to evaluation for special education. The quality of the strategies seemed to vary both by teacher and by team. All too often, the requirement was undermined by teachers' beliefs that they had already done everything needed. Indeed, some had. At one school the psychologist suggested preferential seating, positive reinforcement, and redirection as strategies, yet these were exactly the techniques the teacher had already reported using. At another school, one of the high-referring, strong teachers used a set of strategies that included after-school tutoring and daily progress reports to the parents. She commented at one meeting, "Now I think I've got the whole class on daily progress monitoring." In the best schools, the everyday instructional and behavior management strategies used by teachers simply demonstrated "good teaching," such as working at the back of the room with a small group of children, sending regular notes home to parents, having parent conferences, and using a conference-style method that allowed individualized attention to children's work.

Far more often, however, we noted a tendency to treat the "strategies" as a routine, meaningless requirement. The worst example we saw of this was a conference in which the consultation form noted the following "strategies": "write first and last name without model; identify rhyming words; hold book, paper, scissors"—all of which were simply instructional goals, not strategies. We seldom saw meaningful strategies listed at this school, and all of the six CSTs we observed were focused either on getting permission for evaluation or on discussing whether to retain or send the child to evaluation. In conferences in several schools, the possibility of retention was treated as an alternative "strategy" to evaluation for special education. Perhaps the most telling comment we received from a teacher about strategies came when the researcher asked her about the status of a particular child. She looked across the room at the student and said, "Who? Roberto? Oh, I think he's on strategies now."

"QUALIFYING" FOR SPECIAL EDUCATION: A ROCK OR A SOFT PLACE?

You meet criteria or you don't meet criteria. The testing stands on its own.

—1st-grade teacher

We have shown that the referral process was more of a reflection of teachers' and administrators' personal beliefs and practices than of children's performance. However, when it came to the moment of psychological assessment, school personnel expressed confidence in the gate-keeping role of this event. The preceding quote typified this view, and dissenting voices were rare.

Elsewhere (Harry et al., 2002), we referred to the widespread perception of the psychological assessment as the idealized "rock" of special education; the point at which hard science determines whether a disability is present. We recall the statement in Bronfenbrenner (1977) that researchers who do not attend to ecological validity get caught "between a rock and a soft place, the rock being rigor and the soft place being relevance" (p. 15). This is exactly the error of the belief that fixed "criteria" can ensure an empirical determination of essentially intangible, hard-to-measure human processes. We believe that traditional psychology, no matter its pretensions, is a "soft" science, whose softness is an advantage in teasing out the ambiguities and contradictions of human thought and emotion. This does not mean that psychology's outcomes are not valid, but they must be understood within the confines and the possibilities of an informed uncertainty. In their statements to us, some psychologists expressed their awareness of this. Regardless of what they told us, it was evident in their practice.

When a child's referral actually got to "the table," it was clear that neither "rationality" nor "science" were in control. Rather, we noted six "soft places" that informed, influenced, and at times distorted the outcomes of conferences on eligibility and placement: school personnel's impressions of the family, a focus on intrinsic deficit rather than classroom ecology, teachers' informal diagnoses, dilemmas of the disability definitions and criteria, psychologists' philosophical positions, and pressure from high-stakes testing to place a student in special education. We will treat some of these in depth here, but will hold specific discussion of others until later, when we show how they applied to individual children.

School Personnel's Impressions of the Family

We have already devoted an entire chapter to the power of school personnel's explicit belief that "dysfunctional" families were the chief cause of children's school difficulties. Despite the presence of some sympathetic voices, this belief often made it difficult to disentangle views of the family from views of the child. As we also showed, these views sometimes directly affected referral, assessment, and placement outcomes for children.

Classroom Ecology

Perhaps the most detrimental practice we observed was that CST conferences typically took no account of the ecology of the classroom from which
the child was being referred. The assumption seemed to be that the problem
was necessarily in the child, not in the environment. Typically, no one asked
whether a teacher's instruction or classroom management might be an important contributor to a child's difficulties. This was a serious omission, as was
evident in the referrals of two of our case study children, Kanita and Robert,
whose classrooms were so ineffective that children had little alternative but
to be, at best, inattentive, and at worst, troublesome. We will say much more
about the absence of attention to these contexts later.

Overall, it was ironic that school personnel readily sought the source of
children's problems in their home environments but seldom in their school
environments. As we show elsewhere in this book, all too often we saw the
latter as a powerful contributor.

Teachers' Informal Diagnoses

Mehan and colleagues (1986) found that the psychologist was accorded the
greatest status in placement deliberations. However, literature on the effects
of teacher referrals points to teacher judgment as one of the most influential
factors in assessment outcomes (Gerber & Semmel, 1984). In our study, these
two patterns seemed to converge, in that, although the psychologist's judgment was definitive, there was considerable team pressure on psychologists to
meet their colleagues' expectations.

As full members of the referral and placement teams, psychologists had
to balance their role as an expert with their role as a team member. We observed different approaches to attaining this delicate balance. Some psychologists engaged in an interactive style with team members that included casual
conversation about cases before or after conferences. Others seemed to maintain some distance. More specifically, the most interactive of the psychologists whom we observed would sometimes directly invite teachers' opinions
about the source of a child's learning difficulties, for example, asking, "Do
you think the difficulties are just a reaction to the home situation, or do
you think there's an intrinsic problem here?" This approach indicated the
"expert's" respect for the opinion of those who knew the child better, implicitly acknowledging the limitations of formal testing. The downside of this
approach, of course, was the likelihood of undue influence of the teacher's
opinion. Occurring at a preliminary CST conference, this conversation affected whether the child's referral would go forward to evaluation or go back
to the classroom for "alternative strategies." It also affected the psychologist's
expectation regarding the child's condition.

When psychologists did not agree with, or act upon, the views or recommendations of the referring teacher, team relationships could become strained.

For example, on one team, faculty dissatisfaction with a psychologist's finding that a child had attention deficit/hyperactivity disorder (ADHD) rather than an emotional disturbance was followed by an outcome that smacked of considerable manipulation. Robert's behavior had been perceived as so troublesome that he was placed on a program of half-day school attendance that lasted 5 months. Neither teachers nor administrators could fathom how Robert could fail to qualify for an EH placement. The psychologist's determination of ADHD resulted in Robert's eligibility for services under Other Health Impaired (OHI), which meant that he would be served in a part-time, pullout program in his home school. However, Robert's IEP failed to include any specification for a behavioral plan, and the placement soon proved unsuccessful. The psychologist felt impelled to "update the psychological" and qualify Robert for a self-contained EBD placement. Without systematic behavioral support, Robert didn't have a chance to succeed in the pullout placement. We suspect that this was an example of the considerable, though covert, power of the team. He was ultimately moved to an EBD program at another school. We will tell more of Robert's story later.

Psychologists' Philosophies

Psychologists evidenced three main philosophical orientations that had powerful implications for their practice: their preferences for some testing instruments over others, their beliefs about the importance of cultural and linguistic diversity in their testing, and their beliefs about the efficacy of special education.

With regard to assessment of children suspected of having an emotional disturbance, this school district required the use of projective tests such as the Roberts Apperception Test, the House-Tree-Person, and others. We have referred before to the unreliability and subjectivity involved in projective testing (Gresham, 1993; Knoff, 1993; Motta et al., 1993). Our discussions with psychologists revealed that, while they generally had confidence in the tests, their approaches to administration varied. For example, those who used the Thematic Apperception Test reported using it in different ways, such as using all items in the test or using only a few selected items. Similarly, some would routinely complete a battery of four or five tests, while others would select one or two and terminate the testing if the child seemed to be scoring well— that is, not indicating signs of emotional disturbance.

With regard to IQ testing, psychologists' selection of instruments reflected their beliefs about the nature of their craft. Despite current understanding in the field that IQ tests assess children's learning, one psychologist, who used the WISC-III, offered the opinion that the IQ tests do measure "inborn intelligence." In contrast, many expressed concern about the applicability of these tests to culturally and linguistically diverse students. Some of these psychologists selected instruments such as the Kauffman Assessment Battery for Children (KABC) or the Differential Ability Scales (DAS), which, by being "less verbally loaded," are thought to be more appropriate for children from diverse cultural and linguistic backgrounds.

Psychologists' preferences for certain tests were intertwined with their views of the relationship between testing contexts and children's cultural and linguistic experiences. Some psychologists spoke of the limitations of standardized American tests in assessing the capabilities of children from low-SES backgrounds or from localities such as Haiti and parts of Central America. In the case of Haiti, for example, quite apart from cultural differences, poverty and limited schooling made these tests particularly inappropriate. Further, the American practice of placing children in grades according to their chronological age meant that Haitian and other immigrant children were often placed at a level far above the level they had been at in their home countries. This presaged certain failure, which, after a short time, would come to be interpreted as an indicator of disability. Psychologists' attempts to give such children the benefit of the doubt often resulted in what teachers perceived as a juggling act, whereby "easier" IQ tests would be used to allow the child to earn a higher IQ score, so as to gain the required discrepancy between IQ and academic achievement. Gaining this score, the child could "qualify" for an LD program rather than the more stigmatizing ID program.

The foregoing concern was related to psychologists' third philosophical orientation—their view of the efficacy of special education or their preferences for one categorical placement over another. One psychologist said that she often put children in special education to "save" them, because she trusted that the smaller class size and relative individualization would improve the child's rate of progress. To the contrary, another psychologist believed strongly in keeping children in the mainstream wherever possible, especially those with behavioral problems, because placement in an EBD program would almost always be very restrictive. She was also very reluctant to designate children as ID because of the high likelihood of mistaking the impact of poverty and diverse cultural and social experience for evidence of low intelligence. This psychologist also emphasized the effect of the relativity of standards across schools and neighborhoods.

We concluded that many of the processes we saw were truly professional, with psychologists bringing extensive information, responsiveness, and insight to a difficult task. In all cases, the outcomes we saw varied with the three sets of beliefs outlined above and with the other pressures described in this chapter. Some psychologists seemed unduly influenced by preconceived beliefs about children and families. Some were more influenced than others by their colleagues. We saw some prejudice, much concern, and many social pressures that ran in different directions. *Overall, the arbitrariness of the process was frightening. We did not see science.*

Skrtic (1991) defined professional work as "complex work . . . that is too ambiguous, and thus too uncertain, to be reduced to a sequence of routine subtasks." Agreeing with this, we do not argue that special education decision-making ought to be "scientific." We do not believe, in fact, that there is a rock. Rather, we believe that an informed and caring subjectivity should guide well-trained professionals in making decisions about services for children. We note, however, that much of the arbitrariness we saw in the process is the result of the unnecessary requirement for the assigning of a categorical disability.

High-Stakes Testing as a Filter for Disability

During the years of this research, special education students' scores on statewide testing were not included in the state's rating of schools. These rankings bring sanctions and rewards in the form of funding, vouchers for children to be moved to other public schools or private schools, and, no less important, perceived status in the community. Thus, it became important for school personnel to identify those students whose performance might "bring down our scores."

A new definition of disability. The policy in place during our research made a mockery of the construct of disability as the criterion for placement in special education programs. It demonstrated two points we made in Chapter 1: First, it is paradoxical that costly, specialized services, attained through powerful parent and professional advocacy, should come to be seen as detrimental to minority groups because of stigma and questionable efficacy. This paradox becomes more intense when the low achievement of minority students results in their being seen as "having" disabilities, instead of their receiving instruction appropriately tailored to their needs.

Second, we referred to the trajectory of special education and the education of minority groups as reflecting a "collision course." In this district, high-stakes testing and special education had become the crossroads for this collision. Many administrators openly discussed changes they had instituted because of new accountability measures. For example, when one principal was asked whether she thought the state testing and the state grading plan had actually influenced the referral process, she replied:

> Yes. Very definitely it has because when we looked at our scores this year we had no zeros, thankfully. We will take writing for an example—we had no zeros, scored on a zero-to-six scale. But we had ones across the board—*those are our special education students who have not been identified.* Those kinds of scores count in our school's [grade]. They pull our score down, just one factor in the total of the 4th grade, and it brings your score down. *And one student can make the difference between one letter grade and another*, and then that stigma is attached not only to that classroom, to the students, but to the entire school. Where it might be one or two students that if they had been identified early enough, [their scores] could have been factored out of the total results. So that is a very telling statistic and yes, it does emphasize our

making sure that we identify children with special needs prior to the fourth grade. (emphasis added)

The notion that struggling students are actually "our special education students who have not been identified" represents, in essence, a new definition of disability. By this reasoning, *low achievement came to be synonymous with special education eligibility—in short, with disability.* The drive to identify special education students prior to the year they would first take the state's high-stakes tests was described explicitly by principals determined to improve their schools' grades. Though we have multiple examples of this, we will focus on one inner-city school principal who predicted at the beginning of the project that the state's accountability plan would affect referrals:

> I think you're going to see a greater number [of students referred]. I think that principals are going to feel their backs against the wall and whatever it's going to take to make sure that the school is achieving, that's what they're going to do. . . . I know as a principal I'm looking at all options at this point. Where can we see growth and where are we going to put our energies and what must be done in order to do this . . . looking at everyone.

A year later, soon after schools' "grades" had been announced and this school had earned a D, the same principal said:

> I've told the teachers that we've got to identify those children who should be getting special education help and get them over there. We know darned well they should be there, so let's get on with it. . . . This is the reality. It's a matter of survival now!

A teacher in that school reported that there was "a big push to test as many as possible so they won't qualify for the [high-stakes tests] in a couple of years." At the end of the final year of our research project, the school's ranking had moved up to a C. An interview with the principal confirmed that she had set out to ensure that children who needed services were tested to see if they would qualify for special education. She felt that the effort had been successful and that "it was about time," since too many children previously had been left in general education long after it was evident that they were years behind. She believed that this strategy had contributed to the school's new ranking.

This principal's efforts were admirable in many ways. She instituted a program of testing every child at the very beginning of the school year to determine their reading and math levels, followed by weekly testing and official posting of scores. This was supported by intensive small-group instruction, described as follows:

> We took the teachers who did not have classroom responsibilities . . . the reading leader, the Success for All reading tutor, the system locator,

the computer facilitator. . . . Each was assigned a classroom and they
went with the teacher and took 10 to 15 children or however many and
took them out of that classroom and they worked with them on those
skills. We double dosed them in reading or math. Everyone has reading
for an hour and a half, from 9:00 to 10:30. From 10:30 to 11:30 every
day, the children receive [high-stakes-test] reading skills. And those are
the skills that they need to pass. Then 4th grade receives another hour
in writing. Math for 5th grade was done differently because they receive
their hour and a half of reading and then they receive a double dose
of math, regular math, and then [high-stakes-test] math. . . . That and
prayer!

A serious limitation to the program described above was that, while general
education students received more intensive, small-group tutoring, the opposite occurred in special education classes. The reassignment of general education and special area teachers to reading instruction for extended periods
meant a reduction in the resources that usually allowed for small-group special education instruction. Special education teachers found themselves with
groups of students larger than the groups in general education.

Overall, high-stakes testing actually changed the nature of the referral
process in schools in which principals took such actions. Normally, the process placed the responsibility for referral in the hands of teachers. As we have
explained, however, teachers showed great variability in their willingness to
refer. Principals who were trying to "identify" all the special education students before they were tested felt vindicated in their efforts when they discovered that there were children in the 4th grade in their school who could not
read, and whom everyone seemed to have ignored up until then. The principal cited above simply took this matter into her own hands:

A lot of teachers don't like to [refer]. What we have done this year,
we've tried to have patience with them. But we know that they are a
problem and we have our AP go in and we do it for them.

This process, then, directly affected referral rates. Yet when asked if it would
be correct to say that the high-stakes-testing demands had actually increased
special education placements, this principal replied that since the children
"had to qualify" for those services, this qualification would confirm that
they really needed them. She then noted the excellent skills of their psychologist. This psychologist, however, had been observed to be under considerable
pressure to place a child in an LD program even though the child had not
met the "discrepancy" criterion. This was one of the ironies in our findings:
Principals and teachers felt justified in increasing their referrals because they
thought psychologists would only identify those students who actually met
criteria. Yet it was evident that some psychologists did succumb to the administration's pressure to place students. One told us that she did her best to
respond to this pressure by choosing instruments that would be more likely

to "find" the suspected disability. One of these, a test commonly reputed to be unreliable and biased, she referred to as "her secret weapon."

It was not only the failing schools that felt this pressure. In one of the highest-achieving and highest-income schools in the sample, a special education teacher told us that there was a significant increase in the number of 4th-graders entering the special education program. When asked why, she replied, "[High-stakes] testing, of course. The teachers are under a lot of pressure."

Do the ends justify the means? The intensive search for failing children was not without some strengths, since it provided principals with a lever to force attention onto students who previously had been "passed along" without ever attaining grade-level academic skills. Some principals described this pressure as an opportunity to redress this disservice to children. If children did improve, then it is difficult to argue that the ends do not justify the means.

In contrast, our observations of special education classrooms indicated that there was little reason to believe that such placement would be more appropriate than most effective general-education classrooms. As described earlier, in one school, an excellent remedial program for general education students took away from the promise of small groups in special education classes. Ironically, if not for the desire to remove failing students from the mainstream, the remedial program could have been used for everyone. It could have become, simply, the model of general education implemented in that school by a bright and motivated administrator. It could have been accomplished without the need for an arbitrary border between normalcy and disability. Instead, the model that emerged resembles the UK system described by Gillborn and Youdell (2000) as "a form of educational triage, a means of rationing support so that some pupils are targeted for additional teacher time and energy while others are seen as inevitable casualties of the battle to improve standards" (p. 14).

The "accountability" pressure on schools in this state is tremendous. As educators, we agree that some version of this type of accountability is needed and appropriate. However, the extent of pressure placed on schools by the state-ranking plan, tied to the results on high-stakes tests, is extreme. All too often, we saw clear examples of many teachers' statement that they no longer had the professional autonomy to adjust either the content or pace of the curriculum to the needs of their students.

CONCLUSIONS

In concluding our consideration of the discourse by which schools constructed "disabled" student identities, we find that the work of both Mehan et al. (1986) and Skrtic (1991, 2005) point to central ironies and paradoxes in special education service provision. Skrtic (2005) maintained that the goals of special education are essentially those of an "adhocracy"—which should be "premised on innovation rather than standardization, on the invention of personalized practices through organizational learning grounded in collaboration, mutual adaptation and reflexive discourse" (p. 150). However, Skrtic (1991) argued, two other models have affected special education: the culture of a professional bureaucracy, in which highly trained individuals work alone to perfect standard goals, and a machine bureaucracy, which attempts to further standardize by developing "an organization in which worker behavior is controlled by procedural rules" (p. 184).

In our research we saw the interaction of these competing models at work. Psychologists' professional interpretations of children's complex needs were hamstrung by fixed "criteria" for categorical placements. Placement specialists' attempts to develop individualized educational programs were defeated by a climate that emphasized only compliance with legal requirements. School administrators, trying to keep their schools and reputations afloat, created "triage" sorting systems to decide which children could be saved and which sacrificed. General education teachers, stressed by large class sizes and inequitable administrative practices, put their faith in an idealized vision of special education that was very unlikely to be realized. And family members were largely excluded from the discourse because of negative stereotypes and because seeking their genuine participation might further complicate a process that everyone wanted to simplify.

The impact of high-stakes testing on special education referrals was one more example of the machine bureaucracy at work. In this case, the extreme sorting process mandated by the NCLB act worked against the best interests of children whose achievement was toward the weak end of the learning continuum. The drive to find "our special education children who have not been placed" resulted in appropriate interventions for some and very inappropriate interventions and placement for others. Indeed, to frame the issue in terms of that quotation was to confound low achievement with disability.

In an adhocracy, it would be appropriate that decisions should reflect what Mehan et al. (1986) referred to as "everyday" rather than "scientific" reasoning. Everyday reasoning, as long as it is well reasoned, would be a natural part of problem-solving. We understand that the variable, often inequitable, circumstances of schools will limit the possibility of systematic decision-making that proceeds from clear premises and principles. However, that very inequity and variability is the reason for the field to move toward the most flexible service provision possible. Perhaps learning disability should not be conceived of as a condition that can be measured by the same yardstick for all children. Perhaps troublesome behavior cannot be categorized as either disturbance or deliberate noncompliance. Perhaps mental or developmental delay does not mean that children need to be in separate programs. Perhaps there is no rock.

The introduction of the RTI model brought great hope for a more flexible and targeted approach to instruction and evaluation of children's learning needs, but as always in special education, the challenge lies in transforming an idea into reality. In the introduction to this third edition, we outlined what we were able to learn about the current implementation of RTI in this school district. The information we gleaned from the district's official RTI documents and from anecdotal conversations with a well-informed school district staffing specialist suggested a stark contrast between the official model and real-world practice. Typical of the implementation of most school reforms, RTI has been conceptualized as a step-by-step process that can be monitored by "purely technical solutions" (Bal & Harper, 2014), which, on paper, guarantee a rational process. However, we believe that this does little to address the deep understandings of those who must implement the change. Unfortunately, research by Cavendish (2013) and Cavendish and colleagues (2016) in this school district suggest that lack of adequate personnel preparation for RTI has resulted in minimal change of mindset regarding referral practices. It seems also that actual implementation of the model leaves open the question of whether RTI documentation should replace a comprehensive psychological evaluation (Gartland & Strosnider, 2020; Reschly, 2014).

Certainly, one size should not be expected to fit all in a multicultural, multilingual, society where wealth is so inequitably distributed and where the legacy of centuries of racism is still palpable. For the most vulnerable of children to be placed at increased risk of decisions that may negatively affect their educational careers, indeed their identities, is to impose upon them one more inequity.

CHAPTER 8

Bilingual Issues and the Referral Process

It's easier to determine if a disability exists in a bilingual program.

—Counselor in a bilingual school

In this culturally and linguistically diverse school district, careful attempts have been made to address the challenge of ensuring that language learning processes among children whose native language is not English are not mistaken for learning or other disabilities. The referral process for these students is similar except for the additional involvement of a bilingual assessor, an ESOL teacher, and a Committee focusing on children with Limited English Proficiency (LEP) (which would now be referred to as English learners or emergent bilingual students).

As with the district's official referral policies, the written guidelines for English learners (ELs)—that is, bilingual students not yet fully proficient in English—were excellent. However, our findings regarding the efficacy of this system were quite mixed, suggesting that, once more, much had to do with the quality of the school, the knowledge of key players, and the culture of referral. Although school personnel seemed quite knowledgeable about the district's referral policies for native English speakers, and could explain them articulately, we noted much more confusion regarding the process for ELs.

THE RATIONAL MODEL

One AP explained the process clearly:

> The first thing to do with an English language learner is address his language proficiency. Is it a situation where a child is having difficulty with language? So at the LEP committee [the committee set up to monitor ELs' progress], we look for alternative strategies, and we try to get the parent involved in any tutoring that the child might need. . . . We consider whether or not we need to reclassify the child's ESOL level, or that he needs a little more time, some strategies, some alternatives,

and then we continue monitoring him. Children aren't just dropped when they exit ESOL, but they are monitored for 2 years. And during that time they still have to be going to the LEP committee before they go to a child study team (CST), because it might still be a language issue. After a certain amount of time if we see that the child is still having difficulties then we ask for assistance from the CST.

At the first CST, if the child is at an intermediate level of English proficiency (ESOL Level 3 or 4), he is referred to the bilingual assessor for evaluation in English and his native language. The students who are in ESOL 5 and are at the 32nd percentile in reading or lower and have been exited from the program for less than 2 years are also evaluated. According to one bilingual assessor, the reason for this is that

> if a child is brand new, and is an ESOL Level 1 or 2, they do not need to be evaluated by the bilingual assessor. . . . You cannot evaluate them based on their English, you have to go based on their home language. So, if the child has not been here a sufficiently long time to acquire the second language, the evaluation must be based on information or the input that you have on their home language. A bilingual psychologist tests them in their native language only.

However, this policy not to refer students at ESOL Levels 1 and 2 to a bilingual assessor was changing during the years of our investigation. We were told that schools now had the option of asking for a bilingual assessment for students who are ESOL 1 and 2.

The report from the bilingual assessor is supposed to be completed and sent to the psychologist before the second CST meeting. Bilingual assessors administer the Brigance Inventory, written and oral narratives, a social-language inventory, and perhaps additional standardized tests. A bilingual assessor explained:

> You have to look at it holistically, and ask when the child arrived, where was he born, how long has he been in ESOL, what kind of support he has received, is he attending the bilingual programs? Is he in an ESOL self-contained class versus a pullout program? You need to look at all of these things.

The required process is based on Cummins's (1984) well-known distinction between cognitive academic language proficiency and basic interpersonal communicative skills. Thus, the bilingual assessor's evaluation determines whether the child is still in the process of learning formal academic language and whether the child's academic difficulties might be caused by other factors in addition to those associated with language learning. The psychologist takes this into account in assessing the child.

As explained by Hoover et al. (2018), the outcome of an adequate as-sessment should be the development of an individual education plan (IEP) that attends specifically to the language-learning needs of the student, such as attention to the child's academic English, vocabulary development, and accommodations such as native language materials, peer interactions in the native language and incorporation of the native language into instruction. Hoover's list of "red flags" indicating weak planning for bilingual learners were evident in our data.

INADEQUATE ASSESSMENT

The preceding description reflects an idealized version of a process that we rarely saw implemented in this form. In reality, the bilingual assessors were backlogged, and we detected little direct evidence of their influence. We never saw a bilingual assessor attend a CST meeting or placement conference. When questioned about this, we were told that this was "because of the level of work to do. We have over 200 referrals per person in the office per year." This heavy workload was reflected in the very long waiting periods typical for bilingual assessments. The presence of these professionals at CST and place-ment conferences was sorely missed. Even when it had been determined that a child could be tested in English, this did not negate the fact that English lan-guage learning issues were still relevant to understanding the child's problems. We rarely heard any mention at all of the bilingual evaluations. And with the exception of one psychologist who frequently questioned teachers and others about issues related to language acquisition, we rarely saw evidence that these factors were considered when referral or placement decisions were made.

Our research site was not unique in this regard. A survey of 859 school psychologists by Ochoa, Rivera, and Powell (1997) indicated that they fre-quently omitted critical factors such as consideration of the student's native language and the number of years of English instruction. Only 1% attempted to determine if a discrepancy occurred in both English and the student's home language. A review of literature by Rodriguez and Rodriguez (2017) sum-marized numerous flaws in prereferral interventions and assessment prac-tices, and low priority on the provision of teachers, classrooms, and material resources for EL students. Sullivan (2011) detailed these factors and warned against the use of special education as a replacement for appropriate lan-guage support, instruction, and curriculum.

STAFF CONFUSION

Another barrier to effective implementation was confusion among those responsible for carrying out the process. Although some school person-nel seemed quite knowledgeable about district requirements, many seemed uncertain. At one school, the AP who was in charge of the referral process did not seem to know the difference between the bilingual assessor and the bilingual psychologist, referring to them interchangeably. When asked for the name of the bilingual assessor, she provided the name of the psychologist instead. Other personnel also seemed confused about the role of the bilingual assessor and the purpose of testing. At a CST meeting at another school, we noted the following:

> I asked the counselor to clarify the role of the bilingual assessor for me. She says he will test the child's academic skills in Creole, to see if he has learned them in his native language. She explains this for a couple of minutes, then pauses and looks a bit doubtful. Then she turns to the team members and comments that maybe that's not right, since he may not have learned those things in Creole yet. They nod. The conversation drifts off.

At a third school, the psychologist stated emphatically, "The district will not allow psychological testing of young children at ESOL Levels 1 and 2." At yet another school, the psychologist explained to a CST, "He can't be referred anyway until he's ESOL Level 4." The teacher asked if the child could be referred for a bilingual assessment, and the psychologist responded, "No, his ESOL level is too low; they won't accept it."

This issue of when to refer a child certainly caused confusion. When we questioned the district administrator responsible for establishing EL policy about whether there was a rule stipulating that beginning-level ELs should not be referred, she responded, "No, not at all. No, no. At every meeting, in fact at every regional or AP meeting that we have gone to, we say it. All children have access to any categorical program." At another point in the conversation she said:

> One of the issues in terms of ESOL students is that we [in general around the country] wait until the students become proficient in English. But that doesn't happen too much in this district. We sometimes don't really have "underreferral." I think that on the average schools overrefer. That is my perception of what we have out there.

An additional challenge seemed to be the beliefs of individual practitioners. Although the professionals with whom we spoke were knowledgeable about Cummins's (1984) assertions that it takes up to 7 years for a student to acquire cognitive academic language proficiency in English, some confided that they did not really think it took that long. When questioned about this, one bilingual psychologist explained,

> It depends. If they've been taught and if you ask me about an immigrant, a Colombian who is coming without the language, by

the 3rd year they should be able to have social[-language proficiency in English] . . . . So if they have started here since kindergarten and they have heard the language every day, they should be able to learn it like any other student. So even though they switch [to using their native language] at home, it doesn't matter. You see, I was born in [a Spanish-speaking country] but I went to an American school all of my life. So I know what it is like [to learn English]. In my head I have the experience, so I expect [students to acquire English quickly].

DIFFERENTIATING BETWEEN ENGLISH LANGUAGE ACQUISITION AND LEARNING DISABILITIES

It is notoriously difficult to differentiate between normal second language acquisition and learning disabilities (Gonzalez et al., 1997; Ortiz, 1997; Rodriguez & Rodriguez, 2017). This distinction is particularly problematic among children who do not seem strong in either their native language or English. One bilingual assessor explained how challenging the process is:

My role as a bilingual assessor is to determine if the child's difficulties are due to [learning a second] language or due to other factors. Sometimes it might be something I don't know. Sometimes I don't have all of the facts in front of me. Sometimes the discrepancy is so thin. Maybe if they give him more time, he'll make it. Maybe we will give him 2 years and with more time we'll see a change. Maybe sometimes we know that 2 years will not help. Sometimes it is just kind of struggle to see.

In part, placement decisions are difficult because no test of language proficiency has yet been developed that can adequately let us know when a child whose primary language is not English is ready to be tested only in English (Figueroa, 1989; Ortiz, 1997). Even children who demonstrate English proficiency on language assessment measures still typically demonstrate a low Verbal IQ and high Performance IQ profile. If a child was transitioned prematurely, for example, from a bilingual or ESOL program to a regular classroom, this is likely to have had a negative impact on achievement and also depress scores on tests of intelligence. Authors such as Trueba (1989) have challenged the practice of blaming low achievement on low IQ, stressing the importance of looking further at the context within which underachievement occurs. Yet, as described in earlier chapters about our case study students, we saw little evidence of such considerations. Although the bilingual assessors seemed quite knowledgeable about these issues, because they did not attend CST meetings or staffings, they were not in a position to share their expertise.

Personnel at our school with a full bilingual program expressed the opinion that it is easier to identify students with learning disabilities when they are in a bilingual program, "because you can tell if they are having difficulties in Spanish, their native language, as well as in English. You can determine if the child's difficulty is due to confusion learning a new language, or something broader that is apparent in both languages." In addressing this issue, one psychologist explained:

> At [ESOL] Level 3, you start forgetting the native language so the child may have poor vocabulary in both languages, so it is hard to tell if it's a learning disability. Then the tests that are in Spanish are based on norms for monolinguals and these kids are not. So you just do the best you can. . . . The kid falling between proficiency in both languages does poorly. Only in a full bilingual program is the kid likely to adequately maintain both languages.

VARIABLE REFERRAL RATES

The phenomenon of "high-" and "low-referring" schools applied as much to schools with high percentages of EL children as to those with mainly monolingual populations. Indeed, among the four predominantly Hispanic schools, LD placement rates ranged from 4.2% to 12.5%. In the two predominantly Haitian schools the rates were 6.8% and 3.5%.

The most common explanations for varying placement rates had little relevance to differences among children. Rather, they reflected differences in school personnel's beliefs about special education, beliefs about English language acquisition, knowledge of the process, and also how busy the person was. The district-level administrator quoted earlier noted that school-level administrators have a lot of control over how the process is actually carried out in their schools. The issue of "high-referring" versus "low-referring" was tension filled. At one of the high-referring schools, the counselor believed that its rate should be viewed positively:

> We are considered a high-referral school. The district was saying that there were too many referrals. . . . But if the teachers identify more kids that they suspect may have a problem, then they have to work harder because they have to do a lot of paperwork. We have to work harder because we have to do more meetings. But we are trying to help the kids so we don't mind. But then, by the same token, the psychologist needs to test more. The staffing specialist needs to do more staffing, because it affects everybody. When you are considered high referral, it's not good. You are definitely not looked upon favorably.

By contrast, district personnel shared concerns about other schools they considered to be low-referring. One bilingual assessor expressed the view that at some schools "not enough" children were being placed. Another said that for a few years they had received no referrals from one of our schools—"Zero!"

The bilingual assessors with whom we spoke speculated about why some schools are reluctant to refer:

> There are many reasons. Sometimes they are cautious to refer a child . . . because they don't want to do all of the paperwork and find out that the child doesn't meet criteria for services. And there are a lot of cases like that. . . . Maybe it has to do with the person in charge of the referrals. Some people do not believe that the child belongs in special education and say, "Let me give that child a chance." Some people see special education as a negative thing.

PARENTS' ROLE IN THE PROCESS

We were also told that parents' reluctance to place their children in special education and parents' misunderstandings about the process were additional challenges. Issues we noted concerned the use of translators, as well as parents' beliefs about their heritage language.

Misunderstandings Due to Inadequate or Sporadic Translation Services

Despite the great presence of Spanish speakers and Haitian Creole speakers in this region, the district provided translations of some, but not all, official documents. Translation of CST and placement conferences generally was provided by the classroom teachers who were present; the counselor; or, at some schools, the community involvement specialist. However, this depended on the population in each school. In one 99% Hispanic school, all members of the CST, with the exception of the AP, spoke Spanish. This presented a tremendous advantage for parents; all the conferences we observed were conducted in Spanish. It was rather awkward, however, for the AP and severely limited her role.

In most schools it was not difficult to find a Spanish interpreter, but interpreters for Haitian Creole were much harder to come by, and occasionally no one was available to translate. From what we could surmise, those who translated had not received any special training in how to translate the results of a psychological evaluation. We noted that there were misunderstandings when adequate translation services were not provided, even when parents seemed to speak English well, as in the example below from a CST meeting with a Haitian Creole speaker:

> The AP reviews the information on the form. She asks if this was Antoine's first time here at school. The father replies yes. . . . They seem to misunderstand him to be saying that Antoine just started

here this year. So the teacher asks, "Didn't he come to kindergarten here last year?" The father asks the interpreter, "What she say?" She translates and he tells her, "Yes, Antoine was here last year." [Later, the translator needed to leave and the meeting continued without translation services.]

A community involvement specialist who was the usual translator at her school spoke about her scheduling difficulties:

I went to about three [CST] last week. They had already scheduled the time and they never let me know beforehand. . . . It is a scheduling issue; it is hard, when you schedule a parent to come to a CST, that takes parents from work and you cannot ask them to come back. So when they are there they are trying to do as much as possible. But usually I am there to translate or Mr. M. He's the Creole-speaking visiting teacher, and some of our teachers are also there and they speak Creole.

Parents' Attitudes Toward Their Home Language

Information on the attitudes of some Haitian parents toward the importance of Haitian Creole was a poignant reminder of how societal attitudes toward devalued minority groups can be internalized by group members. In this city, where Spanish is a highly accepted language, we never heard of Spanish-speaking parents denying their home language. We heard this only in the case of Haitian Creole speakers who sometimes would indicate to school personnel that their children spoke only English when in fact the children spoke both Creole and English. The following conversation is about parents' attitudes toward speaking their home language and letting their children participate in the Home Language program. The Haitian community involvement specialist reported that some parents only wanted their children to learn English but that she was able to change their minds by pointing out the benefits of being multilingual. She explained:

Oh, definitely, yes. We have some of them like that. The first time they really don't know what is going on, they are like, "Haiti, I am ashamed of it, so I don't speak Creole; Creole never helped me and I don't need Creole when I come here." . . . But when they come to register, they are asked, "Do you speak another language at home?" and then they put "yes." . . . If you have "yes" . . . the child needs to go to ESOL, then they need to go to Creole classes. But some of them when . . . they put the "yes," we put the child in those classes and then they come back and say, "My child doesn't speak Creole, why did you put him?" "But that is what you answered in your form." And then they say, "No, I don't want them to speak Creole." Once,

I remembered that she couldn't speak English and I asked her why she didn't want her daughter to learn Creole. She said, "No, because Creole is not important for my child, she will stay in the United States. She needs to speak English." And then I told her, "To me it is an opportunity to learn another language. She knows how to speak English but as a parent it is good for you to teach the child Creole because when you go back home one day that child will not want to speak to your mom, to the grandparents, to the friends." And she was taking it in, and I said, "You see where I am now, why do you think I am here? That is because I speak Creole, I speak French, and I speak English. If I didn't know how to speak Creole they would have never put me in a position like this." And I told her, "And we have a Creole class at night, and we have a lot of professionals, doctors and lawyers, in that class because of the needs of the community and they need to speak to the community. They have to learn the language." . . . She was like, "Oh, that is true." They said that they didn't know, and then they want their child in that classroom. . . . If it is good for their child then they are OK. Once I explain it to them then they are OK with it.

CONCLUSIONS

Overall, we noted several instances of concern. Although personnel appeared to be well trained, individual children's language needs were not as central to the referral process as they should have been. We noted that even in schools in which bilingual issues seemed to be well understood by key players, children's language needs and the influence of their limited proficiency on learning and behavior were not discussed at CST meetings or placement conferences; nor were they written into evaluation reports. We detail specific examples of this in subsequent chapters. It seemed that personnel felt that once a child had been through a bilingual assessment, there was no more need to attend to this feature.

Although, nationally, ELs are only marginally overrepresented in LD categories, emerging evidence suggests that subgroups of ELs may be particularly vulnerable to misclassification. In their study of the placement rates in special education of EL subgroups, Artiles and colleagues (2002) found that those students classified as lacking proficiency in both their first language and in English were heavily overrepresented. However, as indicated in Table 2.2 and 2.3 in Chapter 2, this district reflects the national pattern, with Hispanic students only slightly overrepresented in the LD category. It is possible that further research sorting placements by Latinx/Hispanic subgroups could yield interesting information given the considerable differences in national and language backgrounds of students identified as "Hispanic" in this school district.

We have focused in these past two chapters on the discourse by which children's school identities were officially determined. Although we noted many informed professional opinions that were appropriate to such discourse, it seemed that decisions were all too often undermined by the tension between professionalism, administrative and workload pressures, and the demand for categorization of students. In the following three chapters, we narrow our focus to detail the processes by which individual students were determined to be eligible for special education services. We focus also on the outcomes of those decisions.

CHAPTER 9

Constructing Intellectual Disability
Cracks and Redundancies

The placement specialist informs Mrs. Carey [the referring teacher] that Mercedes does not qualify for any special education program. The school psychologist tells Mrs. Carey about Mercedes's achievement and IQ scores. One is too high and the other is too low. Therefore, she doesn't qualify. Mrs. Carey says that she doesn't believe that Mercedes is not EMR. The psychologist tells Mrs. Carey that she gave her the test that would render the lowest scores (trying to qualify her for special education services). Mrs. Carey is visibly upset. She says that . . . special education is "all backwards. Basically, you mean to tell me she is too low to qualify for the LD program and too high for EMR? So, she is just going to fall through the cracks? Then what is she going to do in middle school? I won't be there to watch over her anymore." Mr. Talbot explains that they have the same [placement] procedures in middle school. The best he can do is write a note for them to look over her case in middle school. . . .

Mrs. Smithe, the special education teacher, states that Mrs. Carey's extra help with Mercedes probably led to an increase in her achievement scores. The school psychologist agrees. . . . Mrs. Carey responds incredulously, "Are you saying that it is my fault!?" She continues about the nightmare she has about these students being overlooked. The special education teacher says, "You taught them too well." Ultimately the team recommends peer tutoring for Mercedes.

In this and the next two chapters, we address the cracks and redundancies that plague the high-incidence categories in which students of color are over-represented. Although the acronym EMR (Educable Mental Retardation) was the term in use at the time of the study, it is now generally out of use and we will use the current term Intellectual Disability (ID), except when using direct quotations. We begin with the placement process for this category, looking at the dysfunction that arises from overly rigid diagnostic criteria and from the inability to provide special education services without "proof" of disability.

"FALLING BETWEEN THE CRACKS"

The conundrum faced by Mercedes's assessment team captures two essential shortcomings of the categorical construction of ID, LD, and EBD: First, these disabilities are conceptualized as fixed conditions whose distinctive characteristics will lead to the correct diagnosis. Second, children cannot receive specialized services without "qualifying" for one of these categories. This medical model of disability does not translate well into the complex and social contexts of education. A number of obvious contextual issues arise: Did the child have adequate opportunity to learn or to correct early learning difficulties? Is the child's social behavior a temporary expression of emotional distress? How consistent and how severe does this behavior have to be to be considered a disturbance? Are peer-group pressures contributing to the problem? Can parents be of assistance? As in the case of Mercedes, could a teacher such as Mrs. Carey make a difference?

Unfortunately, the field has not sought answers in the social contexts of schools (Artiles et al., 2010; Keogh & Speece, 1996). Rather, in support of the categorical medical model, it has turned to definitions, operational criteria, and futile efforts to measure intangible context-free and race-neutral characteristics (Carter et al., 2017; Freedman & Ferri, 2017). These attempts continue to fail. As explained in Chapter 2, efforts to crystallize the distinction between LD and ID have historically focused on identifying a discrepancy between academic achievement and cognitive potential (as measured by an IQ score) and on ruling out competing etiologies such as other impairments or environmental disadvantages. But identifying the discrepancy required for an LD diagnosis means waiting until the child is old enough to demonstrate academic competency, which also means waiting until the child is old enough to fail. Appropriate interventions may be introduced too late. These criteria also mean that children from low-income circumstances may not be considered for the category partly because of the exclusionary definition and partly because the cultural content of IQ measures may make it difficult for them to score high enough to achieve the required discrepancy (Collins & Camblin, 1983).

Mercedes's case presents a somewhat convoluted version of the LD/ID conundrum. In her case, although the psychologist gave Mercedes an IQ test on which she expected her to gain a low score, Mercedes did better than expected and scored too high to qualify for ID. It seems that an effective teacher had interfered with the profile by teaching Mercedes so well that her academic scores were too high for her to display the "discrepancy" required for LD eligibility. This case illustrates perfectly Gergen's (1994) argument that the "increasing entanglements" (p. 143) of the mental health professions often defeat the best of intentions.

For decades, the discrepancy criterion and the exclusion of "environmental disadvantage" resulted in Black and low-income students being more likely to be designated ID than LD (Blanchett, 2010; Collins & Camblin,

1983; Sleeter, 1986). In recent years, however, the IND-LD shift has resulted in the use of LD as a catch-all category and a diminution of the use of ID across the board (MacMillan et al., 1998; Ong-Dean, 2009). Indeed, in the four decades since its introduction, LD identification rates have increased almost six-fold, while the rates of placement for all ethnicities in ID have been reduced by almost half (Donovan & Cross, 2002). Despite the reduction in numbers, the ID category continues to display severe overrepresentation of African Americans, who are more than twice as likely to be identified in this category than are students of other ethnicities (Donovan & Cross, 2002; U.S. Department of Education, 2020).

CROSSING THE BORDER: FROM DELAYED DEVELOPMENT TO INTELLECTUAL DISABILITY

It is well known that children found eligible for the ID category nowadays are likely to be more impaired in overall cognitive development than were those children represented by cases such as *Larry P. v. Riles* (1979). The criterion of an IQ score of 70 as an indicator of "significantly subaverage" general intellectual functioning, accompanied by impairments in adaptive behavior, are much more stringent than was the pre-1970s cutoff point of 85 on an IQ scale. With the current standard, it is expected that children identified as ID will show significant differences from their peers who are labeled LD.

In our study, we did find that the children labeled ID seemed to reflect that qualitative difference, but this observation was sometimes called into question, by late educational intervention, inadequacy of the assessment, or poor teacher quality in either general or special education, which resulted in limited opportunity to learn. Each of our four case studies in this category illustrated at least one of these limitations. Leroy, an African American kindergartener, represented an exemplary placement process, including early referral in kindergarten by an excellent teacher, a thorough assessment, and placement within the kindergarten year. Leroy did seem to meet the academic and functional criteria for ID services. The downside to this case, however, was the final phase—extremely poor quality instruction and classroom management in his special education classroom. In contrast, Bartholomew, whose first language was Haitian Creole, was not referred until the 3rd grade, when an excellent teacher expressed intense frustration at the fact that this child had been passed along the grades although, in her words, "he doesn't know his alphabet. He doesn't know the sounds. He knows numbers but he can't add and subtract single digits!" Clearly, lack of early response to this child's cognitive and linguistic needs complicated the apparent evidence of ID. We will focus on the other two children, Clementina and James, whose cases illustrate more mixed configurations of the placement irregularities we noted.

Clementina

Clementina was a 3rd-grader of Puerto Rican parentage at an inner-city, pre-dominantly Black school with a growing Hispanic population. It is not clear what her ESOL level was when she was in her 3rd-grade ESOL class, but by the time of her placement conference in the 4th grade, she was considered fully proficient in English and was evaluated only in English. According to her mother, she had spoken only Spanish at home until she started school at age 5.

We observed Clementina over a period of 2 years. In her general educa-tion 3rd-grade class, she impressed us as a child who was minimally inter-ested in her schoolwork and only occasionally participated in class activities. Each of the following examples is from a different day's field notes during that year:

> The teacher asks Clementina, "What are you writing about?"
> Clementina responds, "I don't have no journal." The teacher says,
> "This is not an art class. You'd better write."
>
> I go over and check Clementina's work. She smiles mischievously
> and says to me, "I'm not doing my work." I ask her, "Why not?"
> She says, "I don't feel like it." . . . She is just sitting now, looking at
> Floyd. . . . Clementina is still sitting at her seat, doing nothing.

The 3rd-grade teacher was concerned about Clementina, saying that she "has really changed, become very aggressive, and is not the sweet little girl she used to be." Clementina was absent for weeks at a time because of head lice and, at one point, because of ringworm. The teacher perceived the family circumstances as very detrimental, saying: "The mother is retarded, and can't even sign her name, and she has eight kids. Her older sister is 14, and now having a baby. The grandmother takes care of her."

Our observations of Clementina in her 4th-grade general education class showed her performing much the same as in the 3rd grade. She participated only minimally and when she did join in she appeared to be parroting what her peers were saying. The teacher expressed puzzlement and frustration over the fact that she had been promoted to the 4th grade, saying:

> Last year Clementina got all Fs in reading but then she received a C
> [at the end of the year]. A D is passing, so she got promoted. I don't
> know how, for Clementina reads on a 1st-grade reading level. She is
> low. . . . I've been trying to help her with her writing, getting her to use
> the prompt when she writes the answer on the [statewide test]. In that
> way she can get a one and not a zero. The whole process I find very
> frustrating.

The outcome of Clementina's evaluation in the 4th grade was an ID place-ment, with a full-scale IQ score of 51 on the WISC-III. Her academic work was assessed to be at the kindergarten level, with some letter recognition but no word recognition, and simple addition but no subtraction skills. The psychologist commented that there was "nothing remarkable, no mental delays, she smiles when you look at her but she does not speak. She forgets things very easily." We found this description of Clementina as having "no mental delays" rather curious, because "mental delays" are precisely what a score of 51 and other aspects of her profile would indicate.

Despite the fact that Clementina's family members agreed that she had "mental problems," other aspects of her case compounded the picture of an inappropriate placement process. First, it turned out that Clementina had been referred by her kindergarten teacher and it had taken 3 years for the first CST to be held and 4 years for her to be placed. Another problematic aspect was the excluding behavior of school personnel toward Clementina's family members at the CST conference and the unsatisfactory nature of the information shared at the placement conference. The CST conference lasted about 5 minutes. When questioned about this, the classroom teacher said, "They rushed through it because they figured the parent wouldn't understand anyway," explaining that they thought the mother herself was "retarded." The following notes are from the placement conference:

> The classroom teacher said, "Let me see the record." Clementina's cumulative file was passed to her. As she looked through the papers, she exclaimed in surprise, "The kindergarten teacher referred her! Clementina was referred at kindergarten!" . . . The placement specialist asked, "Is this the first time she's been staffed [placed]?" She then looked at the AP. The teacher responded, "Yes." The placement specialist said (incredulously), "Clementina was referred a long time ago. But the placement conference just took place today?" Once again she looked to the AP for a response. The AP said, "It's because of the bilingual assessment. You know how long those can take. We were waiting for that to be done." The placement specialist responded, "So the bilingual assessment is what held up the process."

Despite the casting of blame on the bilingual assessment, neither the results of that testing nor information on her ESOL level were mentioned at the conference. Nor could we locate these reports in Clementina's files. By the time she was formally evaluated, she was considered fully proficient in English and the bilingual assessment was not required. Also missing from the conversation and from the files was a record of her scores on the Scales of Independent Behavior, a test of adaptive skills required for ID eligibility.

The missing information and the shocking delay of 4 years in following through on this child's referral casts doubt on the entire process and on the ultimate label of ID. Recalling Mercedes, the student whose story opens this chapter, the question arises of whether Clementina would also have improved in the hands of a Mrs. Carey. Of course, if she had, she might simply have become one more casualty of the ID/LD "crack." Our point is that if there were no categories, there would be no cracks in the system, and such children as Clementina and Mercedes could have been provided appropriate interventions as soon as the need was identified.

James

James, whose primary language was Haitian Creole, was referred early. The 1st-grade teacher who referred him, however, was the same one whom we previously described teaching an ineffective lesson on the five senses. This was a self-contained ESOL class in which no ESOL strategies were observed. The teacher told us that James had never been in school before and that "he wasn't learning anything." By the spring, she was quite concerned that he had not yet been evaluated. She told us that his pediatrician had asked if he was in a special education class yet and had said, "You know, he needs to be." The teacher also thought he needed to be in a full-time ID class and was frustrated with the slowness of the CST process. The school recommended retention, but the teacher thought James would only see this as a punishment and "might totally turn off, whereas now he at least tries."

James's first CST meeting was held in April of his 1st-grade year. He was not retained, after all, but by the end of his 2nd-grade year, he still had not been evaluated, and his 2nd-grade teacher was quite frustrated. Showing us a sample of his work, she pointed out that "he could barely write" and said that she "didn't know why the first-grade teacher sent him like that."

Our testing of James on the Woodcock Johnson-R in the spring of his 2nd-grade year revealed skills in the kindergarten range and in a chrono-logical-age range from 4½ to 6. The tester noted James's distractibility and apparent incomprehension of many of the questions. However, noting that James had a bad head cold and also his status as an English language learner, the tester commented that factors such as the possibility of ear and upper-respiratory infections and second-language acquisition issues could be complicating the picture. He concluded, "There is not enough information to make a clear judgment as to the cause."

During our observations of James throughout his 1st- and 2nd-grade years, we seldom saw him engaged in academic work, but his classrooms were so chaotic that many other students were not engaged either. In his 1st-grade class, he was typically one of the students who was yelled at and sent to stand in the corner for being inattentive and off task. Regarding his behavior, one researcher wrote, "He appears very eager to please. He likes receiving extrinsic reinforcement: praise and tokens. Every time he appears to have gotten into trouble, it can be attributed to someone else doing something to him." We did observe him engaging in tasks such as playing a matching game on the computer, copying words and their definitions out of a children's dictionary, and copying math word problems from the board. Neither of the last two seemed meaningful to James and he was not expected to solve the math problems.

James's history revealed indicators of developmental delay. According to his mother, he was "born at 6 months; he walked late and talked around age 3." She said that she took him to a psychologist, who asked if he was in a special class and was surprised that he was not. The mother was receiving Social Security Disability Income (SSDI) for James, which would indicate that he had already been diagnosed with a disability.

James was finally tested and placed in ID during the fall of his 3rd-grade year. We believe that James was functioning at a lower-than-average cognitive level and that services at the ID level were appropriate. However, we have concerns about the referral and placement process. The instruction and classroom management in the various classes in which we observed James (including his Success for All [SFA] reading classes) were not conducive to learning—thus we doubt that he received adequate opportunity to learn. He certainly started school behind his peers, but it appeared that little was done to help him progress. Also, as with other case study students whose home language was other than English, it seemed that language and cultural issues were not sufficiently considered or addressed. This was James's first year in school, and he was still at a beginning level of English proficiency. The following excerpt from his CST meeting illustrates the inadequate attention given to these considerations:

> The teacher continues with information about some of James's academic difficulties and the AP joins in quickly and says that "a lot of the children in ESOL" have these difficulties. The teacher interjects, "But I think it's more than that. It's more a matter of higher-level thinking. . . . My real concern is that when I give a direction he gives me a blank look, like he doesn't understand . . . he's lost." She adds, "His behavior isn't one of the worst, but he has a problem sitting still. . . . I don't push him too much." The AP nods, saying, "He's probably working to his potential."

We are not convinced that the circumstances of James's instruction were adequate to support knowledge of what his "potential" really was. The teacher's lack of understanding of the needs of second-language learners leads us to ask, for example, whether James's "blank look" was, simply, incomprehension of English.

CONCLUSIONS

What is needed in education is a seamless system that is prepared to respond to children at their level when they enter school. Certain assumptions of the American school system present particular challenges for immigrant children performing at the weak end of the cognitive abilities spectrum. In the case of children coming from Haiti, many are disadvantaged by the lockstep, chronological-age-based system by which children are placed with their age group regardless of their educational levels. Many such children may not have been to school prior to their arrival in the United States, and Haitian personnel explained that even for those who were in school, it cannot be assumed that they were learning at the grade level expected for their age, since in the Haitian school system students are not promoted until they have mastered the required level of each grade.

James was a Haitian American boy who had not had the benefit of preschool or kindergarten; nor had he spoken English upon entering school. Yet he was placed in the 1st grade in a regular class of up to 30 children, with ESOL support of questionable quality, and was expected to rise to the occasion. We contend that whether or not James "had" ID should not be the issue. Indeed, his progress was further delayed by the fact that he had to show evidence of this disability in order to receive placement in a smaller class with a specially trained teacher. While James was referred in a timely fashion, the weak instruction he received from his referring teacher in the 1st grade gave him minimal opportunity to begin to catch up. A similar year in the 2nd grade only compounded his problems. In Clementina's case, the bureaucratic process was even more detrimental, making it impossible to know what her potential really was.

There are many possible reasons why the determination of these children's eligibility for special education instruction was so delayed. It may have been because of some school personnel's desire to protect children from the stigma that comes with the ID label, or their reluctance to engage in the arduous paperwork required for the referral. It could also be because of an overloaded system that makes process delays inevitable.

In commenting on these cases, we may be accused of being too critical. It may seem that we are seeking perfection, always offering caveats to any positive conclusions. The truth is that we seldom saw exemplary practice in relation to special education placement. Either early instruction was poor, limiting children's opportunity to learn, or the placement process was faulty, through delays or inadequate assessment procedures, or the special education class into which the children were placed proved to be of minimal benefit.

Beyond those cases that did "cross the border" were the many students like Mercedes, who fell between the cracks, becoming what one administrator referred to as the "PDK" (pretty dumb kids) group, whom she perceived as needing a program of practical "survival skills." Another teacher, referring to this group as the "borderline retarded child, who doesn't qualify for any program," asserted, "It is the responsibility of the regular education teachers to fill those gaps." We believe that this is one more group of children to whom the current categorical system does a grave disservice.

Constructing Learning Disabilities
Redundancies and Discrepancies

> I can qualify Germaine for LD. . . . His reading was OK but his math was very low. His Verbal IQ was low. He doesn't really have a learning disability, but with this [special education] teacher, he'll get the nurturing and individual attention he needs.
>
> —Psychologist

The quote above captures precisely the point made by Artiles et al. (2016) that, building on the intersecting histories of ableism and racism, special education has served the dual purposes of protection and discrimination. Our case studies in this and the next chapter demonstrate the nuances of both sides of this paradoxical coin as professionals engage in the "boundary work" (Artiles et al., p. 786) required for the provision of specialized services to children who do not fit the norms of schooling.

In the case of Germaine, the psychologist sought to "protect" a vulnerable child from falling through the cracks of the education system. Germaine was referred with suspicion of an emotional disturbance, based on the classroom teacher's skeletal anecdotal report of "strange" behaviors, which were listed as "playing with pencil," "looking at pencil," "smiles to self," "talking to self," "writing on desk," "fingers in mouth," "sitting on feet in chair." The teacher's awareness that the child had a parent with a psychiatric illness seemed to have played more of a part in her suspicions than did the child's actual behaviors.

The psychologist quickly discerned that the child's answers to projective tests were clearly within the realm of typical, middle-class norms for child rearing: Germaine reported appropriate discipline from his parents and showed a clear sense of responsibility for his actions. But he was slightly behind academically and his occasional misbehaviors in class indicated that he was very sensitive to teasing by his peers. Our observations of Germaine in the LD class into which he was placed indicated that the psychologist's expectation was correct: He did flourish in the hands of an excellent, nurturing special education teacher. However, this placement was truly an anomaly for the teacher, since Germaine was on grade level in reading and less than a year behind in math. In fact, his reading was so ahead of the rest of the group that he had to be sent to the intermediate special education class with 4th- and 5th-graders. Nevertheless, at the end of the year, the special education teacher felt that he should remain in special education for the supportive small class, in which he would be under less social pressure from his peers.

In effect, the protective strategy of LD placement succeeded in providing this sensitive child with small-group instruction tailored to his learning and behavioral needs. Germaine's father, who was the primary caregiver, was very pleased with the outcome and felt that the school had indeed done the very best for his son.

DILEMMAS OF DEFINITION AND ASSESSMENT

Germaine's story reflects what has come to be referred to in the field as the "comorbidity" of learning disability and emotional disturbance: the fact that children often present behaviors and learning patterns indicative of both disabilities. Throughout this text, we have used the term "EBD" since it is the federal category and would be recognizable to readers across the country. However, at the time of our research, concerns about definitional ambiguity in the category of Emotional/Behavioral Disorder were reflected in the state's establishment of two categories—Serious Emotional Disturbance (SED) and Emotional Handicap (EH)—in an attempt to determine the intensity of service needed. The SED label, seen as a subcategory of the EH umbrella, was reserved for students thought to require comprehensive mental health and psychiatric supports within a psychoeducational program. The distinction was introduced primarily to allow for additional funding for the more intensive category (Hart, 2003). Thus, it was the milder category of EH that represents the "high-incidence" category in this state. Currently, however, the state has opted for only the more generalized category of EBD.

A key issue with eligibility for the Emotional Disturbance category is that the disturbance must be creating an "inability to learn." Meanwhile, for the child to qualify for services under the Learning Disability category, there must be evidence that the child's inability to learn is not caused by other conditions, such as emotional disturbance or ID. Because of this categorical construction of learning difficulties, one of these conditions must be identified as the primary cause.

School personnel turned to a number of strategies to solve this classic "chicken or egg" dilemma. The psychologist referred to above, using judgments that seemed to be based on commonsense middle-class norms for social behavior and attitudes, was impressed by Germaine's openness to personal questions about his family and by his clear-cut answers to questions about right and wrong and about appropriate punishments. By contrast, in the case of Kanita, the African American 2nd-grader whose strong extended family had supported her through her mother's incarceration, the same psychologist was suspicious of the child's reluctance to discuss her family, of her indications that corporal punishment was appropriate, and of references to "hitting" in some of her projected interpretations. Based on these responses, the psychologist found Kanita eligible for services in the EH category. However, as we will detail further in Chapter 12, Kanita's immediate change in behavior in her EH class, along with her rapid academic progress and subsequent placement in a gifted program, indicated that all she needed was a solid, structured teacher who challenged her strong intellect.

As outlined in Chapter 1, our research was conducted during a period of increasing uncertainty among scholars and policymakers about just what the criteria should be for qualifying students as having learning disabilities. The report published by participants in the Learning Disabilities Summit (Bradley et al., 2002), the report of the President's Commission on Excellence in Special Education (2002), and Donovan and Cross (2002) all recommended looking closely at current eligibility criteria. Since that time, the introduction of RTI procedures for identification of Specific Learning Disability (SLD) should have reduced the likelihood of the "between the cracks" phenomenon. However, a study by Cavendish et al. (2016) highlighted the challenges of systems-change that plagued the district during the first years of RTI implementation, including many school personnel's difficulty in making the transition from discrete categories to a more fluid understanding of children's learning difficulties. During the time of this study, the categorical system ensured that children who did not meet criteria often fell between the cracks and were left to languish in unresponsive general education classes.

In this school district, there was an attempt to avoid the implication of intrinsic deficit through framing the question in terms of whether the child would "qualify" or "be eligible" for special services. This language allows that there could be any number of reasons why the child has come to this pass and that the school's purpose is simply to provide appropriate services. As one psychologist in our study explained, his job is not to diagnose a disability but to determine what services, if any, the child needs. The school district uses the language of "services" and "placements," not of "disabilities."

In day-to-day professional and family discourse, however, qualifying for special education services is seldom conceptualized in this way. For most people, the meaning of the event is the discovery of a disability within a child, proving that the child's failure reflects some deficit that makes the child qualitatively different from others. This was the common understanding among the school personnel in this school district, who did not express any awareness of the controversy over the discrepancy criterion for LD.

CROSSING THE BORDER: FROM LOW ACADEMIC ACHIEVEMENT TO LEARNING DISABILITY

Our information on children across all the schools presents a portrait of tremendous variability in the types of learning difficulties and in the reasons for, and the processes by which, children were placed in LD programs. Three issues predominated: the comorbidity of behavioral and learning disabilities, along with school personnel's preference for the LD category as a protective device; the influence of local (within-school) norms for academic achievement; and, related to the local norms, the absence of any clear criteria for referral. We will illustrate each of these with exemplars of children we followed closely, noting, once more, that these represent only a fraction of the cases examined.

Learning Disability as a Protective Strategy

As in the case of Germaine, cited above, the comorbidity of behavioral and academic difficulties was a common theme across the schools. Most often, the outcome seemed to be mainly a matter of psychologists' preference. In this section, we describe the situation of Paul, a kindergartner who, like Germaine, displayed reading achievement close to grade level and indicated no sign of either processing deficits or an IQ/achievement discrepancy. Both children's referrals occurred because their behavior was seen as troubling, though not severely noncompliant. In both cases, the psychologists' determination of SLD reflected a desire to protect these children from the pressures of a general education classroom and from the stigma and isolation of an EBD classroom.

Paul was a 6-year-old Hispanic 1st-grader at a school serving a predominantly middle-income, Hispanic population. At ESOL Level 4, Paul was referred at the end of kindergarten primarily for concerns about his emotional and behavioral functioning. Two child study team (CST) meetings were held for Paul during his kindergarten year, at which his kindergarten teacher described him as impulsive, distractible, and needing constant supervision. At his second CST meeting the psychologist strongly recommended that he be seen by a medical doctor regarding medication for hyperactivity. When Paul was evaluated at the end of the year, however, a different psychologist, though also noting hyperactivity and possible depression, explained that she did not write the latter in her report because of a reluctance to see the case "go EH," which would mean a "more restrictive" placement. At the placement conference, she stated that Paul had been referred for "poor academic performance," when in fact this was not the case, and that he qualified for LD because of "learning process deficits," despite the fact that Paul displayed an IQ/achievement discrepancy that went in the opposite direction from the one required by eligibility criteria. That is, his academic achievement as tested by the Weschler Individual Achievement Test (WIAT) was higher than his composite IQ score, as follows:

WISC-III: Performance 90, Verbal 83, Composite score 85
WIAT: Reading composite score 98, Basic reading 94, Reading comprehension 97, Spelling 101, Math composite 85, Math reasoning 84, Numerical operations 97.

Further, the fact that Paul's primary language was Spanish and that, at the time of testing, his ESOL level was 4, was not mentioned in the evaluation report.

Our administration of the Woodcock-Johnson scales confirmed that Paul was at or above grade level in all but Applied Math Problems, where he scored at mid-kindergarten level. Observations of Paul over a 2-year period revealed that he did have trouble concentrating and was easily distracted and frequently out of seat. We saw widely varying behavior and task accomplishment by him, and it seemed that his completion of tasks depended on how well he could concentrate on any given day. Eventually his parents withdrew him from this school and placed him in a private school where he did not receive special education services. We were not able to follow him to that placement.

Like Germaine, Paul's case revealed explicit manipulation of assessment findings to fit the psychologists' judgment of the most appropriate placement. Neither child met the criteria for LD. In Germaine's case, we know that the psychologist's good intentions had the desired results. Both cases illustrate professionals' attempts to find the best solutions for children but, in doing so, prove the incompetence of the categorical system to meet children's needs. As we have argued before, children, particularly those who belong to an already stigmatized group, should not need a false disability label to receive appropriate instruction.

Learning Disability as Relative to the Peer Group

Although we have argued that diminished opportunity to learn placed children in the inner-city schools at risk of school failure and unnecessary special education placement, this was not the only source of risk. On the contrary, in schools that had higher academic standing and expectations, we saw referrals of children who would most probably not be referred in schools with lower academic standing. Ironically, the raising of the bar in the "better" schools, along with school personnel's belief in sorting children by presumed ability, meant that being in a "better" school did not protect children from unnecessary special education placement. The cases of two children in such a school reiterate the issue of comorbidity, but also illustrate our second issue regarding LD: the influence of local norms on referral and placement practices.

Matthew and Austin, two African American 2nd-graders in a high-achieving, high-SES, predominantly White school, were referred by an African American teacher with strong instructional skills and a warm but firm management style. Besides being the only African American boys in the class, Matthew and Austin stood out by virtue of always being seated separately from the rest of the class—Austin next to the teacher's desk and Matthew at the back, sometimes with an aide working with him for part of the time.

The two boys were very different in all aspects. During the period of our research, Austin lived with a relative who had a terminal illness and who died some years later. Toward the end of our research, Austin's father also died. In class, Austin was very attention seeking, seeming to use an exuberant personality to cover insecurities about his work. Whenever he paid attention and understood what was happening, he worked well, but he could be quite disruptive both verbally and physically. Matthew was much quieter, but was generally inattentive, easily distracted, and often out of seat. We learned that he had witnessed the death of a sibling and had received some counseling services to help him deal with this trauma. The teacher was very patient with both boys and tended to ignore consistent out-of-seat behavior from Matthew, but not from other members of the class. She described him as a "sad child" who could not concentrate and needed a smaller class.

Matthew and Austin differed from their peers in terms of their academic levels. Austin's scores stood out because they ranged widely, suggesting that he would do well when he tried and very badly when he didn't. Matthew's scores were more consistent but were the lowest in the class and he was always behind the rest of the class in completing his work. Of four math test scores posted on the wall, Austin's were 90, 9, 62, 4. Matthew's were more consistent—70, 74, 72, and 0 (we do not know if he was absent for this last test). Most of the other students regularly scored between 75 and 100 and each tended to have consistent scores, whether higher or lower.

Official referral records noted that both boys were referred mainly for behavioral difficulties, but the placement outcomes represented the opposite of the teacher's expressed concerns: Austin, whose referral statement cited "disordered school behavior," was given a battery of tests usually used for children suspected of having an emotional disturbance. He did not qualify for EH, however, and was placed in a pullout LD program in the same school. It was noticeable that the language in his record changed distinctly after the evaluation results were in, stating that he had been tested in order to assess his poor general academic performance and his difficulty in specific learning areas. Matthew's evaluation report stated that his academic achievement was found to be average but that he showed "serious learning difficulties." This statement was puzzling, since his academic scores were higher than his IQ scores and he was not found eligible for LD services. Given the same battery of projective tests as Austin, Matthew *was* found eligible for EH services in a self-contained class. He was moved to another school.

Matthew settled quickly into his EH program. Writing samples of his work demonstrated appropriate conceptual, writing, and spelling skills for a child just beginning the 3rd grade. We have already introduced the reader to Matthew's "I have a dream" composition. His composition about his summer plans was equally appropriate both conceptually and technically:

My summer
Week 1: June 18th–24th

I will be with my nephew having so much fun playing game and riding on bikes but he's not riding one because he's just 2 year old.

Austin's work was not as impressive. Most of our samples were of routine work rather than creative writing, perhaps because he often left his work unfinished. His handwriting was more uneven than Matthew's, sometimes mixing upper- and lowercase letters. It showed spelling errors but no signs of letter reversals or difficulty forming letters, although his sentences were poorly structured. The following excerpt is from his notes on two science experiments. Writing within the confines of a dittoed sheet with rectangular frames, Austin seemed to be working carelessly, "squishing" his answers into the frames:

> I noticed that the potting soil
> see a litte white thing in it . . .
> Tap the Baking tray softly, the harder
> Baking tray was tapped softly it was Doing No happened
> call through the tube softly, then louder
> I noiced when the baking tray Was tapped louder happed
> I was juimp

In contrast to this, a copy of Austin's freehand drawing of the globe with the lines of latitude and longitudes was excellent, showing no signs of difficulties with visual perception. He earned an A for that assignment.

In comparing these two students, our observations of Austin pointed more to inattention and insufficient practice than to a learning problem. Behaviorally, he was certainly the more troublesome student, and it seemed that his need for attention was what deterred him from making better progress. We would not have been surprised to see him placed in the EH program. Matthew, by contrast, was not very disruptive at all, although it was reported that he occasionally had tantrums and seemed to "shut down" whenever he was confronted. We believe that he would, as the report said, have benefited from a smaller class in which he could get more individual support. Although it seemed clear that he did have some emotional difficulties, he seemed to fall into a more gray area, and his rapid progress in the behavioral program suggested that he had adequate control over his behavior once individual support was provided.

Matthew's and Austin's peers in the 2nd grade were generally performing well above average for the grade. By this standard, these two students' achievement just below grade level appeared low. Although we were not able to ascertain whether there was any explicit attempt to use special education as an alternative to having low-scoring students "bring down" this school's state ratings, this seems quite probable in light of the fact that it was common practice in many schools. Alternatively, it is also possible that the high-achieving norms of the school simply infiltrated teachers' consciousness, with the effect of an implicit raising of the bar regarding general education expectations. That low-income African American students might become ready targets in the sorting process would not be surprising in view of their differential preparation for schooling. Matthew and Austin's teacher would likely be as affected by these standards as would any of her colleagues, even though she was herself African American.

What was quite certain was that Matthew's and Austin's scores and classwork were well above those of 2nd-graders referred for learning difficulties in our lower-income schools. We turn now to some illustrations of this point.

Learning Disability as Anything

The influence of local norms on referrals is one specific example of a widespread issue concerning the lack of clear criteria for referrals. Our examination of children's work indicated that there was no stable pattern of learning difficulty among children designated as LD. Rather, the children referred seemed to reflect four "types" or profiles. We have already illustrated the type characterized by comorbidity of LD and EH characteristics. The other three types did not typically display social or behavioral difficulties, but showed a variety of academic profiles, as seen in the following: first, those children who fit the classic definition of LD, showing severe discrepancies between their academic progress and their overall cognitive functioning; second, children whose work was characterized by low overall achievement and slow, steady progress; and third, those whose academic achievement seemed to be more of a lag, possibly related to absenteeism or other contextual circumstance.

True LD. The term "true LD" was used by several school personnel to refer to children whose learning difficulties resulted in "unexpected underachievement." Some personnel felt that the "true LD" kids represented only a small portion of those who were placed. We concurred with this opinion.

Jonas, a student in a school serving a predominance of Hispanic students of mid-SES level, was an example of a child with "true LD." Entering the 2nd grade unable to read, Jonas was described by his teacher as having trouble "learning little simple things," and his writing showed minimal understanding of the phonetic code. In response to a written prompt for a letter, he wrote:

> Dear Madeline, Ae hop bat uo foe god and uen uo sen pop bat us fone and uoo ro ros seen on tehr and a uen e un to the fr and the bods lapr et us fn un ur uf mi and a col a hap uo feo god.

He was found eligible for LD services in a pullout program when he started 3rd grade.

Manuel, a Hispanic 3rd-grader at a school with a predominantly Black, low-income population, had good listening-comprehension and verbal skills, but was quite low in reading and writing. Manuel was a quick study, as long as no reading or writing was required. His auditory comprehension was among the quickest in the class, and his keen attention and verbal articulation contrasted greatly with his weak reading. His barely legible writing showed some mastery of common words and of an attempt to spell phonetically:

> I will like to be a DocTor because you can wen A los of mune and dey can heg you win you siTsk and you can breeing The kids to The DocTor win dei or siTsk And You cAn hAs fun.

Manuel participated actively in class discussions. This excerpt is from an SFA lesson that the teacher said was supposed to be on Level 2.2 (the second half of the 2nd grade). Manuel, she said, was "way below that." The lesson was about a boy whose grandfather was coming home from the hospital after having a stroke, which had affected his memory and his initial recognition of his grandson. Toward the end of a very lively lesson, our field notes read:

> After they've read for a bit, the teacher starts some more questions. "How would you feel if you were his grandchild?" There is silence for a few seconds. Manuel offers, "I'd be upset 'cause he might be sick and I'd get sick and I can't go to school." The teacher says she understands this because Manuel may be thinking that his sickness is catching, but really it's not. Other kids say, "I'd be sad 'cause he wouldn't know me"; "Scared, that he might say something awful and sound like a monster." Then she asks, "As a child, what would you do?" Manuel says, "Give him his medicine." Others say, "Take care of him"; "Give him soup." The teacher comments supportively on just about every opinion. . . . The story goes on: "A tear is coming down Bob's [grandfather's] face when he watches the boy playing with blocks." The teacher asks them why. Manuel says, "'Cause . . . my opinion is, he's remembering him as he sees him play with blocks."

Low average but making steady progress. In contrast to Manuel's display of a discrepancy between oral and academic performance, we observed children, such as Delia and Marc, who typified more of a "low average" profile. We will focus on Delia, a quiet, diligent 2nd-grader in a predominantly Hispanic school, who was similar to Manuel in that her compositions showed weak attempts at phonetic spelling, with some apparent reversals, but her handwriting was neat and legible. She wrote:

> I will met wtet ther in the manu oufes gras. (I will meet her there in the main office.)
> Did the hrse fyl aseep uend are the tree waey eating har? (Did the horse fall asleep under the tree while eating hay?)

Unlike Manuel, Delia's comprehension was evidently lower than that of her peers, as exemplified by the following field observation:

> In this class, Delia was still quiet and studious, but not very participatory in question-answer sessions. When she did respond, her answers tended to be a bit off target. It was not clear whether this was a matter of poor comprehension or poor verbal expression. For example, when asked to give a sentence with the word *Braille*, she hesitated a long time and when the teacher prompted her by asking what kind of person uses Braille, Delia finally said, "They can't see but they listen." This answer contrasts greatly with the succinct reply offered by another child: "Blind people use Braille to read." In reading out loud, Delia read quite well but with a couple of mistakes such as saying *she* for *his* and *through* for *though*.

A native Spanish speaker, Delia attained an ESOL level that was documented at Level 4, but that was found by the bilingual psychologist to be at Level 5. Using the Differential Ability Scales (DAS), the examiner found Delia's general cognitive ability to be in the low-average range, but noted that these scores might be an underestimate of Delia's global intellectual skills. Delia's scores on the Woodcock Johnson placed her word recognition and math calculation in the low-average range and her written skills also in the low average, with quality and fluency noted as "extremely below average" and lower than expected given her overall cognitive scores. These results, along with findings of a cognitive-processing deficit, qualified her for LD services in the pullout program. By granting that Delia's low cognitive score could have been an "underestimate," the psychologist allowed leeway in interpreting whether the child met the discrepancy criterion for LD. While we cannot say for sure, it seems likely that she was more like those who used to be called "slow learners" in a previous era of special education.

Slow starters. Of our LD case studies, both Miles and Anita exemplified children whom we refer to as *slow starters*. This term indicates that the children seemed to have missed important early opportunities to learn school material, through either excessive absences or ineffective teachers, and were behind academically.

Anita, who was of mixed Hispanic and Anglo American ethnicity, attended a school serving low-income Hispanic and African American children. Her chronic absenteeism in the 1st grade seemed to contribute to her low achievement and she was placed in an LD program in the 2nd grade after repeating 1st grade. Samples of her work show immature but clear handwriting with poorly developed language skills. Using a rectangular writing frame, she wrote:

> Brid live and nest
> Thye have Feather

To FlY and warm the eggs
Brid hav mon in Dad
TheY KeeP They eggs
Warm i Save
Wintiwind TheY KeeP
The eggs warm
When I Write I Should
AlWays make it neat. MY
Teacher will be happy and
My WorK Willook Nice.

Anita's mother, Janey, after several observations in her child's special education class, was dissatisfied with the frequent absenteeism of the teacher and
with the general education teacher's view of Anita as "not her student." Janey
moved Anita to another school at the end of her 2nd-grade year, and we were
not able to follow her further.

Miles, an African American kindergartener in an inner-city school in
which teacher quality was extremely variable was fortunate to be taught by
Ms. L, the African American teacher whose effective strategies for teaching
school culture we cited earlier. She referred him because of his lack of basic
alphabetic and math concepts. On working with Miles, we agreed that these
concepts were missing, but we noted that he had an excellent vocabulary,
which his mother explained was augmented by the family's regular viewing
of the Disney Channel. It seemed that Miles would learn quite quickly with
some individualized instruction. He showed himself to be very determined
to try to complete whatever task he started. We noted that Miles had missed
28 days of his kindergarten year. The decision was to retain him in kindergarten and have him evaluated for special education. The outcome of the evaluation was that he qualified for 12 hours of LD services a week, and he was
described by the psychologist as a "very bright, charming" child who had a
learning disability.

In the fall, the special education teacher started Miles with coloring tasks
that were far below his level. In one of our early observations of him in this
class, he pointed to his 1st-grade classmates and remarked to the researcher,
"I can add and subtract like them but they put me back in kindergarten."
Within a month of Miles's placement, his special education teacher seemed
to agree with him on this. By October he was working on the 1st-grade math
book, and the teacher anticipated that he would soon have mastered his individual education plan (IEP) goal of knowing numbers 1–20, which was a
kindergarten goal. Our end-of-the-year interview with the special education
teacher confirmed that Miles had, as expected, done very well. His math and
reading were then on 1st-grade level. He had mastered his IEP goals and was
by then doing additions up to 20. The teacher thought she would most likely
mainstream him for reading in the fall but keep him in special education for
math to give him additional support.

Overall, we believe that Miles's difficulties in kindergarten/1st grade were related to absence from school. In Miles's case, while we do not believe that he "had" a learning disability, we do think that the intensive instruction by an excellent special education teacher, and possibly his kindergarten retention, made a world of difference to his being able to catch up. On the one hand, this case exemplifies what can happen when appropriate interventions are introduced early, not waiting for the child to fail. On the other hand, there was little reason to believe that Miles needed a special education program. We believe that the kind of "tiered" intervention currently proposed by researchers such as Vaughn and Fuchs (2003), and possibly a repeat of his kindergarten year, would have worked, without need for a disability label.

CONCLUSIONS

We believe that some children have learning disabilities that require specialized interventions. We believe also that most children will benefit from good instruction and supportive classroom contexts within general education. Of all the children described in this chapter, those who reflected features of "true LD" were clearly in need of intensive instruction, preferably through small-group or individual tutoring, or both. The others displayed a range of needs that we believe could have been addressed in the general-education classrooms of strong, nurturing teachers.

Several issues worked against even the best teachers. One was class size—30 being a typical number across the schools. Another was administrative pressure to remove weak students whose scores would depress schools' ratings on statewide tests. Another was the pressure of what we have referred to previously as a "culture of referral" within a school. This feature can be driven by explicit or implicit concerns about standardized testing, or it can be an ingrained belief that children who do not quite fit really "belong" in special education. Delia was such a child. Miles was out of sync with the school's lockstep system.

On the other side of the picture is the likelihood that the protective motive evident in the case of both Germaine and Paul also drove many other referrals and maybe even worked to children's benefit. Paul's parents moved him to a private school soon after his LD placement so we do not know the outcome. Both Germaine and Miles benefited from a program of excellent instruction. The teacher who referred Austin and Matthew was very accommodating to them within her general education classroom and told us that she hoped, as did many teachers, that the smaller class sizes in special education would help.

Despite the benefits of the protective intention for some children, we cannot support the uses we saw of the LD category as a catch-all for students who seemed not to fit. The application of the category was arbitrary and often simply inappropriate, resulting in protection for some and discrimination for others. The apparently clear-cut criteria of discrepant cognition and achievement along with deficient information processing were circumvented or ignored, as desired, by assessors; and the referring teachers' recommendations were as likely to be either overwhelmingly influential or not at all influential. In Germaine's case, it proved beneficial that the teacher's negative view of him had no impact; in Kanita's case, as we will see in the following chapter, teacher negativity was unduly influential. The process was so variable that it was impossible to tell if children were getting what they needed.

We do not know the long-term outcomes for all these children. We know that Austin continued to have problems that were exacerbated by the subsequent death of the caregiver with whom he lived. Given the extreme experiences of family loss experienced by this young boy, we believe that he must have needed intensive emotional support. Not "qualifying" for the EH program, an SLD program was not what he needed, and his special education teacher reported that he was becoming increasingly angry. By contrast, the EH program into which his classmate Matthew was placed emphasized behavior control, not emotional support, so we have no reason to think that it would have been helpful to Austin.

In Matthew's case, the fact that his "emotional disturbance" all but disappeared overnight leads us to the third disability conundrum. In the chapter that follows we focus on the subjectivity evident in four children's placement in the EBD category and on the double-edged sword of their "troubling" behaviors being rapidly removed and then replaced by a stigmatizing cloak that would prove very difficult to discard.

CHAPTER 11

Constructing Emotional/Behavior Disorders
From Troubling to Troubled Behavior

> There is pressure from the administration and teachers to remove kids, who are not EH, who are a pain in the neck. They get into a lot of fights. They are disruptive, but that is not EH. They are conduct disordered. . . . Some kids are so far gone that they are just criminals, instead of kids.
>
> —School counselor

The quotation above calls attention to a crucial concern in identifying students as having emotional behavior disability (EBD): the challenge of distinguishing between behavior that is troubling to those in authority and behavior that indicates that a child is truly "troubled" (Leone et al., 1990). This distinction, as is usual within special education's categorical mindset, results in a need to determine whether behavior reflects a deliberate refusal to conform to behavioral expectations, or whether it is beyond the child's control and beyond normal responses to adverse circumstances.

The means of making this determination vary widely and depend on the preference of psychologists or on state or school district regulations (Hosp & Reschly, 2002). In this school district, projective testing was the required approach. The subjectivity inherent in the process of interpreting the meanings behind a child's stories or drawings was exacerbated by the relativity of local norms. According to one teacher in a school serving a low-income, predominantly African American population:

> Social-emotional problems are difficult. A lot of it depends on the school. You put a child in another school, [gives an example of a higher-SES school]. They would be considered EH. They wouldn't be considered normal if they got into a fight because that's a very upper-middle-class school. They rarely have fights and a deficit problem might be if a child talks out in class and doesn't finish work. . . . [In this school] the only kids I would place would exhibit psychopathology. . . . Then, you have some people who would say that it is unusual for

a child to talk about killing people and drawing guns. Here, that is reality. It is the way they live. It is not EH. If they were to draw pictures of daisies and picket fences, they would be crazy!

This, indeed, was the thinking of the psychologist who inferred that Kanita's reluctance to reveal her family problems indicated a "denial of her feelings," since most children "in this neighborhood," were quite "blasé" about events such as a parent's incarceration. Both the psychologist and the teacher quoted above illustrate the danger of assuming that children's social circumstances will dictate how they think.

Most of the children we saw referred for behavioral problems were of the "pain in the neck" variety. The referral often reflected the teacher's poor classroom planning and management, as in the case of the kindergarten children whose behavior was transformed when they entered the music class. Despite the obvious variability in classroom contexts, the environment of the regular class was seldom taken into account when children were referred for their behavior.

We have already introduced three of the four children who were placed in EH programs: three African American children—Matthew, whom we described in the opening and foregoing chapters, and Kanita and Robert, whose families we described in our discussion of the discrepancy between school personnel's views of families and our own. Additionally, in this chapter we introduce a Haitian American girl named Edith.

The outcomes for the four children placed in EH programs were dramatic: All appeared to have their behavior transformed after placement in these self-contained settings. There are two possible interpretations of this—either the special education programs into which they were placed were exactly what the children needed to address their internal emotional deficits, or there were other competing explanations for their transformation that had to do with social contexts and professional responses and decision-making. Kauffman et al. (2007), in response to the first edition of this book, supported the former interpretation. We responded with our explanation of why we supported the alternative interpretation (Harry et al., 2009). We invite our readers to pay attention to the entire contexts of these cases and judge for themselves. We note also that although all four met the expectations of their behavioral programs, after 3 years of this placement, only one child returned to the mainstream. We will highlight briefly the key aspects of Matthew's story and will then focus on the other three children.

MATTHEW

As was the case for children in all the EH programs we observed, Matthew's entire classroom experience was framed by a behavioral token-economy system. Despite the fact that the teacher and teacher assistant in his EH classes were less nurturing, and instruction was less effective than in the classroom of the general education teacher who had referred him, Matthew settled quickly into the EH program and proved quiet and compliant even when he had finished or was bored with an activity. The only reports of behavioral difficulties occurred in the cafeteria. Nevertheless, our follow-up study indicated that after 3 years of consistently satisfactory behavior, there was still no sign of mainstreaming for Matthew.

It is difficult to know what was really going on with this sensitive child who had experienced serious family loss. It could be that the size and structure of the EH class accounted for his improved behavior. However, there could also have been other social factors at play. For example, in his general education class Matthew may have been affected not only by the high achievement levels of his peers but also by their high income and valued racial status. In his "I have a dream" composition, Matthew's keen perception of "helmets" as symbols of wealth among bike-riding children in the school showed his sensitivity to his social situation. In his general education class, he had been one of only two African American boys in the class and was performing at the bottom of the class, though close to grade level. By contrast, in his EH class, which typified the overrepresentation of his group in this program, 8 of the 10 children were Black, and Matthew's behavior and academic level earned him the reputation of a "star" in the eyes of the teacher.

We acknowledge that it is speculation to wonder if Matthew's progress may have been related more to the familiar social environment of the EH class than to his status as a child with "emotional disturbance." Nevertheless, this question indicates that such contextual information could be more important in understanding a child's difficulties than are decontextualized "tests" through which a psychologist who does not know the child or his family purports to interpret the internal states "projected" by the child onto the external world.

Matthew's record in the EH class was the same as those of the three students we will describe next. Within a very short time, all were functioning consistently at the top level of their behavioral programs. We do not believe that this sudden turn in behavior is consistent with emotional disturbance.

KANITA

Kanita's transformation in her EH program was even more dramatic than Matthew's. In her 1st-grade class, we had observed her to be stubborn, resistant, or even hostile to the teacher, and provocative to her peers. In our first visit after 2 weeks of her placement, Kanita's behavior was so compliant that the teacher asked if we knew why she had been referred.

Unlike Matthew, Kanita had the good fortune to be in the hands of a very good special education teacher who moved her quickly to part-time mainstreaming, where her behavior was seldom an issue. Nevertheless, it was evident that the bar had been raised for this "EH child," to the extent that typical 3rd-grade behaviors such as passing notes or making fun of other kids were enough to warrant a report to the EH teacher and, at one point, a return to the EH class. Because of this, the team decided to keep Kanita for a second year so that she could get the support of the EH teacher. In the third year, Kanita was fully mainstreamed and placed in a part-time gifted program, but her EH teacher managed to keep her on an individual education plan (IEP), "just in case." In our discussing this with the teacher, she commented that Kanita knew when to behave and tended to take advantage of weaker teachers. The teacher acknowledged that Kanita's behavior was actually no worse than that of many of her general education peers, but the teacher did not want to release her from the program, only to "see her back in my classroom the next year."

In contrast to the EH teacher's misgivings about Kanita's readiness to be without an IEP, the teacher of the gifted program reported that Kanita displayed no behavior problems and was doing very well in her work. The teacher of that program asked us, "Do you think she was misplaced [in the EH program]?"

How did Kanita get to the EH program? She had had a history of emotional outbursts in her kindergarten year, during her placement in the class of Ms. L, the excellent kindergarten teacher cited earlier. This teacher told us that she saw Kanita's difficulties as being a response to her mother's incarceration, and that the strategies the teacher devised for helping Kanita overcome these outbursts had worked quite effectively and consistently. However, the teacher stated that in Kanita's 1st-grade year she "put the school in an uproar." This teacher said that she had not expected Kanita's difficulties to prove so severe and was surprised when she qualified for EH services.

The environment of Kanita's 1st-grade year was, however, very inadequate for a child with emotional difficulties. The 1st-grade teacher was Ms. E, whom we referred to in Chapter 3 as practicing "passive" classroom management. The first time we observed in her class it was obvious that she made next to no effort to intervene in early signs of misbehavior and typically did not respond to it until it was nearly out of control. Our observation of Kanita in this classroom, around the same time as her referral, revealed a very disjointed lesson to which only a few children seated near the front were paying attention. Most children were restless and distracted, and Kanita and one or two others stood out as verbally oppositional to the teacher, while another student simply stood at her desk with her back to the teacher and appeared to stare at the wall throughout the period without any attempt by the teacher to redirect her attention. The following is an excerpt from the observation field notes:

> The teacher begins a lesson on synonyms. Her voice is loud as she tries to talk over the noise in the class. . . . Soon after she asks a question, students at the computer request help and other distractions occur

so that she is not focusing on any one thing. She then walks out of the classroom for something and when she returns she asks another question about synonyms. During this lesson, there is little student involvement. Some are looking at what their classmates are doing at the computer. At least one student is cutting paper, while others look aimlessly around the room. . . . The boy sitting next to me keeps talking to Kanita, who is at the computer. Someone tells the teacher that Kanita is doing Math Corner on the computer and the teacher tells her not to. Kanita replies that she is going to do it anyway.

A child near me tells his neighbor to behave and says, pointing to me [the researcher], "She writin down what you do." The neighbor looks around and replies, "She ain't writin bout me, she writin bout her!" [pointing to the teacher]. A child at his table starts singing Aretha Franklin's "Respect."

Although we observed this classroom only once while Kanita was in it, we observed the teacher again in the following year with a different group and noted exactly the same (lack of) management style.

Kanita, the only "success story" of our four EH students, exited the EH program when she entered middle school. Nevertheless, we are concerned that a child should have to experience such a stigmatizing label in order to receive an appropriate educational program—indeed, in order to get back on track. Based on our observations of Kanita in her 1st-grade classroom, we concur that she was a "pain in the neck." So was her teacher. In contrast, Kanita's quick perception that good behavior was required in the EH class resulted in an immediate change in her behavior.

We conclude, first, that with an effective general education teacher, Kanita's behavior would not have deteriorated to the point of her requiring a referral. Second, this was a bright child whose scores on the WISC-III defied the sociocultural bias of that test (she achieved a combined score of 107 with 118 on the freedom-from-distractibility subset). Had she been placed in a class with a strong teacher whose expectations were high, she might well have been perceived as "gifted" rather than "disturbed." Finally, the power of the psychologist's preconceived and erroneous belief that Kanita's family was dysfunctional resulted in an evaluation that was truly a travesty. In summary, Kanita's success resulted from her good fortune in being placed in the only high-quality EH program we observed.

ROBERT

As in Kanita's case, the first thing we noted about Robert was that he was referred to special education from a very ineffective classroom. In the 1st grade, Robert had been marked as having behavioral problems that seemed to become worse the following year and resulted in his referral.

Our first recorded observation of Robert was in the fall of his 2nd-grade year. The atmosphere in this classroom was extremely negative and exemplified our concern with the validity of a referral coming from such a classroom. Although the class was team-taught, there was minimal individual attention given to any child and almost total reliance on repetitive seat work, which was seldom monitored. When instruction did occur, it was offered by the younger teacher, Ms. J, who, despite a nurturing approach to some children, was largely ineffective. The older teacher, Ms. P, reserved her participation almost totally for discipline, which usually amounted to harsh reprimands, insults, and threats, such as: "Do you want me to snatch you?" or, yelling at Robert, "I don't appreciate your acting like somebody crazy today! Did you take your medicine? I can't take this every day. I will get on the cell phone and call your momma." Robert first appeared in our observational notes that fall in the following context:

> Marvin, one of the students we have been following from [his first-grade class] last year, is seated at a lone desk facing the wall near the front of the room. He is doing nothing. If he has a reading book it is not in evidence on his desk. He stands and looks around. I go over to him and ask if he should be reading. He shrugs and says no. I walk away and soon he is wandering around the room talking to various children. Ms. P is seated at her desk talking to a parent and Ms. J is standing facing the class. Neither teacher pays any attention to him. The noise level is increasing.
>
> After about 10 minutes, Ms. J starts calling on some children to read their books out loud to the class. Several volunteer, but many do not appear to have heard the request and continue to chatter to their neighbors. After about five children have read their books aloud, the teacher tells a boy to collect the books. The chatter increases even more. Marvin is still wandering around and Jose is also out of his seat. Ms. J reprimands Jose. . . .
>
> Every now and then, Ms. P looks up and reprimands the class sharply . . . they quiet down immediately, but as she returns to her conversation with the mother, they soon start talking again. At one point she tells Jose, "I'll take you to the cafeteria to your momma. That'll stop that smiling!" Another child, Robert, whom we had also noticed in the first-grade class last year, is also wandering around.

Our observations through the fall confirmed that the negative ambience and ineffective instruction were typical of this classroom. In January of that school year, both Robert and Marvin were placed on half-day school attendance because of their behavior, with a referral to the child study team (CST). Marvin's mother became angry and pulled him out of the school, while Robert's mother accepted the decision and he remained on this arrangement for 5 months. In our earlier discussion of families, we explained that the arrangement for Robert to attend school only from 8:30 to 11 A.M. continued for 5 months, until his mother, Jacintha, refused to come for him at 11:00 A.M. any more. At that point, he was referred for evaluation. Most shocking was that his records revealed that his mother had signed permission for evaluation in January.

When Robert returned to school in May that year, it was clear that no one, including himself, expected appropriate behavior from him. At this time, Ms. P's approach to Robert's misbehavior was to send him to stand at the front of the room where he did basically whatever he pleased until she noticed him again and offered some reprimand that would quiet him for a few minutes. This teacher was often out of the room, and although the coteacher said she did not agree with having Robert stand at the front, it was not her decision. The following excerpt illustrates the scenario:

> Ms. J is standing behind the screen at the back of the room. I hear her talking to someone and I think perhaps Ms. P is there with her, since I don't see her anywhere else in the room. Soon I realize that Ms. J is talking on her cell phone behind the screen. She remains there for about 10 minutes. I realize that Ms. P has left the room.
>
> There is steady, though not too loud chatter in the room. Robert is at the front, standing and playing around the teacher's desk. Ms. J comes from the behind the screen, still talking on her cell phone as she walks toward the front of the classroom. She puts the phone away and then yells at Robert, "No! Not at my desk!" She tells him to get away from her desk. He moves away from the desk and remains in constant movement, kneeling, standing, then walking over to a girl seated near the front. He stands next to her watching her. He is always on the move but is not really noisy. Soon, he stands at the front, swinging his arms. . . . Then he walks around the front of the room chatting to kids. She tells him to go back to the front. He does, stays for about 5 minutes, then walks around again. Ms. P has not returned.

Our final observation of Robert in this classroom toward the end of the school year noted the following:

> Robert is standing toward the front of the room. He is hopping up and down with his shoes off [all the children have their shoes off to be weighed and measured for some reason]. Then he puts them on and is quiet for a few minutes. Then he starts rocking from side to side, hops, jumps, walks over to stand in line. He looks over at me and grins. . . . Soon after this, Robert is doing flips on the floor and crawls under a desk. The line of standing children blocks the teachers' view of him.

Robert was evaluated twice, which reflected a continuing controversy over what his label and services should be. The psychologist's first evaluation of him determined that he had no emotional disturbance but was exhibiting behaviors typical of attention deficit/hyperactivity disorder (ADHD), such as impulsivity and lack of reflective approach. Because of these findings, the psychologist referred Robert to a doctor and he was designated as having ADHD. This allowed him to be served under the category Other Health Impaired (OHI), and placed, within the same school, in a pullout class that served children eligible for various high-incidence categories. His IEP, however, did not include a behavioral plan, and although his behavior proved better in the hands of a skillful special education teacher, it was still challenging, and he was still being troublesome in his general education placements. Some months later, after an occasion when he threatened to harm another child, Robert was reevaluated by the same psychologist. He was found to qualify for an EH placement and placed in a self-contained program in another school. Thus, he proceeded to the most restrictive environment without appropriate behavioral interventions having been tried.

This child's story raises several important concerns. First is the issue of medication. All school personnel who worked with Robert described his behavior as being variable according to whether he was taking his medication, and they expressed the belief that he often was not. His mother supported the medication plan but tended to withdraw the medication when Robert complained that it made him feel ill. The assurance of compliance is not always within the power of the school, and parental ambivalence when children express discomfort with medication is common.

The second issue, classroom quality, certainly *was* in the hands of school personnel. The negative effects on Robert of this unproductive classroom were exacerbated by the third issue, the administration's decision to place Robert on 5 months of half-day attendance at school. From the point of view of the school's responsibility to provide appropriate educational opportunity, this decision was unconscionable. School personnel's awareness of the dangers of the neighborhood was evident in that they did not consider it safe for Robert to walk home alone outside the regular hours, so they requested the mother to come for him personally every day. When Robert returned to full-day school in May, he was more of a "pain in the neck" than ever.

Fourth, despite Robert's obvious need for behavioral support, no behavior plan was written into Robert's IEP when he was placed in the special education pullout classroom. In a class of only about 12 children and a competent teacher, such a plan would have been feasible. Further, the school had Robert's mother's full agreement to the placement, which she hoped would help to curb his behavior.

Finally, the most disturbing aspect of Robert's story is the outcome at the end of his primary-school years. After the end of our funded research project, we did not see Robert during his 4th-grade year. In his 5th-grade year, Hart (2003) obtained permission to resume research on him for her doctoral dissertation. Observations and interviews with Robert, his mother, and his teachers indicated that Robert put out more effort in all areas than did his peers and was consistently compliant with the behavioral program, maintaining full points for extended periods of time. In this program children would lose points for minor infractions such as turning around in their seats, whispering to a neighbor, or asking a classmate for a pencil without permission. Robert's only periods of challenging behavior occurred when he had not taken his medication. Despite Robert's success in this very restrictive placement, he was not mainstreamed for any elective or content-area classes, and at the end of the 5th grade, he was sent to an even more restrictive setting—a totally separate school for students with emotional disturbance.

EDITH

Like Kanita, Edith was a child whose story supports the hypothesis that she had no emotional condition that warranted an EH placement. Of greatest concern was the fact that Edith showed no behavioral problems at home, as explained by her mother and verified by our home visits.

Edith was born in the United States, of Haitian parents. She was a 3rd-grader when we first saw her, and she stood out among her peers because of her height and unusual attire—somber, conservative skirts and blouses required by her religion. These features made her appear quite atypical in her class of African American and Hispanic children. She was described by her teacher as "different" and was referred for evaluation because of poor academic achievement. However, near the time of her evaluation, there was an incident in which she reacted to her peers' teasing by threatening to kill herself. This event caused the psychologist to focus on emotional rather than academic issues in her assessment and Edith was found to qualify for an EH placement.

Since Edith did not stand out in the classroom in terms of her behavior or academic level, her placement in an EH class came as a shock both to us and to the school counselor who told us about it. It was a shock also to her mother, who expressed adamant disagreement with the evaluation:

> Edith is not handicap! [emphasis on *handicap* in a raised voice] I tell them at school, Edith do lots for me at home. I send her to the store, she get everything I need, no problem. She listen at home and do what I tell her. She behave. She have no problem in the brain. She fine. I pray to God and she fine. I have six children. Two in college, two in high school, doing fine. I have a 4-year-old and he doing fine too. All of them fine, Edith too.
>
> There was these kids, bothering Edith every day, that's why. Edith come home, she cry every day. I go to the school, the principal don't do nothing about it. They tell me Edith have problem. So I take her to doctor. He say she fine. No handicap. I take her to another one. Same thing. I take her to three doctor. They all say she fine! They [school personnel] say Edith say she want to die, so she have problem. I tell

them, kids been bothering Edith every day and she cry, she upset. That why she say that. Doctor say she fine. She fine with me at home. She go to church every week. She walk with her cousins. She sing in the chorus at church. She going to be in a play at church in December 25. Edith, she OK. She fine. She need help with her reading and writing, but she not handicap.

I went to the school [placement conference]. I am not agree with them about Edith. They tell me Edith cannot read and write, and she have problem. . . . They say she stay in program one year. She still there. If she need help to read, they should help her.

We began observing Edith again in her self-contained 5th-grade EH placement and followed her into her placement in middle school. Both these placements were extremely restrictive, her only potential contact with children in general education occurring at lunch. Hart's (2003) follow-up study reported that, across 16 classroom observations (including regular education homeroom, special classes, and EH classrooms), and observations at lunch and during transition periods, there was never any sign of Edith's behavior being problematic. The only report we had from school personnel in the elementary education EH setting was that she once had to be "taken down" (physically restrained) for telling lies. State regulations on the use of physical restraint indicate that this was not an acceptable sanction for lying.

The first issue in this case was that the entire placement process reflected family stereotyping. Unfounded assumptions related to Edith's family and culture resulted in disregard of family information. Our visits to Edith's home confirmed her mother's claim that Edith functioned well and normally within her family. On one occasion, a researcher accompanied Edith to Sunday school, which she attended with her cousins and in which she participated fully and appropriately. It is clear that school personnel's perception of Edith was based totally on her social difficulties in school, which defies the requirement that the disturbance should exist across settings or that information given by the family be taken into account.

The second issue was the lack of attention to context in the referral process. It was reported by her referring teacher that Edith was initially referred for learning difficulties, but the psychological assessment, conducted by a Hispanic psychologist, focused on a report that Edith had threatened to kill herself. Without any attempt to investigate or correct the peer-group dynamics that led to Edith's frustration, the assessment "revealed" underlying emotional issues, which resulted in an extremely restrictive placement for this child who, in her home and community, functioned no differently from her peers. The parent attended the conference and expressed her disagreement, but her views concerning Edith's emotional state and needs were disregarded, and Edith was placed in the EH class with promises from school staff that the placement would last "about a year" and would assist Edith "with her reading."

A third issue brings Edith's situation in line with that of Robert—the question of the efficacy of the EH program and its ultimate outcome. Hart (2003) reported extensive evidence of inappropriately restrictive settings and ineffective, rote instruction that did not address Edith's language needs. Although she demonstrated little, if any, propensity toward angry outbursts, she was instructed solely in the EH class because of her "inability to deal with the frustrations of the mainstream." Like Robert, Edith often maintained the top level of the behavioral system and her cumulative file showed no instances of behavior referrals.

CONCLUSIONS

Two overwhelming conclusions emerge from our study of the four children placed in EH classes. First, classroom contexts were most often not taken into account either in the decision to refer or in the assessment itself. The referral processes for Kanita and Robert did not raise questions of whether or to what extent negative classroom environments were contributing to these children's behavior. No one thought to address the extreme teasing that led to Edith's threat to kill herself. And no one raised the question of the potential effects of the busing policy on Matthew, a sensitive African American boy whose on-grade academic achievement seemed inferior in a class of high-achieving, wealthy, White peers.

Second, with the exception of Kanita's program, the EH programs we observed defied the law's requirement for the least restrictive environment. Even in Kanita's case, the stigma of the EH label worked against initial efforts at mainstreaming her and it was only her teacher's persistent protection and advocacy that enabled her eventual return to general education. This very protection, of course, echoes the words of the psychologist who had referred both Kanita and Germaine, who put children in special education "to save their lives." It can certainly be argued that these two children were "saved" by these actions, and it could be that Germaine did need the protection of the nurturing SLD teacher. Kanita, on the other hand, simply needed a good teacher.

Overall, we do not believe that the changed behavior of Robert, Kanita, Edith, and Matthew proved that they needed a self-contained EH class. They needed to be in smaller classes with good teachers who were sensitive to their social and emotional needs and structured in their approach. In Edith's case, the placement was particularly inappropriate from the point of view of the evaluation results. If Edith's threat to kill herself had been serious, she would have needed a much more supportive environment than the "file the line" classroom into which she was placed. Conversely, Austin, whose case we reported in Chapter 10, was truly in need of emotional support, but was placed in an LD program.

Kanita was the only student whose EH placement was helpful to her, and she was the only one who exited the EH program. Kanita's "success" story points to the power and the pain of special education. A good teacher, small class size, a structured but challenging curriculum, individualized supports, and an openness to recognizing the child's strengths are all within the purview of the IDEA. We believe that Kanita benefited from, but did not need, this classroom. Two years after the initial placement, she functioned without a hitch in a classroom of about 22 children designated "gifted," in the same school from which she had been referred. We believe that she could have done that in the 2nd grade.

These students' stories underscore the negative results of a construction of disability that focuses on identifying within-child deficits. As we argued in our earlier discussion of assessment, there is great danger in this approach, especially when it is reliant on controversial, subjective projective testing. Our research dramatically endorses the arguments of scholars too numerous to mention who have called for an emphasis on school response and context rather than child-centered labeling (e.g., Artiles et al., 2012; Carter et al., 2017; Keogh & Speece, 1996; Montague & Rinaldi, 2001; Skiba et al., 2014). Further, the importance of effective classroom management in the 1st grade has been shown to have a lasting effect on children's behavior (Kellam et al., 1998). There has been a great deal of concern with the punitive and "zero-tolerance" approaches to such issues. Skiba and Peterson (2000) and others have argued for zero-tolerance to be replaced with "early response" strategies too numerous to detail here. Central to all these proposals is a preventive principle that combines individualized response with supportive rather than punitive schoolwide policies and a commitment to functional assessment of behavior. Skiba and Peterson state:

> The technology of functional assessment, for example, enables school personnel to better understand the "communicative intent" of challenging behavior (Brady & Halle, 1997). In a zero tolerance environment, however, teachers and administrators may be less interested in understanding communicative intent than in ridding schools and classrooms of troublesome students. (p. 340)

Robert's school exemplified the zero-tolerance approach. This was the school cited earlier as suspending more than 100 students in one year, with a required suspension for fighting. This applied even to kindergarten and 1st-graders.

Finally, we conclude that despite good intentions, the concept of "emotional handicap" as practiced in this state is not tenable. The existence of the EH category encourages school personnel to assume child deficits without examining context and to place children who are troubling to teachers or peers in separate settings that defy the law's call for the least restrictive environment. The reification of these negative labels in the eyes of school personnel results in school careers marked by exclusion.

CHAPTER 12

Into Special Education
Exile or Solution?

> Disproportionate representation is a problem if the quality and academic relevance of instruction in special classes block students' educational progress, including decreasing the likelihood of their return to the regular classroom.
>
> —Heller et al. (1982)

Our research was premised on the argument of Heller et al. (1982)—namely, that overrepresentation of culturally and linguistically diverse students in special education must be considered a problem if either the precursors to, or the outcomes of, placement are inappropriate or inadequate. In other words, how did the students get there? Was it worth it? The preceding chapters have presented our answers to the first question, concluding that the process was so variable and subjective as to be inequitable. We have reserved this chapter for close attention to the second question.

SPECIAL EDUCATION BENEFITS: IDEAL VERSUS REALITY

The two statements below represent the ideal versus the reality of special education in this district:

If you get them placed correctly, and get them whatever they need, early on, they have a chance. You know, get them counseled, or get them reading or doing math and writing, you know, whatever it is that they need. (High-referring, first-grade general-education teacher)

With special ed, there are large numbers in the classroom. And we write these wonderful individual education plans. When I was going into special ed, my professor talked about five kids in a classroom . . . and you'd get to do so much and it all made sense—IEPs, and five kids, and being able to work with them and build them, then let them fly. . . . But special ed teachers have a lot of responsibilities . . . paperwork, authorization, and on and on. And they have no assistance in the classroom, as far as a paraprofessional, you know, it's just them and 20 kids and IEPs. . . . You walk into a special ed classroom and everybody is doing the same thing. So . . . where's the individualization? The material is probably at a lower level, but everybody is doing the same thing. . . . I guarantee you, in more than 90% of the classrooms. . . . How can you expect me to individualize when I have 20, 25 kids? (Placement specialist, former special education teacher)

The first quote above captures the essence of most general education teach-ers' expressed beliefs about the value of special education placement. In a few cases, we saw these expectations realized. More often, we saw the pic-ture described by the special education teacher who had become a placement specialist. Overall, the "big picture" of special education programs was not encouraging: large class sizes, teacher shortages, undifferentiated instruction, poor teacher quality, poor curriculum quality, undue restrictiveness, continu-ing stigma in EH programs, and, at the end, a low rate of exit.

In the previous section, we outlined the basic outcomes for the students we were able to follow closely. To summarize: Of the students designated with Specific Learning Disability (SLD), Miles and Germaine, placed in the same special education class, did well. Miles, described as a "bright" child with LD, exemplified what the psychologist called "early intervention." A slow starter, he caught up in a year, repeating kindergarten with an excellent gen-eral education teacher and spending 12 hours a week with an excellent special education teacher. We do not believe Miles had LD; we believe that excessive absenteeism in his kindergarten year set him back and excellent instruction caught him up. We believe that his need for early intervention could have been met without psychological assessment and without the assignment of a disability label. We believe the same for Germaine, who, referred in the 2nd grade and almost on grade level in reading, was out of place academically in his primary special education class. But, a sensitive child who had experi-enced serious family loss, he benefited from the gentle manner of the special education teacher. Austin, by contrast, did not do well in his special educa-tion pullout program. In fact, he did much better in his general education homeroom of 30 than in the resource room. It seemed that with his extreme experience of family loss, what Austin needed most was a strong connection to his teacher; once more, the teacher made the difference. Marc was in a pull-out program with 16 other students; he was quiet and compliant, and made steady but slow progress in an uninspired, nonindividualized program. We do not know the outcomes for Anita and Paul, since they were both moved by their parents to other schools.

Of the students placed in EH programs, Kanita blossomed in the strict but supportive environment provided by a strong EH teacher who recog-nized her potential for a gifted program. We believe that Kanita would have done just as well in the class of any structured, challenging general educa-tion teacher. Like Kanita, Matthew's and Edith's "emotionally disturbed"

behaviors disappeared upon placement in their EH classes, where they became immediately compliant with strict behavioral management systems.
Matthew, whose work was just below grade level when he entered the program, became a "star" in contrast to his lower-achieving peers. Edith, who
had no behavioral difficulties in her home and community, continued into
middle school in an extremely restrictive setting and never received the appropriate literacy instruction she desperately needed. Robert improved as long
as the program was able to enforce his medication regimen. Despite his progress, he was placed for middle school, in an even more restrictive setting—an
entire school that served only children with emotional disturbance.

The three children placed in full-time ID programs were destined to
remain there. It seemed that Bartholomew developed health problems that
would probably diminish his progress. Clementina seemed much happier in
her well-run special education class. She was an enthusiastic participant in
class activities, and the teacher stated that "Clementina is one of the smartest
in her group. She is a good fit. She will catch up." She stayed in this class for
2 years, but we do not know what happened to her when she moved on to
middle school. Leroy, in a primary special education class where he would
remain for 3 years, was not likely to improve much in the chaotic environment we observed. We were not able to follow James into his special education setting.

This picture of mixed outcomes indicates that there were circumstances
in which special education placement proved a blessing. In others, it was no
worse, and no better, than general education placement. In the worst cases, it
was disastrous. Overall, we concluded that the most important factor in these
outcomes was the teacher. However, there were several factors that mitigated
against this benefit, and others that made it difficult even for good teachers to
perform well in these programs.

Class Size

The belief that special education programs provided small class sizes with
individualized instruction was not generally substantiated by our observations. This was most obvious in classes referred to as Varying Exceptionalities
(VE), which served those children perceived to have a range of high-incidence
learning difficulties. These classes contained a mixture of children designated
as having any of the three high-incidence disabilities, although they were predominantly LD, with a few children labeled ID, and occasionally a child labeled EH. These classes could be self-contained, where children spent most of
the day, or resource classrooms to which students came for up to 12 hours a
week. Most typically, these classes ranged between 16 and 24 children.

In one inner-city school serving a predominantly Black population, the
Intermediate Special Education teacher exclaimed: "At 9:00 A.M., there are
21 to 23 kids at my door." This situation reflected a plan in which all the 4th
and 5th graders who received LD services came to the LD resource room for

2½ hours for instruction in the same Success for All (SFA) reading program used by their peers in general education. Thus, the special education instruction they received was a poor imitation of what they received in the regular classroom. Moreover, students in this class represented five SFA levels, so the teacher had to "juggle instruction and seat work" for her 21–23 students. The theoretical advantage of individualized instruction envisioned both by the SFA program and special education were offset by this large number of students.

In another school, in which the principal was determined, at all costs, to improve the school's grade in the state's evaluation system, an intensive attempt to assist general education students had some very detrimental effects on the special education program. The numbers in the LD program were already very large (9.8% of the school population). Worse, however, was the administration's decision, in the semester prior to the high-stakes testing, to schedule all the special education children to stay with their special education teachers from 9:00 A.M. till noon every day, while all general education teachers would focus on test preparation with small groups of students. This brought the LD students' special education programming to 15 hours a week instead of the 12 required by their individual education plans (IEPs), and some students, who should have gone to LD for reading and language arts only, were required to stay with the LD teacher for math also. The last arrangement reflected the fact that, since those students already had an LD label, their scores would not "count" in the school's assessment. These arrangements shortchanged the special education students of appropriate math instruction, of the least-restrictive-environment requirement, and of the IEP requirement for small-group instruction while in their special education class.

As in our findings about variability in general school quality, class sizes suggested a pattern of socioeconomic (SES) inequity in special education. At the school serving the highest-income, mostly Anglo and Hispanic population, we saw the smallest class size in the entire sample—two resource rooms that ranged from 6 to 12 children each. Paraprofessionals were more likely to be present in the higher-income schools, apparently paid for by money raised locally. By contrast, at one inner-city school serving a predominantly Black population, the average size of an LD class was 13–16. At another in a nearby neighborhood, there were, in the first year of our study, two VE classrooms, a primary and an intermediate. But when one teacher resigned, both classes were combined under one teacher and this remained so for the entirety of the following year. At another school in a similar neighborhood, resource room size was 17–24 students. In some of these inner-city schools, the special education teachers started out with comparable class sizes, but when a vacancy occurred, it was harder to fill, thus resulting in larger classes for varying periods of time.

These classrooms typically had no paraprofessionals. In one inner-city school, the self-contained VE class had 19 students, 4 designated MR and 15 LD, across all grade levels from 2nd to 5th. The principal reported that the

VE class must be up to about 24–25 students to get a paraprofessional and that this self-contained class had never had more than 22–23 students. The principal did not consider this a problem, since the teacher was excellent and there were no "uncontrollable" children in that class. Our perception was that the teacher was indeed excellent and did manage quite well, but that the class size seriously negated these children's IEPs and the law's mandate for individualized instruction.

Classrooms for students designated as having EH or ID generally had smaller numbers, and often a paraprofessional. These classes typically had no more than 12 students, usually with a paraprofessional for at least part of the day. An exception to this was one school serving a low-income, African American population at which the ID self-contained intermediate class included 19 students, with a paraprofessional.

Individualized Versus Undifferentiated Instruction

Specialized teacher preparation is a centerpiece of special education and goes beyond just "good teaching" (Kauffman & Hornby, 2020). As special educators ourselves, the researchers in this study fully appreciated this, but it was also clear that the most effective teachers we saw, whether in general or special education, were not only skilled, but were empathetic and culturally responsive to the children. It was also evident that the fact of special education certification did not guarantee appropriate instruction. In fact, very often instruction in VE and resource classrooms was indistinguishable from that in general education classrooms. The claim of individualized or differentiated instruction was completely negated in schools in which special reading programs such as SFA were used, since reading instruction in the resource room used the same SFA texts as general-education classes. Math instruction also was mostly "whole class," though we did see a few exceptions. The following example of routine, whole-class instruction is from a school with a predominantly Hispanic population, where we generally noted a high quality of instruction and management in the general education classrooms. Students did not appear to be following the lesson at all, since the instruction was so unclear.

> 10:10 A.M. There are 13 students total—aged 6, 7, and 8, in 1st and 2nd grades. The teacher is teaching a whole-class lesson. Students are working at their desks, completing a workbook page—there is some talking. The teacher says, "If you can hear me, clap once. . . ." Walking around looking at students' work, she says, "I told you three times to write your name, you haven't done it yet, now do it." She instructs students to "find the number for your age and circle it" in their workbooks. . . . She then returns to the board and asks, "Who is 7?" and writes the names of students who raise their hands. One student says that he is 9 and another student says, "No, you are 7." The teacher

says, "Ask your mom." Next the teacher writes the names of the 8-year-olds. She makes a bar graph. I hear a student say under his breath, "We don't care about that." . . . The teacher says, "The problem is that you are not listening—it is very important to listen to me so you know what to do."

[Observer's comments: I don't think the students followed this lesson at all—it wasn't clear what the teacher was trying to show, and she didn't really explain it. All students seem to be doing the same thing (no differentiated instruction). Students are quite wiggly.]

Several teachers emphasized that large class size was a serious deterrent to individualized instruction, and our observations showed that the amount of individuation did seem to correlate with the number of students present in the class—the more students there were, generally the less instruction was differentiated. In one of the ID classes we observed we did notice small groups working at different centers and at different levels in a well-structured environment. In the following example of a resource room in an inner-city school with otherwise variable instruction, there were only two students in the room and the teacher provided one-on-one instruction. This was a math lesson; class size was much larger during reading (up to 18 students):

1:00 P.M.: Three students are leaving as I enter the room. One, a kindergartner named Gerald, remains. He's sitting at the kidney-shaped table. The teacher counts with him, pointing to and "reading" large numerals on cards posted over the whiteboard. The 8 is missing. When they get to 8, the teacher acts surprised that it is missing and asks in exaggerated fashion, "Where is the 8?" Another student comes in at this point, and the teacher stops to give him a paper and direct him to sit down and start working. She goes back to working with Gerald. She writes on the whiteboard: "1, 2, 3, 4, 5, 6, 7, 8 [circled]." He is supposed to circle eight animals in his workbook. The other boy asks, "Do I do the back?" The teacher responds, "Um hum," and goes over and checks his work. The kindergartner is coloring the animals on his workbook page. Now the teacher comes back and asks, "Finished?" Gerald nods. The teacher checks his work and says, "Very good." She writes a happy face and Gerald says, "Happy." The teacher says, "OK, now count with me." They count, and this time she circles the 7 and asks Gerald to come up to the board and write a 7. The teacher says, "Very good, that is another star." She draws the star under his name on the board—he now has two. Next Gerald is supposed to color seven balloons out of nine on the page. I ask the teacher if this is how many students she usually has now, and she tells me that one is absent. Gerald has colored all nine of the balloons in his workbook, and the teacher explains to him that he needs to cross out two because he has colored too many. She helps him cross them out, with her hand over his, and then asks him if he understands. He nods. She tells him that now he can play on the computer. She then works with the other student.

This situation represented the placement specialist's ideal vision of special education—"IEPs and five kids." Clearly, differentiated and individualized instruction was possible where there were good teachers and small, even reasonable numbers in a classroom. However, this scenario was rare.

Teacher Quality

In comparison with general education, where we saw a clear pattern of weaker teachers in the lower-income, Black neighborhoods, the pattern was similar but not as clear-cut in special education. While it was true that the schools serving higher-income populations did have consistently more effective teachers, several of the inner-city schools also had some excellent special education teachers. However, they also had some very weak ones.

In one inner-city school, for example, we observed a teacher in a resource room with 10–12 students offer routine, whole-class instruction that resulted in considerable boredom and inattentiveness on the part of the students. The teacher made no effort to improve students' responses by changing seating, adjusting the task, or engaging the children at the back of the room. The researcher's summary notes read:

> Throughout the lesson, only three girls seated at the front were participating. Other behaviors included a boy in the back interacting angrily with a peer, a boy in the front fiddling and failing to respond to specific requests from the teacher. When the lesson moved on to choral reading, I observed that the girls in the front read very well, and actually carried the group reading. Round robin reading also revealed one very poor reader. The lesson was based on an SFA text, with sentences such as "Don gets Pit Pat. He gets the sock." There is so much idling taking place that I can see the overwhelmed look on the teacher's face. . . . She turns to me and sighs heavily, and says "I have a lot of antsy kids."

We were often struck by the rote, low-level quality of some of the instruction we saw. For example, we observed several times in the resource room at another school with a predominantly African American population of higher SES than that of the inner-city schools. The 16 4th- and 5th-grade students with LD in the class were generally on task and well behaved, yet frequently were occupied completing workbook pages and doing low-level work such as coloring. In one observation, the teacher was giving a spelling test of words such as *ran* and *sat*, which seemed to be at an early 1st-grade level, even though the students we were following were working at an upper-2nd-grade level or higher.

At another school, this one mostly Hispanic, we observed Paul, one of our case study children, in his resource room. We were struck by the low level of the work:

> During this single observation, Paul completed two "color and cut" activities (one an alligator to go along with the story "The Lady with the Alligator Purse" and one a Christmas bell). He also took a "spelling test" with the words listed on the board for students to copy, and did a sentence-completion activity, with the answers written next to the sentences that were to be copied. Paul completed all these activities without any difficulty.

Nevertheless, we did see some very effective teaching in some classrooms. One of the most effective lessons took place in a school that was, otherwise, characterized by some of the worst instruction we observed. This was in a self-contained special education class in the predominantly Haitian school featured as providing limited opportunity to learn. The teacher herself was of the same ethnicity as the students. This lesson was characterized by student engagement and higher-level thinking, even though the students themselves seemed to be functioning at a fairly low level:

> As I enter the classroom, one boy holds out his hand and introduces himself. He then shows me a bulletin board about Mexico and says, "The teacher is good and teaches us a lot, like about Mexico and Black people and what they've done, and the rainforest." 8:50: The teacher has written on the board: "May 20, 1999. The destruction of the rainforest cause [sic] Jane to . . ." She asks students to write in their journals. They do so quietly, without a sound, apparently accustomed to this routine. The children are bright eyed, well groomed, friendly. . . . The chalkboard has a poster with rainforest animals on it. Books about the rainforest are lined up along the bottom. . . . 9:06: The teacher asks Joselyn to share and "show her beautiful picture." Joselyn shows the class her picture, then gives me a big smile and goes back to her seat. Charles comes up to read what he has written: "The destruction of the rain forest cause Jane to cry." The teacher tells him that his picture is nice, to show it, but he doesn't want to, saying that his other drawing is better. The teacher says again, "It's nice, go around and show it." She asks, "Anyone else? Don't be shy." . . . Another boy shares and says that the destruction of the rainforest "cause Jane to die." Another student (a girl) adds, "Maybe from stress."

Teacher Shortage

In some of the highest-need schools, teacher shortage severely affected teacher quality. It was in these schools that principals had the hardest time finding permanent replacements, or substitute teachers, when teachers left. As mentioned, some principals solved this by combining two classes under one teacher. Another strategy was to staff the class with a series of long-term substitute teachers. We observed one substitute special education teacher twice during SFA reading instruction. When the researcher entered the classroom, the substitute teacher told her, "I don't know what I'm doing." The room was quite noisy and chaotic, with very few students actually reading.

VARIABLE QUALITY IN EH PROGRAMS

We have already described the main outcomes for the four students placed in EH (currently known as EBD) programs. At one end of the spectrum was Kanita's classroom, in which the emphasis was on work and learning within a structured behavioral program. At the other end of the spectrum was Edith's classroom, where the curriculum was essentially behavior modification—or, to put it bluntly, what we heard referred to as "boot camp." We will detail here some features of Edith's program, to indicate how detrimental such placement can be.

Although Edith was placed in EH because of perceived depression and possible suicidal tendencies, her EH program was of the "boot camp" nature and seemed designed much more for her classmates with acting-out behavioral problems. Our observations of this classroom were rife with negative, even insulting phrases from the teacher's repertoire of reprimands, such as: "Heads down!" "Bury your face!" "File the line!" "You're off level, you just got three extra days!" "PE is canceled!" "Stand in the corner!" "Give him zeroes!" "You and me will be on the floor." Additionally, school personnel were observed imposing physical intimidation tactics, such as walking menacingly toward students, grabbing student's faces, banging a chair or desk en route to deal with an off-task student, and the use of physical restraint with students "for becoming verbally disrespectful." It was evident that this climate was dictated mainly by the lead teacher and aide, but when a new teacher was transitioned and tried a more thoughtful approach, it was difficult for her to be taken seriously either by the students or staff.

Overall, daily instructional and organizational routines removed the locus of control from the students. Such routines included supervised breakfast in the cafeteria at a later time than that of the general education population; supervised bathroom breaks, with teachers accompanying all students to the bathroom at regimented times; the requirement that students "file the line," or keep a specified distance of 3 feet between themselves and the student directly in front of and behind them; and the requirement that students line up for out-of-class activities by behavioral level. It was clear that these 5th-graders were being exposed to a class environment that would in no way prepare them for the normal routines of the mainstream. Edith did not receive specialized instruction in reading or counseling for depression.

Robert's and Matthew's EH programs fell between the extremes of Kanita's and Edith's and were far from exemplary. While not totally reliant on "boot camp" tactics, the curricula in these programs were generally unchallenging and repetitive. Given their main focus on children's ability to earn points in the behavioral program, there seemed to be little emphasis on teaching and learning, and it was all the more surprising to see that the majority of the children in these classes, despite their designation of EH, were able to sit quietly through periods of minimal instruction and boring, repetitive routines. Once more, we were left with serious doubts as to the presence of emotional disturbance in most of these children.

RESTRICTIVE ENVIRONMENTS

School personnel's approaches to mainstreaming children varied from school to school. In general, however, little mainstreaming took place, whether from resource or full-time programs. Self-contained EH and MR programs evidenced significant concerns with meeting the requirements of the least restrictive environment. With just a few notable exceptions, self-contained programs were set up to allow the minimum movement outside the classroom and little if any modification to meet the needs of individual students. The impression given at the placement conferences was that if a child was considered eligible for such a program then it meant that this was the level of restrictiveness needed for that child. Yet our data indicated quite the opposite for some children.

EH Programs

We have already indicated that Edith's placement in the EH program was totally inappropriate for her. Indeed, bearing in mind especially that the designation EH in this state indicates the milder end of the SED spectrum, the restrictiveness of this program was inappropriate for any child designated EH. Students in this program, after eating breakfast separately from their nondisabled peers, returned to their classroom no earlier than 9:05 A.M. and as late as 9:15 A.M. Thus, they had 35–45 fewer instructional minutes than did their nondisabled peers, who were able to eat breakfast in the cafeteria prior to school. Moreover, students in this program attended only PE with the general education students, a privilege that was frequently withheld in order to punish misbehavior. When the students did make it out to PE, the special education teacher accompanied the class to "show his face," thus keeping the students in line. Instruction in music and art was delivered to these students in the self-contained setting. Despite the teacher's protestation that he was "a big advocate for inclusion," none of the 14 students in Edith's class was mainstreamed in any subject area. When asked about Edith's possible return to the mainstream, the teacher said, "Maybe she'll be *partially* mainstreamed by high school."

Fortunately, such restrictiveness was not uniform across all the schools. Kanita's program was quite different. With an excellent teacher in the self-contained classroom, these students "went out" to mainstream settings according to their needs. From the start of her placement there, Kanita was mainstreamed for PE and other special classes. When, after only a couple of months, it was evident to the teacher that Kanita's behavior was fully compliant in the self-contained classroom, the general mainstreaming process began.

Finally, one of the most disconcerting aspects of these programs was that they were often a dumping ground for any child perceived to have behavioral difficulties. Thus, students who were perceived to be depressed and suicidal were "thrown in" with students with conduct disorders and other acting-out behaviors, and then treated similarly, as in Edith's case. We consider this one of the most disconcerting aspects of the EH category.

ID Programs

The ID programs that we observed were also very restrictive in that students were rarely mainstreamed. For example, we have already noted inappropriate restrictiveness in Bartholomew's ID program. In direct contradiction of the recommendation in the child's placement conference, the teacher's insistence that her students "do not go out" deprived Bartholomew of his right to participate in the Creole language program that would have been his only opportunity to use his home language during the school day. This was particularly troubling for several reasons: First, this child was at ESOL Level 2 and it was evident that the teacher (a Hispanic woman) had great difficulty understanding his speech. Moreover, he was the only Creole speaker in his class, all the other children being either African American or Hispanic. During one observation, in response to a prompt of "I love to . . ." Bartholomew dictated to his writing partner, "I love to go to BCC" (acronym for the home language program). The teacher at first did not understand either what he had said or what his partner had written, and when the researcher interpreted it to her she commented, "Bartholomew can't handle going out to other classes. He has to stay here with me."

The restrictiveness of the ID and EH programs reflected and reinforced the reification of these disability labels. One evident outcome was a raising of the bar regarding these children's performance and a pervasive view that the children "belonged" in these restrictive programs. Kanita ultimately succeeded in defying the pervasively low expectations of her as an "EH child" in the mainstream. The other three children designated as EH were not given this opportunity. Hart's (2003) follow-up study of Kanita, Robert, and Edith offers a detailed portrait of the sticking power of this label for the last two children.

LD Programs

Despite the widespread use of part-time programming for students designated as LD, there were also several self-contained classrooms. In these programs, the issue of the "velcro" label was often evident. With the exception of the school with an inclusion model where we saw a great deal of mainstreaming, we noted few attempts to return children to the general education environment. In one inner-city school serving a predominantly Haitian population, a special education resource teacher explained that although they did both partial and full mainstreaming, with a requirement on the IEP to monitor students' progress, there was often not enough time to do this properly. The teacher of the self-contained VE class in the same school reported that she had four students whom she wanted to mainstream, but the principal told her to put them in the resource room program for reading, which she did. The teacher commented, "I don't think that's really mainstreaming . . . but I have to take what I can get—whatever." In the school in which the principal had instituted a rigorous testing-and-placement process in order to improve the school's rank on the statewide grading, a teacher reported that it was becoming increasingly difficult to mainstream successful LD students.

LOW RATE OF EXIT FROM SPECIAL EDUCATION PROGRAMS

The foregoing review of the restrictiveness of special education brings us to the very low rate of exit from special education programs. Those with whom we spoke about this issue told us that students rarely exited from special education during elementary school. One LD teacher shared that she was not in favor of dismissing students until they were at least in middle school:

> Now our policy is to recommend that the parents keep the child [in special education in elementary]. They should spend time in special education classes until they make some kind of adjustment in middle school and if they do really well in middle school then you pull [them out of special education]. Because it is a big adjustment to go from here to there in an environment where they have five or six classes and they go from class to class. I can think of two students in the past that did need special education in elementary, they needed that extra, and when they got into middle school they were dismissed. A couple of them did get promoted into honors classes. So it depends, but that is rare. It really depends on the child and how they push themselves.

In this chapter, we have addressed the issue that was at the heart of the famous decision in *Larry P. v. Riles* (1979/1984)—the judge's concern that special education placement not be tantamount to relegation to "dead end" programs. In this school district, good special education programs did exist and it was evident that children placed in such programs did benefit. "Dead end" programs, however, were far too often in evidence.

CONCLUSIONS

Overall, our main concern was that "special" education was too often not at all special. We observed two excellent special education teachers—Kanita's EH teacher and Germaine's and Miles's SLD teacher. For the most part, the special education programs were marked by routine and generic, rather than individualized, instruction; teacher shortages; widely variable teacher quality; unduly restrictive environments in the EH and ID programs; and unduly large class sizes in classes for students with LD.

In terms of VE classrooms, the best programs we saw were generally in the higher-SES neighborhoods, not necessarily because they had the best teachers but because the teachers in those schools tended to have smaller class sizes and paraprofessional support. Good teachers in lower-income areas were often negatively affected by large class sizes and no support from paraprofessionals. While class sizes were generally more manageable in EH and ID programs, a combination of teacher quality and restrictive philosophies frequently limited the programs' effectiveness. The obvious least-restrictive-environment violations were striking.

Finally, we reiterate that a great deal of what happens in any given school depends on the principal. In our discussion of administrative issues, we reported in detail on what we referred to as the anomalous school (Green Acres) in our table showing the relationship between SES and teachers with master's degrees. In terms of special education quality, we found this school to be, once more, anomalous, with an excellent special education program despite the low-SES population being served. Another anomaly was evident in the predominantly Haitian school that seemed to have the highest percentage of weak general education teachers but effective special education teachers.

It was evident that the general approach to special education was that the child was expected to fit the program rather than the other way around. This was exactly the opposite of the individualization envisioned by the IDEA. The idealized beliefs expressed by many general-education personnel regarding the value of special education were not borne out by our study. To conclude, the likelihood that special education placement would block rather than facilitate students' educational progress undermines school personnel's faith that this program would provide a remedy for the learning and behavioral difficulties of Black and Hispanic children in this school district. This was especially true for those who also experienced economic disadvantage. Moreover, for the ID and EBD categories, special education placement was tantamount to exile from the mainstream of the educational system. These are the categories in which Black children are overrepresented nationwide and in this school district. Such outcomes strongly support our view that patterns of overrepresentation in these categories are, in the final analysis, inequitable.

CHAPTER 13

Conclusions and Recommendations

That would be nice if we didn't "leave no child" behind. But we have so many problems to deal with: low students, home problems, discipline, and behavior.

—2nd-grade teacher in a high-poverty urban school

Three years of intensive qualitative study of the placement process in 12 elementary schools in a large, multicultural, urban school district point to problems at both systemic and individual levels, to the need for refinement of procedures, and to problematic human factors in decision-making. The issue of overrepresentation is very challenging because of its complexity. In all cases, we noted several potential explanations for special education placement that went well beyond the notion of intrinsic deficits or disabilities in children.

Twenty years later, the widespread societal disruptions caused by the COVID-19 pandemic continue to reverberate throughout the education system and intensify the concerns expressed throughout this book. While the literature on this topic is rapidly increasing, we mention here only a few key issues, highlighting the fact that students who experience educational disadvantages, whether through disability or lack of home and community resources, are at increased risk of educational failure, lack of needed services, and/or inappropriate special education placement. However, one ironic outcome reported by parents was that virtual instruction during this period allowed them to see both positive and negative aspects of the quality of instruction that their children were receiving (Ocasio-Stoutenburg & Harry, 2021).

Jameson and colleagues (2020) provided a detailed discussion of the pandemic's challenges to schools' ability to conform to key principles of the IDEA—specifically, a Free Appropriate Education (FAPE) and the provision of individualized education plans (IEPs). Not surprisingly, the National Center for Learning Disabilities (2021) reported a backlog of assessments and intensified learning gaps in both mathematics and reading for students of color and those in low-resource environments as a result of loss of instruction. In an even more urgent vein, the National Association of School Psychologists (NASP) (2020) expressed concern about a potential increase in inappropriate Specific Learning Disability (SLD) referrals and emphasized the need to reestablish core instruction and evidence-based interventions for all students, but especially for those potentially being considered for SLD identification. A trend of increased referrals, especially for incoming 1st-graders, has already been reported anecdotally in the school district studied in this book (staffing specialist Meaghan Chaplin, personal communication).

Perhaps most concerning is a key point emphasized by NASP (2020): Traditional assessments cannot be assumed to be valid or reliable when implemented in virtual settings and with students who have experienced 5–6 months of disruption in their schooling. The NASP brief on this topic included a statement that echoes our central argument that the SLD category is in dire need of revision. They say that the pandemic has provided "a unique opportunity to reconceptualize SLD, which has been a controversial construct since it was first institutionalized in federal law" (p. 6).

FINDINGS AND RECOMMENDATIONS

Our study demonstrated the processes by which 12 schools in this multicultural, multilingual school district contributed to the district's pattern of overrepresentation of Black students in all three high-incidence categories and, to some extent, of Hispanics in the LD category. In the light of the model we adapted from Heller and colleagues (1982), we conclude that disproportionality in this school district is indeed a problem because of the numerous inequitable factors influencing all phases of the placement process. These inequities related to the three main phases of the process: children's opportunity to learn prior to referral, the decision-making processes that led to special education placement, and the quality of the special education experience itself. Specifically, our main concerns were poor teacher quality; large class size; detrimental administrative policies regarding curriculum, instruction, and discipline; subjectivity in psychological assessment practices; pressure for special education placement because of high-stakes testing and the state's grading plan; arbitrary application of eligibility criteria; tardiness in placement processes; and restrictive or ineffective special education programs.

We refer to these negative impacts as inequities not only because they contributed to inappropriate or unnecessary special education placements, but also because there was a clear pattern of their being more in evidence in schools serving low-income, predominantly Black students. This pattern of inequity constitutes a form of institutional bias, wherein schooling reinforces rather than mitigates the effects of poverty and racism. The possibility of personal bias based on racial or social class prejudice seemed to us inherent in certain schooling situations, but was difficult to substantiate. Overall, we believe that what is needed is a firm commitment by the school district to policies and practices that will strengthen schools in poor neighborhoods, standardize the criteria on which referrals and eligibility decisions are made, and ensure an equitable assessment process. We do not deny that some students need more and, in some cases, specialized assistance than others—but we believe that, for the majority of students, this support can and should be provided without having to "prove" a disability and remove the child from general education. Students need, and deserve, a consistently higher level of instruction than we saw in the schools serving low-income populations, whether in general or special education.

While some of our case study students who were placed in special education did display learning or behavioral deficits, the explanations for their difficulties were not simple. There were a few whose deficiencies seemed likely to be inherent in the child's cognitive or socioemotional makeup. For most, however, the school circumstances surrounding their learning and development provided a strong competing explanation. For some, the most detrimental circumstance was inadequate opportunity to learn, resulting from poor instruction and ineffective classroom management and the absence of supportive schoolwide disciplinary policies. For most, decisions were idiosyncratic and arbitrary, influenced by the school setting in which the student was placed and by the student's performance relative to the norms of the local situation. For all, there were systemic influences that filtered down to the individual child through various avenues from the larger society. Indeed, the barriers to the effective implementation of the school district's seemingly sound referral and placement policies were to be found at local, state, and federal levels of the ecology of education. Below we describe these and offer several recommendations for improving outcomes for racially, culturally, and linguistically diverse students at each of these levels.

Federal Level

Findings. Twenty years after the termination of this study, the essential construction of special education services at the federal level has changed little. At the broadest level, the conceptualization of IDEA itself remains, which requires a determination of disability for a child to receive special education services. The 2004 reauthorization of IDEA however, did attempt to respond to concerns about evident inequities related to students of color, as seen in two adjustments in policy: the introduction of RTI/MTSS as an alternative to the IQ/discrepancy model for determining SLD, and the specification of State Performance Plans requiring that states report "significant disproportionality" in identification, placement, and discipline that result from "inappropriate identification."

Despite good intentions, it appears that neither policy has had much impact. While RTI represents an important change in practice, it has not altered the essential criterion of intrinsic deficit, as indicated by the continuing debate over the tier at which identification of a disability should occur and whether comprehensive psychological assessment should still be a requirement for identifying an LD. Consequently, the process is often implemented as simply a modified way of "hunting" for a disability (Baker, 2002; Ferri,

2011; Hoover, 2010; Johnston, 2011). Similarly, the requirement for state reporting and monitoring of disproportionality remains weak because of a permissive posture that allowed the states to determine the numerical criterion for "significance" and the vagueness of how identification practices would be determined to have been "inappropriate" (Cavendish et al., 2014; Voulgarides et al., 2017).

Recommendations. Although we continue to celebrate the tremendous advocacy that brought the EHA/IDEA into existence almost 50 years ago, we believe that it is time for a reconsideration of the relevance of the concept of disability in the case of the high-incidence disabilities. The arbitrariness and confusion evident in these shifting categories cast serious doubts as to their validity. Moreover, a tremendous irony of the entrenched commitment to these ambiguous categories is that countries that look to the United States for models of education, such as some Caribbean nations (Harry, 2019) and India (Kalyanpur, 2022), often try to transport models of disability to their societies, where their implementation is a poor fit for local educational systems and social structures.

We recommend that, at least for children with high-incidence learning and behavior difficulties, special education should be reconceptualized as a set of specialized services that are available to children who need them, without the requirement of a disability label. The conceptualization of special education as requiring a search for intrinsic disability has not succeeded in adequately serving the needs of students who are performing at the low end of the general education spectrum. In particular, we think it is time to relinquish both the concepts of LD and EBD and focus on establishing (1) schoolwide systems of support and (2) individualized, targeted supportive instruction for students with learning and behavioral difficulties within the least restrictive settings possible. This does not mean that one size should fit all: We believe that some students will need individualized instruction and counseling and that schools should provide these without relying on stigmatizing and often unsubstantiated disability labels. Students with ASD, ID, and verifiable sensory or physical impairments should also receive needed support in the general education setting to the extent appropriate. We believe that IEPs should continue to be a central requirement for the provision of specialized services.

With regard to RTI/MTSS, we still have great hope for the potential of this model to ensure high quality instruction for all students supplemented by culturally responsive monitoring of their progress and increased individualization and specialized instruction wherever needed (Klingner & Edwards, 2006). However, implementation of this process needs to go beyond the lock-step, check-list approach noted in the literature and currently applied in this school district. Federal guidelines should include requirements for teachers, counselors, therapists, and psychologists to be engaged in thoughtful considerations of the meaning and purpose of RTI while addressing the range of inertial, technical, normative, and political forces that might undermine their practice (Thorius & Maxcy, 2015). Further, the guidelines should specify that "research-based" should not be taken to mean "one-size-fits-all," but rather should include the systemic application of culturally responsive, research-based principles (Hernandez et al., 2022).

State Level

Findings. At the state level, we identify two key concerns. First, our study raises serious concerns about the unduly negative results of high-stakes testing on children who are performing at the weaker end of the educational spectrum, but who do not necessarily have a disability. Because special education was seen as a way for schools to keep their scores from being depressed by low achievers, many children were inappropriately determined to have disabilities instead of receiving the intensive regular education support they needed.

Second, although this study was conducted prior to the introduction of State Performance Plans citing disproportionality, we see this as an important aspect of the problem. The lack of clarity in federal guidance regarding criteria for reporting disproportionality and inappropriate practices allows states to respond by relying on "race-neutral, technical fixes" (Tefera & Fischman, 2020, p. 6), and by disguising the problem through various strategies such as manipulation of numbers and superficial reliance on checklists that evade the issue of race (Voulgarides, 2021).

Recommendations. We recommend reexamining accountability measures, including how high-stakes test results are used to evaluate schools. It has long been shown that high-stakes testing affects children of color and English learners in disproportionately negative ways (Hilliard, 2000; Kohn, 2000; Townsend, 2002; Valencia & Villareal, 2003). In particular, high-stakes testing of English learners should take account of the primary language in all phases of testing, including the opportunity to learn the material, test administration, and interpretation of the scores (Heubert & Hauser, 1999). Moreover, the IEPs of English learners being served in special education should specifically attend to their language issues (Hoover, 2018). We recommend placing more weight on year-to-year improvement rather than absolute comparisons across dissimilar schools, and we strongly support efforts to include the scores of students receiving special education services when holding schools accountable, which has become the current approach in this district. States that have been cited for disproportionality should demand authentic self-reviews from the relevant districts.

We urge careful scrutiny of governmental policies and mandates related to school financing. As shown in our research and across the nation, educational resources are not equitably distributed across schools and districts and students of color living in high-poverty areas are more likely than their peers to attend schools that are inadequately funded and staffed (Donovan & Cross, 2002; Parrish et al., 1998). As one counselor in our study noted:

> They should give the inner-city schools more, not less—the kids come with nothing, and the teachers need to buy them things. We need more money just to get them the things that they need (that others take for granted). At other schools, if they don't bring their supplies, they get suspended, but you can't do that here.

Finally, we recommend examining preservice teacher-education programs to determine the extent to which they include coursework in culturally responsive pedagogy, quality field experiences in the highest-need schools, and practice within RTI/MTSS models (Cavendish et al., 2016; Ross & Lignugaris-Kraft, 2015). We suggest that all states review their teacher certification/licensure requirements to make sure they include standards specific to teaching children of color and English learners and that they require evidence from teacher-preparation programs indicating they are addressing diversity in significant ways (Miller et al., 2000).

Most important, though most challenging in light of the current ethos of denial regarding the basic tenets of Critical Race Theory (CRT), we echo the work of scholars who call for explicit self-awareness of both racism and ableism in teacher preparation and continuing professional development (Boscovich et al., 2020; Sleeter, 2017), as well as a historical understanding of housing policies, implicit bias, microaggression, colorblindness, and the role of race in disparate discipline practices and educational opportunities (Carter et al., 2017).

District Level

Findings. This large school district encompasses all the counties within the state, so we were informed that the funding is spread equitably across the district, as contrasted with the funding formula by which property taxes affect a district's funding. Nevertheless, our findings point to systemic or "institutional" bias against the lowest-income and, in particular, Black student populations through hiring practices that resulted in inadequate instruction for the very children who had the least preparation for schooling. As we have shown, and as has been demonstrated in decades of research, many schools serving students from racially, ethnically, economically, and linguistically diverse neighborhoods have less-qualified teachers, inadequate resources, and high turnover among administrators (e.g., Ansell & McCabe, 2003; Darling-Hammond, 1995; Krei, 1998; Oakes et al., 2002). Also, we noted a striking need for ongoing professional development for teachers in the highest-need schools.

Recommendations. We recommend that school districts reexamine how they allocate their resources and place priority on the reduction of class sizes and the hiring and retention of effective principals and teachers in the highest-need schools. Such a process of self-examination necessitates asking tough questions about who benefits from current policy and practice and who is being marginalized or disadvantaged (Carter et al., 2017; Townsend & Patton, 2000). Districts should develop a system of incentives and supports for teachers that will attract strong teachers to the highest-need areas, in order to provide more equitable distribution of quality instruction. Extremely weak instruction should not be tolerated and whatever supports or consequences are necessary should be readily available.

To provide sufficient professional development, we see promise in models that go beyond one-shot or short-term professional development efforts that can readily be resisted by school faculty (Tefera & Fischman, 2020). Rather, we recommend a focus on collaboration between school districts and local universities, whether these partnerships are called "professional development schools," "partner schools," or by another name (Klingner et al., 2004; Levine, 2002; Murrell, 2000). More recently, a line of research by Bal and colleagues (Bal, 2012; Bal et al., 2014, 2018) demonstrates a more vigorous type of partnership in which researchers and key stakeholders in the district participate in "learning labs" that explore the sources of disproportionality and develop culturally responsive positive behavioral supports.

School and Classroom Levels

Findings. At the level of the individual school, a variety of detrimental school-based policies and practices worked against the success of the least prepared children. In low-income schools serving predominantly Black populations, commonly noted features included the assignment of weaker teachers to weak students, fragmented and discontinuous instruction, the retention of extremely weak teachers, and the inappropriately extensive use of out-of-school suspension, along with inadequate support to teachers in matters of discipline. In the schools serving middle- to upper-income populations, more equitable opportunity to learn was accompanied by a raising of the bar in response to high local norms and to increasing statewide pressures to excel. This, in turn, resulted in increased pressure to enact the special education placement of children who probably would not have been referred in higher-poverty schools and who could have been adequately served in general education classrooms. In the only school that served predominantly White, high-SES students, the busing of a lower-income African American population resulted in disparate levels of preparation for schooling, and a clear overrepresentation of the latter group was evident in special education programs.

At the level of the classroom, the vast range of instructional quality was the variable of most concern. The inequity of this lay in the fact that the schools serving the neediest children included levels of teacher incompetence that were not evident in schools serving better-off children. When this disadvantage was compounded with stereotypical negative beliefs about families, individual children were at increased risk of inappropriate consequences and decisions. We conclude that, while we could suspect but not document a pattern of individual ethnic bias, the systemic bias of having poor teachers, and teachers who held untested negative preconceptions about families, created an accumulation of negativity that increased the likelihood of special education placement especially for Black students living in low-income neighborhoods.

Recommendations. Our recommendations are primarily derived from what we witnessed in schools that seemed to run more smoothly and equitably than other schools. First, administrators need to take into account how decisions affect all students, including those who typically are marginalized. Effective school leaders must be able to see the "big picture" and ensure that the simultaneous conglomeration of programs and policies they enact make sense and enhance rather than fragment the curriculum. The field has long acknowledged that high priority should be given to quality instructional time in class without interruptions (Berliner & Casanova, 1989; Leonard, 2001). Teachers should be assigned to classrooms in equitable ways that ensure all students have access to the most effective teachers and stimulating instruction.

School leaders should consider alternatives to suspension and put into practice discipline policies that are proactive rather than strictly punitive, such as in-house counseling support for anger management and other emotional/behavioral needs, positive behavioral intervention supports (PBIS) (Sugai & Horner, 2009), and increased relationship building with students and their families (Townsend, 2002; Utley et al., 2002). In particular, we recommend teacher preparation in how to embed culturally responsive practices into PBIS approaches (Bal, 2012). We also recommend implementing alternative programs (other than special education) that provide students with more intensive early assistance within general education, such as by using Title I funds in creative ways (Borman, 2000).

Given the propensity we noted among teachers and administrators to blame families for students' difficulties and to speak in disparaging ways about them, we suggest providing professional development for school personnel in proactive, collaborative models that focus on finding common ground upon which to build and become coadvocates with parents in all decision-making processes (Ocasio-Stoutenburg & Harry, 2021). Efforts should be made to restore the balance of power in parent-professional discourse, with an emphasis on families' and communities' resources and abilities, or "funds of knowledge," which can promote student learning and enrich schools and classrooms (González et al., 2005; Nieto, 1999). Parent liaisons funded in Title I schools can serve as cultural intermediaries who assist faculty in understanding community and family strengths.

Referral Process

Findings. In the referral process, there was a good attempt, on paper, to protect against inappropriate placement. However, it was evident that even full compliance with the letter of the regulations was not always tantamount to equitable or appropriate decision-making. In most cases, the process was not carried out as intended, with only cursory attention given to prereferral strategies. The ecology of the classrooms from which students were referred was ignored. Most students were pushed toward testing, on the basis of an assumption that poor academic performance or behavioral difficulties had their origin within the child and indicated a need for special education. There was tremendous variation in the quality of what transpired during referral or placement meetings, as seen in differential "cultures of referral" across the schools.

Recommendations. Since the time of our study, the practice of "prereferral strategies" has been replaced by the RTI/MTSS process. As outlined earlier, we believe that RTI should work as intended if the larger issues of racial/ethnic bias and assumptions of intrinsic deficit are addressed directly. That is to say, we believe that RTI should be understood as a part of general education, in which general education teachers collaborate with special educators to correctly identify and address children's learning needs. This focus should be implemented in culturally responsive and flexible ways rather than through scripted programs that encourage teachers to simply "check the boxes" on the RTI forms. As mentioned earlier, particular attention should be paid to the needs of English learners, with information from bilingual assessments being built in to instruction.

Of great concern was our finding that almost no attention was paid to the ecology of the classrooms from which children were referred. This concern should be of top priority at Tier 1 of the MTSS process, because it is here that weak classroom management and instruction can set the trajectory toward special education. Observations should be required to take place in the classrooms of referring teachers as well as in different settings. These observations should be completed by someone other than the classroom teacher for the purpose of determining whether the child's difficulties are being exacerbated by the classroom the child is in (for example, with instructional practices or disciplinary styles that are not responsive to cultural differences) and whether the child seems to be receiving an adequate "opportunity to learn."

Special Education Services

Findings. The quality of special education services is the final but equally important aspect of the entire process. As has long been observed by the courts, scholars, and practitioners alike, if special education services were of high quality and were fully focused on the return of students to the mainstream wherever possible, there would be little controversy over placement rates. As in the case of general education instruction, we found great variability in the quality of these programs and, in the schools with the lowest-income students, inappropriately large classes. However, the quality of special education teachers, although exceedingly variable, seemed to be more equitably distributed across schools than was the quality of general education teachers. Finally, a crucial concern was the unduly restrictive placement of students designated EBD and ID. Until special education can develop the reputation of being a set of services designed to support and integrate students with learning and behavioral difficulties, it will continue to be a source of stigma and controversy.

With regard to the least restrictive environment, in the school district there currently has been a strong press for the inclusion of students in the SLD category. The district reports state that the vast majority of these students are served in the regular classroom, with only approximately 17% having pullout instruction (Florida Department of Education, 2020). However, anecdotal information points to concerns about the adequacy of this model and the quality of instruction being provided in inclusive settings for children who need more individualized attention.

Recommendations. In our recommendations for the federal level, we have called for a reconceptualization of special education as a set of supportive services rather than a program for which children are eligible by being determined to have a disability. To be clear, we are not calling for the demolition of special education. We agree with foundationalists such as Kauffman and Hornby (2020), who say that there are specialized instructional skills and therapeutic approaches that many children will continue to need. We also acknowledge that sorting processes are a part of making life manageable, especially in large institutions such as schools. Most important, we support the use of pullout instruction wherever needed; inclusion must be tailored to individual children's needs.

However, we also believe that the high-incidence disability categories of LD and EBD impose unnecessary stigma and often intensify the exclusion of students who already experience social and economic marginalization. We acknowledge that this conceptual restructuring would present a radical departure from the concept of the IDEA, but we see it as a paradigm shift in the way of thinking about diversity in children's learning and behavioral patterns.

In sum, we concur with Kauffman and Hornby (2020), who conclude that "key special education strategies and approaches must co-exist with those from inclusive education . . . within a model of inclusive special education which combines key elements of special education with those from inclusive education" (p. 11).

IN CONCLUSION: ATTENDING TO SCHOOL-BASED RISK

We bring this book to a close with a challenge to those who would argue that disproportionately large percentages of culturally and linguistically diverse students in special education simply reflect disproportionately large problems experienced by this population. Rather than assuming that intrinsic, family, or community risk factors account for excessive special education placement of minorities, we call on the field to attend to and address the prevalence of *school-based risk* for these children. Recognizing that children begin their academic careers with differential preparation for schooling, we contend that schools play a tremendous role in further directing the outcomes of these children. Schools must be prepared to meet children at any point on the continuum of learning, and begin there.

To return to the premise stated in the introduction to this book: To conclude that the children we saw being placed in special education exhibited cognitive or social/behavioral limitations that warranted a high-incidence disability label would require consistent evidence of their failure to progress despite appropriate and adequate instruction in supportive educational environments. This was by no means the case. We found a great deal of evidence of inappropriate and inadequate instruction and school-based decision-making that increased the likelihood of special education placement for some children. In many cases, there was simply no way of knowing how children would have fared in more effective educational circumstances or with intensive instructional supports in the regular classroom. In many cases, also, the lack of standard criteria for referral to special education allowed schools to respond inappropriately to the pressure of local norms and high-stakes testing. We conclude that it cannot be assumed that high special education placement rates reflect genuine learning and behavioral deficits.

We are confident in our finding that the overrepresentation of students of color in special education programs is caused by much more than the existence of intrinsic or family-based deficits. Indeed, the perception that a child is disabled results from a complex weave of widely varying historical and current beliefs, policies, and practices at all levels—family and community, classroom, school, district, state and federal government, and society at large.

In framing the problem so broadly, we run the risk of seeming to frustrate those who are anxious for a quick fix or a clearly identifiable scapegoat. We believe, however, that to frame the problem more narrowly, seeking a simple answer in microlevel interactions or in monolithic constructs, such as racial or class discrimination, is to miss the opportunity to view the big picture. The overrepresentation of students of color in special education is not a phenomenon that exists in a vacuum. Indeed, communities of color are overrepresented in many of society's most detrimental circumstances, such as the justice system and among the homeless, while being underserved by the health care system and underrepresented in the nation's most powerful institutions, such as the U.S. Senate and the leading media outlets.

The sociologist William Julius Wilson (1998) posited that an understanding of the Black-White test score gap must go beyond the assumption that "collective outcomes" are the result of the "properties of individuals" (p. 508). Citing discriminatory patterns in disparate areas such as housing, employment, government taxation policies, and corporate decisions regarding the location of industries, Wilson argued for attention to the "impact of relational, organizational, and collective processes that embody the social structure of inequality" (p. 508).

Clearly, racism is integral to these processes. But in education, as elsewhere, there are other belief systems that intertwine with racism and intentionally or unintentionally perpetuate it. Most detrimental is the hegemony of the norm—the society's determination to sort children by their perceived failure to fit into a prescribed schedule of personal and academic development. *The "normative" schedule, however, is not a matter of intrinsic ability. Rather, it represents the normative pace of children who have been prepared for certain learning milestones.* That norm is then imposed upon all who enter the schoolhouse door, notwithstanding the fact that neither communities nor schoolhouses offer equal opportunities to attain the norm. Special education, built on the criterion of intrinsic deficit, comes to be seen as the place where children who fall outside the parameters of the norm "belong." School personnel, anxious to locate the "right placement" for struggling students, invoke this criterion, expressing the opinion that "maybe there's something else going on"—some deficit, some intrinsic misconnection, some missing piece.

We conclude that with regard to the high-incidence disability categories, special education's lofty intentions have been subverted by the fixation on identifying the "something else" and locating the correct box with the correct deficit label. Fraught with ambiguity and contradiction, the search for a disability results in decisions that have lasting, detrimental effects on children. It is true that some children benefit from special education services as currently constructed. However, children who fall into dead-end special education programs and those who "fall through the cracks" of the categorical system are left to flounder, while well-meaning teachers throw their hands up in frustration. Children who inappropriately receive a disability label are introduced, at best, to what Gergen (1994) described as "a potential lifetime of self-doubt" (p. 151). At worst, these children are relegated to school settings that further isolate them from the world of their "normal" peers while failing to resolve their learning and developmental challenges.

In the case of students who have experienced multiple exclusions and oppressions, the labeling process easily intersects with racial stereotypes, as was illustrated in Banks's (2017) study of the experiences of African American male college students who had been labeled with learning disabilities in high school. Frustrated by pressure of intersecting stereotypes regarding gender, race, and disability, the participants' perspective was captured by the exclamation, "these people are never going to stop labeling me!" (p. 96). Similarly, Boskovich and colleagues (2020) presented poignant narratives of how the self-doubt initiated by disability labeling can lead to enduring internalization of ableism and racism.

Because of the nation's continuing social structure of inequality, children at the receiving end of these errors are disproportionately children of color groups. These structural inequalities belie the nation's wealth and global status, as does the overrepresentation of students of color in categories of deficit. We contend that special education should be an addition to, rather than a replacement for general education. We recommend that special education relinquish its search for intrinsic deficit and, in Lisa Delpit's words in the Foreword to the first edition of this book, "just teach children what they need to know" (Harry & Klingner, 2006, p. xi).

Research Methods

Who Are We, and How Did We Do This Research?

When the phone rang in my Minneapolis hotel room* at 6:30 in the morning and my roommate said, "It's for you," I expected the worst—either someone was sick at home or my copresenter at today's conference session was about to cancel. Peeking out from under my pillow, I put the receiver to my ear: "I hear you guys got the grant!" gasped a throaty voice on the other end. I tried to focus, fighting off a rising tide of panic. My inside voice said, "Oh no!" The voice she heard said, "Wonderful! I'll call you back," as I buried my head once more under the pillow and pulled the sheets up to my ears.

My ambivalence around the news that I'd get to conduct 3 years of research on the topic that concerned me more than any other in the field of education was partly the daunting thought of the amount of work that would be involved. However, it was also related to the intimacy of the topic I had chosen to study up until this time—the experiences of culturally and linguistically diverse families of children with disabilities. The topic of this new grant would be more controversial—the disproportionate placements of students of color in special education disability categories. For me, it was all quite personal, stemming both from my experience as a parent of a child with cerebral palsy and my identity as a person of color in the United States. These aspects of my identity result in an intense sensitivity to issues of race and disability, and a strong tendency to side with families of color as they navigate special education services in the United States. Becoming immersed in this research would require a heightened awareness of all my biases on the topic and a firm commitment to a habit of self-reflection in the research process. Fortunately, this being the fourth research study I would conduct on such topics, I had developed a strong consciousness of my positionality as a researcher.

---

* This epilogue was written by Beth Harry.

QUALITATIVE RESEARCH AND THE RESEARCH QUESTION

Nature/Purpose of Research

The inductive nature of qualitative research requires a stance of relative neutrality, in which the goal is to describe and understand, rather than to evaluate, patterns within and across cultures. In this research, we followed basic principles and traditions of ethnographic data collection and grounded theory process and analysis (Bogdan & Biklen, 2007; Charmaz, 2014; Corbin & Strauss, 2008; Glaser & Strauss, 1967; Strauss & Corbin, 1998). According to methodologists Bogdan and Biklen (2007), a typical ethnographic question might be "What's happening here?" This open-ended approach comes into conflict with the goals of educational research, which, typically, include stating specific questions designed to evaluate educational programs and processes. Moreover, ethnographers traditionally attempt to study cultures relatively foreign to them. This differs greatly from the typical educational researcher who comes to the work with a wealth of knowledge and, inevitably, preconceptions about the topic. Grounded theory methodologist, Charmaz, explains that while ethnographic work tends to describe the broadest landscape of the research question, grounded theory methods begin with a broad view but seek to explain, rather than simply describe, specific social processes in the setting being studied.

Janette and I, the lead researchers in this project, certainly fit the educational researcher profile, while Keith Sturges, the third researcher, had been trained in ethnography and had no experience as an educator. This difference proved helpful in our process as we tried to contain our preconceptions and personal—as well as professional—biases. Specifically, as educators who had either taught in special education classrooms or studied the placement process, Janette and I were steeped in experiences that pointed us in certain directions and provided us with certain assumptions about "what's happening." The most obvious assumption we shared was that many of the children being placed did not have intrinsic deficits worthy of being designated as "disabilities." We held assumptions that the cause of this possibly lay in school-based processes, specifically, several components of the placement process, such as poor instruction prior to referral, bias or inadequate information in decision-making about whether a child should be referred for evaluation (i.e., the referral process), or bias in the evaluation process. These assumptions were based not only on our own observations over the years but on well-established literature on the topic (e.g., Heller et al., 1982). We were also concerned about whether the child's placement in a special education program would be beneficial. Of course, focusing on school-based causes did not mean that we were not aware that there might be home- or community-based problems contributing to the child's learning difficulties; however, our focus was on whether and in what ways schooling contributed to the problem. Thus, we stated the question as: "Do school-based processes contribute to disproportionality? And if so, how?"

From the Question to the Method

Based on an ecological model (Bronfenbrenner, 1977) of the many levels at which social conditions and pressures could affect the phenomenon of overrepresentation, we designed the research as a funnel that moved from a review of nationwide statistics and policies to state and district policies and practices, and ultimately to classrooms and individual children within those classrooms. The data collection proceeded as follows:

Data Collection Phases and Strategies

> Phase 1 (September–December): Overview of district data and official process
> Phase 2 (January–June): Initial interviews with 71 administrative personnel
> Phase 3 (August–December): Interviews and observations across 12 schools

- Observations of review and placement conferences
- Observations in all K–3 classrooms
- Observations in homes as feasible
- Observations of psychological evaluations
- Interviews with school personnel
- Interviews with parents where feasible

> Phase 4 (December–June): Selection of two target classrooms per school

- Interviews and observations focusing on two classrooms per school
- Examination of documents/student work

> Phase 5 (August–May): Selection of 12 students for case study

- Observations and interviews: general and special education classrooms
- Home visits and interviews
- Examination of documents/student work

Sample Selection: How Did We Choose the Schools, the Classrooms, and the Case Study Students?

Phases 1 and 2 of the process were conducted between September and June of the first year of the project, providing us with information that helped us select 12 schools that reflected a range of ethnicities and referral rates. (See the description in Chapter 1 of initial selection of schools.) To begin phase 3, district administrators introduced us to the principals of the schools we were interested in and, in the fall of Year 1, we conducted what we referred to as a "blitz" of one-shot observations in virtually every K–3 classroom in all 12 schools as well as interviews with the principals regarding referral rates in various classrooms. Based on this overview, we began phase 4 by select-ing, in each school, two classrooms that seemed to evoke concerns about the referral process. These decisions were often complicated, sometimes based on our observations of individual students who were about to be referred, and sometimes on peculiarities noted about the referral process. For example, in Sunnybrook, the highest-performing school, the referral rate was consider-ably lower than in the low-performing schools, but African American stu-dents represented 50% of the special education program while their presence in the school population stood at only 17%. Further, some of the children being referred were achieving within the average range and would not have been referred had they been in one of the low-performing schools. In this case, we decided on a classroom that reflected this pattern in order to under-stand what drove the referral process.

Throughout the selection process in phases 4 and 5, we engaged in an ongoing dialogue about the balance between open-ended and focused data collection. Below, we cite a slightly reconstructed version of a conversation among the three lead researchers:

Dialogue From a Research Team Meeting

> *Keith:* So, in selecting cases for the in-depth case studies, should we be driven by a pure grounded theory approach, that is—tentative hypotheses arising from the data—or more eclectic—on issues that have been identified as problematic in the extant research literature or that are seen as general and relevant "issues out there" in the field?
>
> *Janette:* Well, we are already committed to some issues a priori, such as to examine race/ethnicity and to examine certain disability categories. So those are issues that are out there, that we need to look for.
>
> *Beth:* OK, but does it really matter? I mean, don't you think that the important thing is if the issue is present in our data? Whether we set out to look for it or whether it "arose"—dare I say "emerged"—from the data and hit us in the face? I mean, to assume that we're to be grounded theorists doesn't mean we don't bring ideas to the table. If we see the issue there, it's there!
>
> *Keith:* Yes, but whether we see it or not is influenced by who we are and whether we're looking for it! You guys are educators so you think like educators and look for issues that you've known to be

> important. But if I'm a grounded theorist I want to be open to
> what's there, not imposing my own preconceptions.
> *Beth or Janette:* Yes, but still—you're not a tabula rasa! None of us is!

I believe that these conversations helped us maintain a critical consciousness
about our decision-making and, overall, we were guided by the main research
question, seeking children whom the data suggested were at risk for inappropriate referral and placement. In following them through the process, we
would be asking, "Why was the child referred?"; "What was the quality of
the instruction the child received prior to referral?"; "What was the nature
of the evaluation process?"; and "What was the quality and outcome of the
child's special education placement?"

Sample Size: Overly Ambitious!

One of the first challenges of all research design is to decide on the sample
size. In qualitative research there is no clear guideline regarding power in
analysis, as one must rely on in statistical studies. Rather, the concept of
power relies on the authenticity of the report (Guba & Lincoln, 2005), and
authenticity is intangible. Oh, to be a real ethnographer like Ann Ferguson
(2000), whose three years of "hanging out" in one elementary school resulted
in an in-depth and thoroughly persuasive portrait of the processes by which
Black boys became "bad boys!" Studies like this can truly attempt to capture
the social nuances needed to answer the question "What's happening here?"
This approach requires a very small sample size, and the true ethnographer
is comfortable with learning everything possible about even just one setting.

So why didn't we write this proposal as a "true ethnography"? Mainly
because we would probably not have received funding! Although this grant
proposal predated the establishment of the Institute for Education Sciences
(IES) in 2002 and was being offered by the Office for Special Education
Programs (OSEP), which had previously been quite open to qualitative designs, the trend was already moving toward a preference for experimental designs. Proposing a qualitative study, therefore, we felt pressured to propose a
design that would indicate our appreciation of the importance of larger numbers and the concept of reliability inherent in the idea of trying to show that
findings were consistent across a number of schools. However, we believe
that just as important as perceived external pressure are the conflicting value
systems of educational researchers themselves. We suspect that we are more
influenced than we like to acknowledge by the all-encompassing discourse of
"evidence-based" experimental designs and "empirical" findings.

Overall, in trying to prove that we could "do numbers" too, we went for
breadth that would allow a range of comparative data. What was lost by this
decision? First, data collection across the 12 schools was uneven in quantity,
although I believe that quality of what we did collect was generally solid.
No doubt, the schools that were more accessible in terms of dependability

of schedules and availability of teachers produced more data. For example, classrooms where teachers were frequently absent or schools where parent conferences were frequently canceled meant thinner data and fewer points of triangulation. Also, we had envisioned following each of our 12 case study students into their special education placements or other school transitions, but this was not always possible both because of the difficulty of adding yet another school and because by the time some of those students were finally transitioned, we were near to the end of the study. Nevertheless, our richest case studies were outstanding! For example, for one child, Robert, we conducted 27 points of data collection, which included 15 classroom observations, three parent-teacher conferences, four home visits/interviews, five interviews with his teachers, and a full review of his cumulative school file. In this way we gained perspectives on his teachers, mother, child study team (CST) personnel, and our own observations. We simply could not do this much data collection for all 12 children.

In the long run, we believe that had we studied six schools, we would have had essentially the same findings, but supported by more points of triangulation. Given a chance to do this study again, a better model might be to align it more closely to the ethnographic mode, perhaps spending 6 months to a year gaining an overall impression of six schools, and then selecting two contrasting schools serving similar populations, for example, Green Acres, a high-performing school with a low rate of referral, serving a population of low-income, predominantly Hispanic children from recently immigrated families; and Palm Grove, a low-performing school with a high rate of referral, which served low-income, predominantly Haitian children from recently immigrated families. Despite similar demographics, the main differences evident in these schools provided a drastic contrast: At Green Acres, there was much higher quality teaching, a principal who said she had her pick of whom to hire, a teaching faculty and office staff that was predominantly the same ethnicity as the children, and a new, attractively laid out school building. The typical attitude of the teachers at Green Acres toward the school community was one of respect and empathy, while at Palm Grove it was one of impatience and pity. More depth in these two schools would have provided the field with a deeply convincing portrait of the way one set of children came to be seen and treated as "needing time" to improve and the other as "deficient."

DATA COLLECTION METHODS

Our interviews and observations were based on the ethnographic model of open-ended interviewing and participant observation (Spradley, 1979, 1980). While originating in ethnography, this approach may also be referred to as "naturalistic" (Lincoln & Guba, 1986), meaning that it occurs in the natural setting, and in a manner that least disturbs or alters the usual flow of social interaction. While we developed guiding questions for the interviews the process was essentially conversational, deliberately following the interviewee's lead and coming back to our planned questions at moments that seemed to fit the flow of the interview. The same was true for our observations. For example, we did not approach classroom observations with a fixed frame for what to look for; rather the observer, from a relatively removed position at the back of the room, would start with a focus on the teacher and follow the teacher's actions and interactions with students and, to the extent possible, scan the classroom for student behaviors and activities. Interviews were transcribed verbatim, with interviewer comments where appropriate; observation notes, taken briefly during the observation, would be written up in narrative form with as much descriptive detail as possible, following a chronological flow from the start to the finish of the observation. These documents, along with students' school records, became the "data" of the study.

Establishing Trustworthiness and Credibility

We faced two obvious challenges in using an open-ended approach to data collection: First, that researcher bias might determine what is to be observed and which aspects of interview information should be pursued; second, and related to the first, the data may be incomparable across interviews and observations, since it is true that different observers might focus on different things. One way around this is for two observers to conduct some observations in tandem, which we did for approximately 20% of the observations. Most important were several strategies for ensuring credibility, which were central to our entire research process. First, the principles of prolonged engagement and persistent observation throughout Years 2 and 3 of the project were enhanced by the fact that each pair of researchers was assigned to only four schools, allowing them to become immersed in these settings. Second, self-critique practices were built into our team meetings, with a strong focus on peer debriefing and review of data, including code-recode strategies, discussions about potential researcher bias, and examination of "negative" (apparently contradictory) cases. Above all, our use of thick description and triangulation of data enabled us to be confident in the trustworthiness of the information gained. We will discuss these two principles in more depth.

Thick description of naturalistic settings. Despite the exigencies of naturalistic observation, we consider the use of thick description in field notes vastly superior to annotated observations based on a preconceived set of observation points. The behaviors in a classroom involve a social flow that cannot be put into preconceived boxes. The value of our descriptive field observations became evident when we came to select field data to illustrate various points in the book. For example, Chapter 5, which we titled "In the Classroom: Opportunity to Learn," provides descriptions that demonstrate beyond doubt that children were exposed to vastly different opportunities, both across schools and within schools from classroom to classroom, depending on the teacher. In that chapter also, the power of field notes is demonstrated in the description of children who went from full engagement in the story "I am special" in their kindergarten classroom to totally chaotic behavior in their music class. Similarly, a description of what we called a "passive" style of classroom management in Chapter 4, "Cultural Consonance, Dissonance, and the Nuances of Racism," showed the steady deterioration of children's behavior after the entry of Larry, a student whose increasingly disruptive behavior was totally ignored by the teacher.

The power of triangulated data. Triangulation is a central tenet of qualitative research. Being able to gain multiple perspectives on a situation is the main way that we can have confidence in our data. Our data were very well triangulated both in terms of methods and sources. First, our interviews gained a range of perspectives from all stakeholders. Second, our observations included classrooms, school-based conferences, and visits to several students' homes. A difference between interview and observation data is worth some discussion here: Interview data essentially reflects the perspectives of the study participants, while observational field notes yield the researchers' perspectives. In analyzing the former, we were learning what school personnel and parents thought about our topic, while in the latter we were analyzing our own emerging perspectives on the topic. This combination of interviews and observations is a key advantage in qualitative research, in that it provides the researcher with the opportunity to compare what they are told to what they see for themselves.

The third point of triangulation comes from the review of documents—another key source of information, which serves mainly to corroborate or extend data gleaned from interviews and observations. For example, as described in Chapter 4, our observations in Ms. Q's 2nd-grade classroom in South Park Elementary revealed little difference in behavior between the Hispanic and the African American children. Ms. Q, however, described the Hispanic children as "generally calmer and better behaved" and was delighted to find that, because she had been assigned an ESOL class, her group was approximately 50% of each ethnicity. Moreover, Ms. Q's descriptions of the children's academic skills also proved discrepant from what we found in their records: Specifically, she expressed sympathy for Juan's and Francisco's behavior problems, attributing them to frustration because of learning problems; she did not express sympathy for the behaviors of two African American boys, Andre and Jimmy, whom she described as having behavior problems. Yet both Juan's and Francisco's records showed SAT scores that were well above those of Andre and Jimmy, casting doubt on the idea that learning problems explained the Hispanic boys' behavioral difficulties.

The power of triangulation to explain discrepancies became particularly important at the third level of analysis, when we worked at comparing data within a given theme. So, for example, in the theme Family and Community Circumstances, there were cases in which there was a strong contrast between school personnel's and researchers' perceptions of family involvement or family circumstances. Edith's teacher described the family as "children raising themselves," but a researcher's visit revealed an effective system of older sibling responsibility and authority while the parents were at work, and even neighborhood responsibility in the fact that a neighbor, upon seeing the researcher arrive at the home in the mother's absence, immediately came to the door to find out who the researcher was and remained there until she left. In the case of Robert, during the researcher's visit to the home at the end of the summer vacation, Jacintha, the boy's mother, showed the researcher the tins of Slim-Fast that had helped her to achieve her weight-loss goals, yet, the following week, at Robert's school, the counselor expressed the firmly held opinion that Jacintha's weight loss proved that she was "back on drugs." All of the examples of such discrepancies had one consistent pattern—that school personnel, who had never visited the families' homes, based their negative views on assumptions of family deficiencies that seemed to emanate from generalized stereotypes about Black families living in poor neighborhoods. While there was often a kernel of truth in the assumptions, such as the knowledge that Jacintha had in fact had a history of drug abuse, or that the parents in Edith's home were often not home because of long work hours, an informed interpretation of these limited facts was sorely lacking.

GAINING ENTRY AND BUILDING RAPPORT (YOU WANT TO STUDY WHAT? WELL, YOU WON'T SEE OVERREPRESENTATION HERE BECAUSE ALL THE KIDS ARE BLACK!)

Gaining entry to a school district can be a tricky business. Prior to submission of the research proposal, we had talked with the special education superintendent about disproportionality and found that he was absolutely on board with the proposal. When we received the grant award, he literally opened the doors for us by arranging a meeting with the directors of the six regions of the county, who, in turn, helped us identify schools and introduced us to the principals.

Getting In and Staying In

Getting your foot in the door of a research setting is simply the first step. After that, researchers must walk a fine line between being outsiders and insiders, developing a posture that Agar has called "the professional stranger" (Agar, 1996). First, we must acknowledge that building rapport requires a mix of authenticity and deception on the part of the researcher. Below is a summary of my field notes on a situation like this:

Ms. P, second grade teacher at South Park elementary school, was an African American veteran teacher of 34 years. She wore a daunting expression of boredom and annoyance and her carefully coiffed hair and brilliantly painted talon-like fingernails added to the impression of someone you just don't want to mess with! I had been introduced to Ms. P briefly by the assistant principal, and Ms. P had affirmed that it would be alright to come in any time. Upon my arrival for the observation, Ms. P greeted me with a frown, and waved me toward the back, where I took a seat and observed as both teachers circulated, handing the children purple folders and instructing them to go ahead and get started silently on their work. As she circulated, Ms. P focused on whether the children were silent or not, exclaiming "Scuse me!" whenever she heard a child talking, and at one point delivered a lecture about the fact that the classroom pencils belong to the school and are only "on loan" to the children. She did not stop to look at or assist the children with the work. When all the children had completed their tasks, Ms. O collected the folders and took over the class, beginning a lesson about the weather. At that point Ms. P came to the back of the room and sat beside me, still frowning, but asking what I needed to know.

Where do you begin an interview with someone who clearly doesn't want to be interviewed? With a compliment, of course! I began by commenting on the orderliness of the classroom, to which Ms. P replied, "Well, they have to be orderly. I just can't stand the confusion!" I replied that I had also taught 2nd grade and totally understood what Ms. P meant. I commented that Ms. P's experience was evident, and asked her how long she had been teaching. She opened readily to this question, explaining that she had been at this school for most of her 34 years of teaching and had taught the parents of many of the children currently in the school. I asked her to talk about the children she might be considering for referral for special education evaluation. By this time, there was no hesitation as Ms. P pointed out several children and moved into a lengthy and detailed complaint about the new principal, whom she described as "a mean person," who started "picking on" Ms. P as soon as she took on the position of principal last year. This year, she had given Ms. P the "lowest" 2nd-grade class instead of her previous 6th-grade placement. At the end of the class period, Ms. P exclaimed that she had enjoyed the conversation because I was "a very relaxing person to talk to." My field notes ended with the following Observer Comment (OC):

> The change in Ms. P's demeanor between my arrival in the room and her gradual opening up to me was very marked. She presents herself in the room as a very strict person with a tight, somewhat annoyed expression. In talking with me she relaxed a lot and seemed to start trusting me.

Throughout the conversation I was conscious of my own efforts to connect with what seemed to be a reluctant participant: the use of professional compliments, the attempt to connect with her on the level of shared teaching experience, and even my language register, by which I used some aspects of language to make an ethnic connection with Ms. P, such as a style of emphasis that was distinctly African American (mm . . . mm . . . mmm) rather than a more mainstream version (mmhmm). I do not consider the latter strategy as a "deception" since I consider myself generally bicultural and I do use both forms depending on the social group I am in. On the other hand, my compliment about Ms. P's classroom management style was distinctly inauthentic, since, although I do appreciate the need for order in the classroom, I did not at all like Ms. P's very authoritarian manner with the children.

The Real Power of the Naturalistic Setting: Minimizing Observer Effects

We were surprised at the candor with which school personnel answered our questions about very controversial issues of race and social class. Some of the extreme biases expressed seemed to pop right out of the interviewees' mouths without any awareness of the impression they might make on the hearer. For example, when Ms. Q, a White Hispanic 1st-grade teacher listed the deficiencies of the African American children in her class, including the dialect they spoke and that they did not "know how to walk or sit in a chair," her conclusion that "it's cultural" was said in a tone that indicated no doubt whatsoever as to the self-evident truth she was expressing. Similarly, our presence as observers did not stop Ms. J from talking on her cell phone in class, or Mr. R from making empty threats about making the children miss lunch, or a school counselor from making disrespectful gestures behind Robert's mother's back, indicating that the mother was lying.

We concluded that, in naturalistic settings, people will generally do (1) what they are accustomed to doing, (2) what they think is right, or (3) what they feel they must do to produce outcomes that they themselves will have to live with. The actor in a natural setting has to live with the consequences of each action and decision, and therefore cannot afford to change his behavior in order to impress an outsider who happens to be observing. This is quite different from a contrived experimental situation, where the outcomes may or may not be important to the actors.

This does not mean that observer effects will never occur, although they may come in a form not obvious to us at the time. Further to the comment above regarding the importance of building rapport, effects on setting may come not so much as a result of the fact that we are observing, but because of how we conduct our observations. For example, in the third year of the study, we discovered that the note-taking strategies of one of our observers had contributed to a very negative effect on the progress of the research in that school. On meeting a new assistant principal in one of our schools, I noted his facial expression growing steadily more disapproving as he listened to my description of the research project, until finally he exclaimed, "Ah! So you're the same researchers that came to my previous school two years ago!

Your observer sat in an IEP conference and wrote copious notes, hardly ever looking up! Naturally, we figured he was writing about us and we found this very offensive!" It was suddenly clear why our research team in that school had found the administration so uncooperative that we had little choice but to withdraw. Fortunately, this was early in the project, and we had actually included two extra schools before finalizing the list of 12 schools. The lesson learned here is that the observer/interviewer must achieve a fine balance between presenting a nonthreatening, friendly demeanor and maintaining a certain amount of social distance.

NOW WHAT TO DO WITH ALL THIS DATA? GROUNDED THEORY DATA ANALYSIS

Analyzing qualitative data is not a cut-and-dried process. There are no buttons to push that will tell us whether the findings have enough power, differences are significant, or the size of any effects are large enough to be meaningful. It is all a matter of judgment, based on data that seeks to represent as faithfully as possible the explicit and implicit meanings of individual statements and social interactions. Grounded theory method is essentially inductive rather than deductive and typically requires at least three levels of analysis. Figure E.1 displays the overall flow of our analysis, reading from the "ground" (bottom), and moving "upward" as each level of interpretation becomes more abstract.

Level 1 Analysis: Open Coding

We began by naming (coding) what we see or hear in the data. In the summer of phase 1, I, as the lead researcher, conducted phases 1 and 2 of the analysis of the 71 interviews with administrators in the school district. These phases we refer to as *open coding* and *coding by conceptual categories*.

Grounded theory analysis seeks to maintain authenticity by starting as "close to the ground" as possible. Initial, "open," coding, because it is not determined by a preconceived category, is concrete, reflecting the actual action observed. For example, in coding children's behavior, we began by specifying actions such as "out of seat," "gazing around," or "off task," and all examples of these behaviors would be compared and coded accordingly. Sometimes a vivid description offered by an interviewee might capture the meaning so persuasively that the researcher may decide to use that actual phrase as the code. This is referred to as an "in vivo" code, such as "go the extra mile!" or "the parents are the problem!" The purpose of this approach is to avoid interpreting before adequate data are gathered and compared. The process of "constant comparison" across initial codes forces the researcher to determine the similarities and differences and to decide on the most accurate name for any chunk of data. This process resulted in 125 open codes.

Figure E.1. Data Analysis Chart

6. Theory:

Influences—A complex set of negative influences contribute to the overrepresentation of minorities in special education. Predominant contributors are the assumption of intrinsic deficit and the requirement for a disability categorization; inequitable opportunity to learn, resulting from poor teacher quality in lower-SES schools and higher standards in higher-SES schools; negative biases against families perceived as dysfunctional; external pressure from high-stakes testing; and subjectivity in referral and assessment practices.

5. Interrelating the explanations:	Family stereotyping and intrinsic deficits		Inequitable opportunity to learn	
4. Testing the themes (interviews, observations, documents):	Family, community challenges and strengths	Deficit assumptions, low expectations, culture of referral	Standards, local norms, state grading of schools	Policies on hiring, firing, curriculum, class size, discipline
3. Themes:	Family/community influences	Deficits seen as intrinsic to child	External pressures on schools	Teacher skills/biases limit achievement
2. Categories:	Families Community	Student Language Disability	Society/Outer Circle	Classroom/Teacher
1. Open Codes:	Based on initial interviews.			

Level 2: Clustering Codes Into Conceptual Categories

After the open codes have been compared and refined, the next level of coding takes a step forward in interpretation, grouping all similar behaviors into a conceptual category or "family" that imputes meaning to the behavior. However, the very act of interpreting brings challenges that require vigilance on the part of the researcher. For example, in grouping codes related to children's problematic behavior, we started by asking, "What do these behaviors represent conceptually?" "Should we name them 'negative/positive,' 'unacceptable/acceptable,' 'troubling/acceptable,' or 'noncompliant/compliant'?" All of these terms are based on a value judgment regarding the behavior,

Figure E.1. Data Analysis Chart, Continued

Theoretical Statement

6. Theory:

Outcomes—The outcome of the process is placement in special education programs of variable quality and, especially in the case of Emotional Behavioral Disability and Educable ID, unduly restrictive environments. Such placement is often detrimental because of stigma and limited opportunity to exit. Low-SES, African American populations are particularly vulnerable because of the accumulated effect of biased institutional practices. (Outcomes are represented at far right, below.)

◄─────────►

5. Interrelating the explanations:	Pressures on referral process	Negative assessment practices	Limited Outcomes	
4. Testing the themes (interviews, observations, documents):	Statewide testing: exclusion of sped student scores	Pressure to place, family stereotyping, instruments, disability criteria, subjectivity, ignoring of classroom context	Inadequate attention to language proficiency	Outcome: Teacher and program quality, class size, restrictiveness, teacher shortages, low exit rate, stigma, routine vs. individualized instruction
3. Themes:	School system/ administrative decisions	Errors/bias in psychological assessment	Errors/bias in bilingual assessment	Outcome: Special education services
2. Categories:	Administrative Policies CST	Testing	Language/ Dialect	Outcome: ESE (Exceptional Student Education) Effectiveness/ Outcomes
1. Open Codes:				

but the question is, "Whose judgment?" The term "negative," we decided, was too sweeping, insinuating some indisputable deficiency; "troubling" or "unacceptable" would most likely be inferred to mean that the behavior is troubling to the teacher, but it is still up to the researcher to determine that the teacher sees it this way. How does one find a truly neutral term that also implies a judgment within a specific context? As Keith argued, "Well, what's negative behavior on the part of a student? As an ethnographic observer, what I see is compliant or noncompliant behavior, not good or bad behavior."

That kind of neutrality is important for a researcher. So, although as educators, we saw certain behaviors in the classroom as simply unacceptable, we decided on the more neutral terms—"compliant/noncompliant"—since we could usually determine what expectations the teacher had established for behavior and whether children were complying.

In doing the level 2 work, and still using the "constant comparison" method (Glaser & Strauss, 1967), I identified 21 conceptual categories across the 125 codes. At the end of this process, I met with the team and shared the analysis, starting with a general discussion of the coding and then moving to a focused exercise in which a sample set of transcripts were read and analyzed by three pairs of readers. The entire team met twice a week for 3 weeks to compare their separate coding of the same data. Through constant comparison of codes, the process resulted in some codes being changed and new codes being added to the analysis. The goal of this process was to modify and refine the initial analysis until consensus was reached among the team members; we did not aim for a numerical reliability rating as would be required in a statistical study.

A concern arose regarding the decision that one researcher would do the initial analysis and then invite the rest of the team to engage in an exercise to test and compare the application of the codes across a sample of interviews. The fact that I was the most senior member of the team raises the question of potential undue influence over the first and most formative stages of the analysis. Certainly, I acknowledge this possibility and I would describe this process as less than ideal, yet totally pragmatic in the light of the size of the project and our time constraints. The body of data collected between January and June was already large (71 interviews), and the idea of engaging in a collaborative analysis was unimaginable. Despite the theoretical preference of grounded theorists (e.g., Charmaz, 2014; Strauss & Corbin, 1998) for an ongoing analysis side-by-side with data collection, there was no way our team could have accomplished this while also collecting the data. Thus, the summer break presented a much-needed opportunity for analysis, but was also the time when we had no paid assistants and only one fully paid coinvestigator. However, I believe that not only did our testing process serve to refine and strengthen the coding frame, but the care and rigor with which we approached the subsequent analysis ensured a continuing critical examination of the entire process.

Figure E.2 displays the 125 open codes and the 21 categories into which they were grouped.

Figure E.2. Initial Categories and Codes

Administrative Policies: Concerns Of, Concerns About, Support, Initiatives

Classroom/Teacher: Class Size, Paraprofessionals, Expectations, Rewards, Bias, "Chaos/Mayhem," Behavior Management, Stress, Planning, Culture, Instruction, Relationships with Students

Community: Demographics, History, Cultures, Community Support, Socioeconomic Status

CST (Child Study Team): Process, Records, Strategies, "Qualify," Data, Timelines, Race/Ethnicity, Referral Reasons, Members, Paperwork, Retention, Staffing, Student Participation, Effectiveness, Grade at Referral, EBD Referral

Disability: "True LD," "True ID," "True EBD," EBD-LD Interaction, LO-Language Interaction, "PDK"

ESE (Exceptional Student Education) Effectiveness/Outcomes: Programs, Instruction, Effectiveness, Regular Ed Collaboration, Mainstreaming, Gifted, IEP

Ethnicity: African American, Hispanic, White, Haitian, "Islander"

Families: Attitude to Testing, Participation, In Denial, Labels, Assistance, Problems, Family Structure, Ethnicity, Education, Poverty

Language/Dialect: Limited English Proficient, Dialect, Culture, Race, Interpreter, Deficit

Overrepresentation Theories: Broad Theory (multifaceted, often lengthy opinions on overrepresentation, from which specific excerpts were coded discretely, using codes in this list)

Professional: Role, Experience, Attitude to Researcher/Research, Attitude to Profession, Development, Stress, Personal

Programs/Academic/Nonacademic: SFA, Summer School, ESOL, Home Language Arts

Research Procedures: Sampling, Observing, Incentives, Research Purpose, Researcher: Level of Comfort, Input, Role, Impressions, Expectations, **Resources:** Materials, Computers, Textbooks

School: History, Demographics, Scores, Attendance, Funding, Mobility, Safety, Maintenance

Setting and Location: Any factual description of physical characteristics

SLP (Speech/Language Pathology): Therapy, Caseload, Race, Types, Pragmatics, Articulation

Society/Outer Circle: Societal Problems (Crime/Poverty), Political Decisions (High-Stakes Testing/Vouchers)

Student: Gender, Readiness, Social/Academic Skill Deficits, Strengths, Culture

Testing: Standardized, Psychological, Adaptive, Bilingual, EBD, SLP, FAB, Academic, Medical

---

Note: Bold expressions are categories; each category is followed by the code or codes (roman type) that it contains. Expressions enclosed in quotation marks represent the word choice of the interviewee. LD = learning disability; ID = intellectual disability; EBD = emotional/behavioral disorder; "PDK" = "Pretty dumb kids"; IEP = individualized education plan; "Islander" = student from the English-speaking Caribbean islands; SFA = Success For All; ESOL = English for speakers of other languages; FAB = functional assessment of behavior.

Level 3: Thematic Analysis: Answering the Research Question

Seeking the underlying importance or meaning of each category brings us solidly into the realm of interpretation, as does the fourth level, in which we try to interrelate these meanings. Looking at Figure E.1, we urge readers to bear in mind that the linear impression represents an attempt to force our thinking to stay grounded until it's solid enough to yield to interpretation. This is, of course, a goal rather than a fact of the process, since we do not normally think in a linear fashion! It is only natural to start making connections based on our previous knowledge or on our memory of the data at the time it was occurring, but we work to hold back these interpretations until we are sure we have coded accurately. Moreover, we naturally make mental leaps that bring to the forefront a possible interpretation that actually runs ahead of the data but seems to make perfect sense intuitively. One way to slow this down is to write a "memo" noting the thought and putting it on hold until there is more data to support it.

We approached the task of thematic analysis by identifying and summarizing information in those categories that were predominant in the data, that is, Classroom/Teacher, CST, Families, Community, Society/Outer Circle, and Administrative Policies. Additionally, although there was minimal data on the categories Testing and Disability, we decided to summarize this also, since the argument that biased testing contributes to inappropriate placement is common in the literature. (We will comment on this further later in the chapter.) Summaries written by each team member were shared and discussed by the team, and the outcome was a set of seven central arguments attempting to explain overrerrepresentation. We called these arguments "themes," as follows:

1. Family/community influences (including parental participation in children's schooling)
2. External pressures on schools (school district, state, federal)
3. Deficits intrinsic to the child
4. Teacher skills and/or biases
5. School system and/or administrative decisions
6. Errors/bias in psychological testing
7. Errors/bias in bilingual assessment

Level 4(a): Testing the Themes

In quantitative research models, researchers often begin with one or more hypotheses, which they proceed to test. In qualitative mode, the inductive principle requires us to seek the hypotheses within the data, rather than imposing them. In this study, we treated the participants' explanations for overrepresentation as emerging hypotheses (Charmaz, 2014), which we would "test," using them as a lens through which to examine new data. Thus, the seven themes became the analytic frame for most of the next 2 years of data.

In other words, our analysis from here on would ask the question, "To what extent do these data support the seven themes/explanations?" That is, would we hear more from participants about how these explanations contribute to overrepresentation? Would we see, through our own observations, evidence of these themes at work? Would we find new explanations? From here on, both interview and observational data would be subjected to analysis using the seven-theme frame. This process exemplifies what is often referred to in qualitative research as the "iterative" nature of the method.

In addition to applying the seven themes to all interview and observational data thereafter, we applied the thematic frame to our exit interviews with the 24 teachers in our target classrooms. By the end of the second year of the study, we had observed in each of these rooms on eight to 12 occasions and had talked with the teachers both informally and in taped interviews. The exit interviews took the form of a "card sorting" procedure, in which we printed each theme on a separate index card and asked each teacher to sort them into piles of "agree," "disagree," and "irrelevant." Not surprisingly, the teachers consistently agreed with the themes of "intrinsic to child" and "family/community" and disagreed with those pointing to "teachers"; opinions were split half and half with respect to school system and external pressures.

Emic versus etic perspectives. As noted earlier, we added the issue of testing to the explanations derived from the initial 71 interviews. We did this very conscious of an uncomfortable feeling that we were going against the inductive principle of grounded theory, that is, inserting into the analysis a theme that was more of our own belief than that of the participants. That is not to say that there were no comments about testing in the data but, to be specific, only three interviewees out of 71 expressed the opinion that unreliable testing contributed to overrepresentation. All the rest expressed the opinion that "You meet criteria or you don't meet criteria. The testing stands on its own." Psychological testing (in this study most psychologists used the WISC-III) was seen as the gateway to special education placement; students either "qualified" or they did not. Nevertheless, the three participants who expressed dissenting views on this topic spoke their opinions so strongly that they represented a minority voice not to be ignored. In addition to the fact that the literature is so full of both pros and cons to this argument, there was no way we could have ignored it.

Our concern about including what seemed like an "etic" perspective, nevertheless, was so great, that when we developed the card-sort technique for the exit interviews, we decided not to include the testing themes, so determined were we not to "bias" the teachers' responses by introducing our own concerns. In retrospect this was a mistake, because we robbed ourselves of the opportunity to find out what these teachers, who had not been in the initial set of interviews, thought of the role of testing. Fortunately, the rest of the data from these 2 years gave numerous examples of participants' views of testing as well as of our own observations of testing practices and effects. I believe that this dilemma reflects the importance of gaining a balance between being true to the principles of grounded theory method and being true to our own knowledge. In fact, it's also an example of how important it is to be true to the data, by not ignoring a minority voice.

Level 4(b): Applying the Explanatory Themes to Subsequent Data

Applying the themes as a frame for the rest of the data moved our analysis forward in a profoundly rigorous but exhausting process. We did not simply apply each theme to chunks of data; rather, we sought to specify details of the themes so as to produce a fine-grained set of codes that captured the nuances of each theme. Figure E.3 shows selected examples, such as the theme *Family and Community Circumstances*, which we reanalyzed into a subset of nine codes; *Administrative Policies,* which we broke into two subsections—*Administrative* and *Curricular,* each with its own specific codes. The theme *Teacher Skills* was particularly interesting because of the value judgments involved, and was reminiscent of the discussions we had had regarding how to code children's behaviors. Specifically, how should we classify teachers' behavior management strategies? What one observer considers unduly punitive might be seen as appropriately authoritative by another observer. In this case, we turned to our in-house consultant, Bob Moore, who teaches classes in behavior management, to remind us of the key approaches in the behavior management literature and derive our code names from there, rather than from our own value judgments. At level 4, we also integrated our descriptive codes, such as "physical setting," "location," "classroom/school demographics," and so on into the analysis.

Level 5: Analysis

The strong triangulation of data and our careful sorting out of details of data in each theme persuaded us of the power of the themes to explain patterns of disproportionality in these 12 schools. At this point, therefore, we felt confident in referring to the seven themes as "explanations"—the beginnings of a theory of disproportionality. The next challenge was to see how these explanations related to each other.

Looking at our analysis map in Figure E.1, we like to think of the process as moving mostly in an upward direction from levels 1 through 4, and then spreading out horizontally across the explanations at level 5. As we mentioned previously, this is not a rigid pattern of linear thinking, as we will inevitably have been making horizontal connections all along. However, at the fifth analytic level, we deliberately began to seek explicit interrelationships across the themes. In other words, how does the theme *Family Stereotyping* relate to *Belief in Intrinsic Deficits*, and how does the theme *Teachers' Skills and Biases* interact with these other two themes? Continuing across the top

Figure E.3. Refined Coding System (Selected Examples)

Category: Family and Community Circumstances
Caregiver Perceptions (of schools and services)
Caregiver Practices and Knowledge
Community Differences
Cultural Knowledge Set
Economics (micro or macro)
Family Crisis
Family Setting
Family Structure (includes descriptions of family members)
School Perceptions (of caregivers and community)

Category: Teacher Skills
Instructional Skills
Pedagogical
Socioemotional
Style/Personal Expression
Technical
Management Skills
Behaviorist Techniques
Group Management
Socioemotional
Style (overlaps with instructional style)
Unwritten Curriculum

Category: Policy
Administrative
Administrator Perceptions (perceptions of or by administrators)
Assignment of Students
Assignment of Teachers
Class Size
Full-Service School
Interruptions (includes students and adults entering, leaving)
Others in the Room (other than teacher and students)
Retention Policies
Scheduling
Specific Policies
Teacher Out
Other
Curricular
Computers
Math
Reading Programs
Other Curricular
Other Required Classes

row, how do the evident negativity in those three themes relate to the fact that some principals report freedom to hire the teachers they want and others report severe constraints on their autonomy? And how do all of these relate to the theme of *Inequitable Opportunity to Learn* and pressures on the referral and evaluation process? Finally, at the far right of the model, how do the curriculum and instruction in special education programs and limited opportunity to exit relate to all the prior explanations?

Level 6: Delineating the Theory: Complexity as the Centerpiece

As we explain in Chapter 13, our analysis resulted in a resounding statement that the overrepresentation of minorities in special education was the result of "a complex set of negative influences" at every phase of the process of instruction, referral, evaluation, and placement. Despite the apparent ambiguity and "softness" of this conclusion, one point was crystal clear: Evidence of the power of these inequities far outweighed any evidence of within-child deficits. Most important, no single influence could stand alone. The data showed interrelationships that were so intertwined as to be inseparable: A child living in a neighborhood such as Robert's was at tremendous risk of being stereotyped as a behavior problem; of his mother being seen as incompetent; of being placed in Ms. P's class where the only apparent goal was to keep him in his seat; of being subjected to the unreasonable punishment of being excluded from full-day school for 5 months with no remedy; of being determined to be emotionally disturbed despite the psychologist's belief that the problem was ADHD; and of being placed into a severely restrictive program designed to send him, ultimately, to a middle school that served only children with behavior disorders.

Finally, do we believe that the theoretical level of our data analysis constitutes a theory? Using Glaser and Strauss's (1967) distinction between substantive and formal theory, we certainly feel that our theoretical statement represents a substantive theory of disproportionality in the schools we studied. For our explanations to attain the level of a formal theory they would have to be tested in various situations to see whether general statements could be made about how this process occurs regardless of setting.

CONCLUSION

In concluding, I take our readers back to the beginning of this chapter. Our research project began, officially, in March 1999. It ended officially in August 2003. However, for me, the official beginning represented only a moment in a long trajectory of wondering why there were so many Black children, mostly boys, in the special education classroom of a predominantly White elementary school that I visited in Syracuse, New York, soon after my arrival in the United States in 1986. While the official end of the project—and the writing of this book's first edition—represented the culmination of that wondering, it also gave momentum to a question that remains to a large extent unanswered: What were the outcomes of this study for the professionals, children, and families who participated?

We have good reason to believe that our work had some positive influence on local policy. We shared our findings with key special education administrators and were gratified to learn that some changes were gradually instituted in the referral process—in particular, a teach-test-teach model that came to be the precursor to the RTI process now used in the district. We know too that our concerns about assessment were brought to the attention of school leaders.

Our most enduring concern has been what we were not able to do for the children and families in the study. Since this was not an intervention study, we did not have to worry about hurting children or families by doing the wrong thing. However, not doing the right thing is another matter! As researchers, we were unable to intervene when we thought children were receiving inappropriate treatment in school. Being convinced that no illegal decisions had occurred, we had no reason to attempt to intervene and little hope of success if we did.

Some questions created more nuanced concerns. First, how do we withdraw from the careful relationships we had formed with the families who had welcomed us into their homes and shared extensive narratives? We conducted exit meetings in which we summarized what we had learned about the referral and placement processes related to their children, but that left us with the dilemma of how much of the findings to share explicitly. For example: Should we provide them with copies of the publications? Would it be helpful for parents or caregivers to learn how much they had been disrespected by some school personnel, or how inappropriate we thought some assessment or placement decisions had been? Would such knowledge contribute to further souring their relationships with school personnel and possibly to detrimental outcomes for the siblings who would go to the same neighborhood schools? Perhaps most important, if parents were to confront school district personnel with our findings, the confidentiality/anonymity agreements we had made with school district personnel would be broken. My answer to these questions is that family members' full knowledge of all the circumstances we had studied could do more harm than good, so we did not share the written findings with them. This decision does not sit comfortably with me, but I believe that it was the best we could do. With regard to the school district, we did provide the administrators and school principals with an executive summary, (written, of course, with pseudonyms of persons and places), and offered to send the full summary on request. We received no such requests.

I do have one regret: that we did not plan for longitudinal follow-up of our case study students. We have anecdotal information on only two—Kanita, who is employed and holds an associate degree from the local community college, and Robert, who, at our last update, ran into trouble (shoplifting) in his teenage years and was placed in a residential school for juvenile offenders.

These dilemmas highlight some of the personal and ethical challenges that typify ethnographic research. The use of vivid descriptions of settings and events can make situations and individuals recognizable, regardless of careful anonymity protections. With the researcher fully present in the work, the creation of personal relationships is an inevitable part of the process, leaving the reflective researcher with the hardest questions: How do I withdraw from this relationship? What is the extent of my responsibility beyond the purposes of the research? Can I be sure that I have done no harm?

OUR LAST WORD

Our goal in writing this chapter on methodology is to present readers with a peek inside the processes that produced this research report, in order to provide a frame for evaluating its credibility and persuasiveness. While we hope to provide insight into both the power and the perils of these methods, we emphasize that rigor in qualitative work is, at once, essential and attainable. Although tolerance for ambiguity is a hallmark of the method (Charmaz, 2014; Corbin & Strauss, 2008), in the end, the researcher must be confident that every conclusion is supported by richly described data, and that the process of analyzing that data has been conducted under a gaze marked by critical self-awareness and iterative scrutiny. We believe that we can claim such confidence in this work.

References

Agar, M. H. (1996). *The professional stranger: An informal introduction to ethnography.* Emerald Group Publishing.

Albrecht, S. F., Skiba, R., Losen, D., Chung, C., & Middleberg, L. (2012). Federal policy on disproportionality in special education: Is it moving forward? *Journal of Disability Policy Studies, 23*(1), 14–25.

Algozzine, B. (2015). Waiting for the change: A long and disappointing search for multiculturalism and inclusion. *Multicultural Learning and Teaching, 10*(2), 231–253.

Algozzine, B., Christenson, S., & Ysseldyke, J. (1982). Probabilities associated with the referral to placement process. *Teacher Education and Special Education, 5,* 19–23.

Algozzine, B., Wang, C., White, R., Cooke, N., Marr, J. B., Algozzine, K., Helf, S. S., & Duran, G. Z. (2012). Effects of multi-tier academic and behavior instruction on difficult-to-teach students. *Exceptional Children, 79*(1), 45–66.

American Recovery and Reinvestment Act of 2009 : Law, Explanation and Analysis : P.L. 111-5, as Signed by the President on February 17, 2009. Chicago: CCH, 2009.

Annamma, S. A., Ferri, B. A., & Connor, D. J. (2018). Disability critical race theory: Exploring the intersectional lineage, emergence, and potential futures of DisCrit in education. *Review of Research in Education, 42*(1), 46–71.

Annamma, S. A., Morrison, D., & Jackson, D. (2014). Disproportionality fills in the gaps: Connections between achievement, discipline and special education in the school-to-prison pipeline. *Berkeley Review of Education 5*(1), 53–87.

Ansell, S. E., & McCabe, M. (2003). Off target. *Education Week, 22*(17), 57–58.

Anyon, J. (1981). Social class and school knowledge. *Curriculum Inquiry, 11,* 3–41.

Anyon, J. (1997). *Ghetto schooling: A political economy of urban educational reform.* Teachers College Press.

Anyon, J. (2005). *Radical possibilities: Public policy, urban education, and a new social movement.* Routledge.

Anyon, J. (2014). *Radical possibilities: Public policy, urban education, and a new social movement* (2nd ed.). Routledge. https://doi.org/10.4324/9780203092965

Artiles, A. (2009). Re-framing disproportionality research: Outline of a cultural-historical paradigm. *Multiple Voices for Ethnically Diverse Exceptional learners, 11*(2), 24–37.

Artiles, A. J. (2003). Special education's changing identity: Paradoxes and dilemmas in views of culture and space. *Harvard Educational Review, 73,* 164–202.

Artiles, A. J. (2011). Toward an interdisciplinary understanding of educational equity and difference: The case of the racialization of ability. *Educational Researcher, 40,* 431–445.

Artiles, A. J. (2019). Re-envisioning equity research: Disability identification disparities as a case in point. *Educational Researcher, 48,* 325–335.

Artiles, A. J., Bal, A., & Thorius, A. K. (2010). Back to the future: A critique of response to intervention's social justice views. *Theory into Practice, 49,* 250–257.

Artiles, A. J., Bal, A., Trent, A. C., & Thorius, K. K. (2012). Placement of culturally and linguistically diverse students in programs for students with emotional and behavioral disorders: Contemporary trends and research needs. *Advances in Special Education, 22*, 107–127.

Artiles, A. J., Dorn, S., & Bal, A. (2016). Objects of protection, enduring nodes of difference: Disability intersections with "other" differences, 1916 to 2016. *Review of Research in Education, 40*(1), 777–820.

Artiles, A. J., Kozleski, E., Trent, S., Osher, D., & Ortiz, A. (2010). Justifying and explaining disproportionality, 1968–2008: A critique of underlying views of culture. *Exceptional Children, 76*, 279–299.

Artiles, A. J., Rueda, R., Salazar, J., & Higareda, I. (2002). English-language learner representation in special education in California urban school districts. In D. J. Losen & G. Orfield (Eds.), *Racial inequity in special education* (pp. 117–136). Harvard Education Press.

Artiles, A. J., Trent, S. C., & Kuan, L. A. (1997). Learning disabilities research on ethnic minority students: An analysis of 22 years of students published in selected refereed journals. *Learning Disabilities Research and Practice, 12*, 82–91.

Ashby, C., White, J. M., Ferri, B., Li, S., & Ashby, L. (2020). Enclaves of privilege: Access and opportunity for students with disabilities in urban K-8 schools. *History of Education Quarterly, 60*(3), 407–429.

Baker, B. (2002). The hunt for disability: The new eugenics and the normalization of school children. *Teachers College Record, 104*(4), 663–703.

Bal, A., Kemal, A., & Halil, I. C. (2018). Culturally responsive school discipline: Implementing learning lab at a high school for systemic transformation. *American Educational Research Journal, 55*(5), 1007–1050.

Bal, A., Kozleski, E. G., Schrader, J. M., Rodrigues, E. M., & Pelton, S. (2014). Systemic transformation from the ground-up using learning lab to design culturally responsive schoolwide positive behavioral supports. *Remedial and Special Education, 35*, 327–339.

Bal, A., Sullivan, A., & Harper, J. (2014). A situated analysis of special education disproportionality for systemic transformation in an urban school district. *Remedial and Special Education, 35*(1), 3–14.

Bal, A., & Trainor, A. (2016). Culturally responsive experimental intervention studies: The development of a rubric for paradigm expansion. *Review of Educational Research, 86*(2), 319–359.

Ballenger, C. (1992). Because you like us: The language of control. *Harvard Educational Review, 62*(2), 199–208.

Balu, R., Zhu, P., Doolittle, F., Schiller, E., Jenkins, J., & Gersten, R. (2015). *Evaluation of response to intervention (RTI) practices for elementary school reading.* U.S. Department of Education. https://www.mdrc.org/publications

Banks, J. (2017). "These people are never going to stop labelling me": Educational experiences of African American male students labeled with learning disabilities. *Equity and Excellence in Education, 50*(1), 96–107.

Barrett, C. A., Cottrell, J. M., Newman, D. S., Pierce, B. G., & Anderson, A. (2015). Training school psychologists to identify specific learning disabilities: A content analysis of syllabi. *School Psychology Review, 44*(3), 271–288.

Becker, H. S. (1969). *Studies in the sociology of deviance.* Free Press.

Berkeley, S., Scanlon, D., Bailey, T. R., Sutton, J. C., & Sacco, D. M. (2020). A snapshot of RTI implementation a decade later: New picture, same story. *Journal of Learning Disabilities, 53*(5), 332–342.

Berliner, D., & Casanova, U. (1989). Effective schools: Teachers make the difference. *Instructor, 99*(3), 14–15.

Blair, C., & Scott, K. G. (2000). Proportion of LD placements associated with low socioeconomic status: Evidence for a gradient? *Journal of Special Education, 36*, 14–22.

Blanchett, W. J. (2010). Telling it like it is: The role of race, class, and culture in the perpetuation of learning disability as a privileged category for the White middle-class. *Disability Studies Quarterly, 30*(2), https://doi.org/10.18061/dsq.v30i2.1233

Blumer, H. (1969). *Symbolic interactionism: Perspective and method.* Prentice Hall.

Bobo, L. D. (2011). Somewhere between Jim Crow and post-racialism: Reflections on the racial divide in America today. *Daedalus, 140*(2), 11–36.

Bogdan, R., & Biklen, S. (2007). *Qualitative research for education: An introduction to theories and methods.* Pearson.

Bogdan, R., & Knoll, J. (1988). The sociology of disability. In E. L. Meyen & T. M. Skrtic (Eds.), *Exceptional children and youth: An introduction* (3rd ed., pp. 449–547). Love.

Bonilla-Silva, E. (1996). Rethinking racism: Toward a structural interpretation. *American Sociological Review, 62*(3), 465–481.

Bonilla-Silva, E. (2006). *Racism without racists: Color-blind racism and the persistence of racial inequality in the United States.* Rowman & Littlefield.

Borman, G. D. (2000). Title I: The evolving research base. *Journal of Education for Students Placed at Risk (JESPAR), 5*, 27–45.

Boskovich, L., Cannon, M. A., Hernández-Saca, D. I., Kahn, L. G., & Nusbaum, E. A. (2019). Self-study of intersectional and emotional narratives: Narrative inquiry, disability studies in education, and praxis in social science research. In *New narratives of disability (research in social science and disability), vol. 11* (pp. 215–230), Emerald Publishing. https://doi.org/10.1108/S1479-354720190000011026

Bouck, E. C., & Cosby, M. D. (2019). Response to intervention in high school mathematics: One school's implementation. *Preventing School Failure, 63*(1), 32–42.

Bourdieu, P. (1986). The forms of capital. In J. Richardson (Ed.), *Handbook of theory and research for the sociology of education* (pp. 241–258). Greenwood.

Bowers, C. A. (1984). *The promise of theory: Education and the politics of cultural change.* Longman.

Bowles, S., & Gintis, H. (1976). *Schooling in capitalist America.* Basic Books.

Bradley, R., Danielson, L., & Hallahan, D. P. (Eds.). (2002). *Identification of learning disabilities: Research to practice.* Lawrence Erlbaum.

Brady, N. C., & Halle, J. W. (1997). Functional analysis of communicative disorders. *Focus on Autism and Other Developmental Disabilities, 12*(2), 95–104.

Brantlinger, E. (2001). Poverty, class, and disability: A historical, social, and political perspective. *Focus on Exceptional Children, 33*(7), 3–19.

Brantlinger, E. (2006). Winners need Losers: The basis for school competition and hierarchies. In E. Brantlinger (Ed.), *Who benefits from Special Education? Remediating [fixing] other people's children* (pp. 197–231). Lawrence Erlbaum.

Bronfenbrenner, U. (1977, July). Toward an experimental ecology of human development. *American Psychologist, 32*(5), 513–531.

Brophy, J. (1986). Teacher influences on student achievement. *American Psychologist, 41*(10), 1069–1077.

Brown v. Board of Education, 347 U.S. 483 (1954).

Carbado, D. W., & Gulati, M. (2013). The intersectional fifth black woman. *DuBois Review, 10*, 527–540.

Carter, P. L., Skiba, R., Arredondo, M. I., & Pollack, M. (2017). You can't fix what you don't look at: Acknowledging race in addressing racial discipline disparities. *Urban Education, 52*(2), 207–235.

Cartledge, G., & Kourea, L. (2008). Culturally responsive classrooms for culturally diverse students with and at-risk for disabilities. *Exceptional Children 74*(3), 351–371.

Cavendish, W. (2013). Identification of learning disabilities: Implications of proposed DSM-5 criteria for school-based assessment. *Journal of Learning Disabilities 46*(1), 53–57.

Cavendish, W., Artiles, A., & Harry, B. (2014). Tracking inequality 60 years after Brown: Does policy legitimize the racialization of disability? *Multiple Voices for Ethnically Diverse Exceptional Learners, 14*, 30–40.

Cavendish, W., Connor, D., Gonzalez, T., Jean-Pierre, P., & Card, K. (2018). Troubling "the problem" of racial overrepresentation in special education: A commentary and all to rethink research. *Educational Review, 72*(1), 1–16. DOI:10.1080/00131911.2018.1550055

Cavendish, W., & Espinosa, A. (2013). Teacher preparation for student diversity and disabilities: Changing roles in response to intervention models. *Advances in Special Education, 25*, 189–205.

Cavendish, W., Harry, B., Menda, A., Espinosa, A., & Mahotiere, M. (2016). Implementing response to intervention: Challenges of diversity and system change in a high-stakes environment. *Teachers College Record, 118*(5) 1–36. https://doi.org/10.1177/016146811611800505

Centers for Disease Control and Prevention. (2022). *Racism and health: Health equity.* https://www.cdc.gov/healthequity/racism-disparities

Charmaz, K. (2014). *Constructing grounded theory* (2nd ed.). SAGE.

Clark, K. B. (1965). *Dark ghetto: Dilemmas of social power.* Harper & Row.

Clark, R. (1983). *Family life and school achievement: Why poor Black children succeed or fail.* University of Chicago Press.

Cole, M. (1996). *Cultural psychology: A once and future discipline.* Harvard University Press.

Cole, S. M., Murphy, H. R., Frisby, M. B., Grossi, T. A., & Bolte, H. R. (2021). The relationship of special education placement and student academic outcomes. *Journal of Special Education, 54*(4), 217–227.

Collins, K., Ferri, B., Connor, D., Gallagher, D., & Samson, J. (2016). Dangerous assumptions and unspoken limitations: A disability studies in education response to Morgan, Farkas, Hillemeier, Mattison, Maczuga, Li, and Cook (2015). *Multiple Voices for Ethically Diverse Exceptional Learners, 16*(1), 4–16.

Collins, R., & Camblin, L. D. (1983). The politics and science of learning disability classification: Implications for Black children. *Contemporary Education, 54*(2), 113–118.

Connor, D. J., Ferri, B. A., & Annamma, S. A. (Eds.). (2016). *DisCrit: Disability studies and critical race theory in education.* Teachers College Press.

Corbin, J. M., & Strauss, A. L. (2008). *Basics of qualitative research: Techniques and procedures for developing grounded theory* (32nd ed.). SAGE.

Crenshaw, K. (1989). Demarginalizing the intersection of race and sex: A Black feminist critique of antidiscrimination doctrine, feminist theory and antiracist politics. *University of Chicago Legal Forum, 140*, 139–167.

Cruz, R. A., & Rodl, J. E. (2018). An integrative synthesis of literature on disproportionality in special education. *Journal of Special Education, 52*, 1–14. DOI: 10.1177/0022466918758707

Cummins, J. (1984). *Bilingualism and special education: Issues in assessment and pedagogy.* College Hill.

Darling-Hammond, L. (1995). Inequality and access to knowledge. In J. A. Banks & C. A. Banks (Eds.), *The handbook of multicultural education* (pp. 465–483). Macmillan.

Darling-Hammond, L. (2012). *The flat world and education: How America's commitment to equity will determine our future.* Teachers College Press.

Darling-Hammond, L., & Post, L. (2000). Inequality in teaching and schooling: Supporting high-quality teaching and leadership in low-income schools. In R. D. Kahlenberg (Ed.), *A nation at risk: Preserving public education as an engine for social mobility* (pp. 127–168). Century Foundation Press.

Delgado, R., & Stefancic, J. (2000). *Critical race theory: The cutting edge* (2nd ed.). Temple University Press.

Delpit, L. (1988). The silenced dialogue: Power and pedagogy in educating other people's children. *Harvard Educational Review, 58*(3), 280–298.

Delpit, L. (1995). *Other people's children: Cultural conflict in the classroom.* New Press.

Diana v. State Board of Education, Civil Action No. C-7037RFP (N.D. Cal. Jan. 7, 1970 and June 18, 1973).

Donovan, S., & Cross, C. (2002). *Minority students in special and gifted education.* National Academy Press.

Dunn, L. M. (1968). Special education for the mildly retarded: Is much of it justifiable? *Exceptional Children, 35,* 5–32.

Edmonds, R. R., & Frederickson, J. R. (1978). *Search for effective schools: The identification and analysis of city schools that are instructionally effective for poor children.* Harvard University Press.

Education of All Handicapped Children Act of 1975. 20 U.S.C. 1400 et seq. (statute); 34 CFR 300 (regulations published in 1977).

Eitle, T. M. (2002). Special education or racial segregation: Understanding variation in the representation of Black students in Educable Mentally Handicapped programs. *Sociological Quarterly, 43*(4), 575–605.

Elementary and Secondary Education (ESEA) Act of 1965, Pub. L. No. 89-10, § 79, Stat. 27 (1965).

Erevelles, N. (2017). The right to exclude: Locating Section 504 in the disproportionality debate. In J. Allan & A. Artiles (Eds.), *Assessment inequalities: World yearbook of education, 2017* (pp. 120–136). Routledge.

Ervin, R. A., Schaughency, E., Goodman, S. D., McGlinchey, M. T., & Matthews, A. (2007). Moving from a model demonstration project to a statewide initiative in Michigan: Lessons learned from merging research-practice agendas to address reading and behavior. In *Handbook of Response to Intervention* (pp. 354–377). Springer.

Essed, P. (1991). *Understanding everyday racism: An interdisciplinary theory.* SAGE.

Fass, P. S. (1991). *Outside-in: Minorities and the transformation of American education.* Oxford University Press.

Ferguson, A. A. (2000). *Bad boys: Public schools in the making of Black masculinity.* University of Michigan Press.

Ferguson, R. (1991). Paying for public education: New evidence on how and why money matters. *Harvard Journal on Legislation, 28,* 465–498.

Ferrante, J., & Brown, P. (1998). Classifying people by race. In J. Ferrante & P. Brown (Eds.), *The social construction of race and ethnicity in the United States* (pp. 109–119). Longman.

Ferri, B. A. (2004). Interrupting the discourse: A response to Reid and Valle. *Journal of Learning Disabilities, 37*(6), 509–515.

Ferri, B. A. (2011). Undermining inclusion? A critical reading of response to intervention (RTI). *International Journal of Inclusive Education, 16*(8), 863–880.

Ferri, B. A., & Connor, D. J. (2005). In the shadow of *Brown*: Special education and overrepresentation of students of color. *Remedial and Special Education, 26*(2), 93–100.

Ferri, B. A., & Connor, D. J. (2014). Talking (and not talking) about race, social class and dis/ability: Working margin to margin. *Race Ethnicity and Education, 17*(4), 471–493.

Feuerstein, R., Rand, Y., & Hoffman, M. B. (1981). The dynamic assessment of retarded performers, *International Journal of Rehabilitation Research, 4*(3), 465–466.

Figueroa, R. (1989). Psychological testing of linguistic-minority students: Knowledge gaps and regulations. *Exceptional Children, 56*(2), 145–152.

Fish, R. E. (2019). Standing out and sorting in: Exploring the role of racial composition in racial disparities in special education. *American Educational Research Journal, 56*(6), 2573–2608.

Fletcher, J. M., Francis, D. J., Shaywitz, S. E., Lyon, G. R., Foorman, B. R., Stuebing, K. K., & Shaywitz, B. A. (1998). Intelligent testing and the discrepancy model for children with learning disabilities. *Learning Disabilities Research and Practice, 4*(13), 186–203.

Fletcher, J. M., & Morris, R. D. (1986). Classification of disabled learners: Beyond exclusionary definitions. In S. J. Ceci (Ed.), *Handbook of cognitive, social, and neuro-psychological reports of learning disabilities* (pp. 55–80). Lawrence Erlbaum.

Florida Department of Education. (2010). *2010 LEA profile.* https://www.fldoe.org/core/fileparse .php/7602/urlt/0062270-dade.pdf

Florida Department of Education. (2020). *2020 LEA profile.* https://www.fldoe.org/core/fileparse .php/7672/urlt/Dade20.pdf

Florida International University. (1998, March). *Historical impacts of transportation projects on the Overtown community.* Institute of Government. http://dpanther.fiu.edu/sobek/content /FI/GO/00/02/77/00001/Historical%20Impact%20of%20Transportation%20Projects%20 Overtown%20Community%200001.pdf

Fordham, S. (1988). Racelessness as a factor in black students' school success: Pragmatic strategy or pyrrhic victory? *Harvard Educational Review, 58,* 54–84.

Freedman, J. E., & Ferri, B. A. (2017). Locating the problem with: Race, learning, disabilities, and science. *Teachers College Record, 119*(5), 1–28.

Fuchs, D., Deshler, D. D., & Reschly, D. T. (2004). National center on learning disabilities' multi-method studies of identification and classification issues. *Learning Disability Quarterly, 27*(4), 189–195.

Fuchs, D., & Fuchs, L. S. (2017). Critique of the National Evaluation of Response to Intervention: A case for simpler frameworks. *Exceptional Children, 83,* 255–268.

Gallagher, D. (2010). Hiding in plain sight: The nature and role of theory in Learning Disability labeling. *Disability Studies Quarterly, 30*(2). https://doi.org/10.18061/dsq.v30i2.1231

Gartland, D., & Strosnider, R. (2020). The use of response to intervention to inform special education eligibility decisions for students with specific learning disabilities. *Learning Disabilities Quarterly, 43*(4), 195–200.

Gatlin, B. T., & Wilson, C. E. (2016). Overcoming obstacles: African American students with disabilities achieving academic success. *Journal of Negro Education, 85*(2), 129–142.

Gay, G. (2010). *Culturally responsive teaching: Theory, research, and practice* (2nd ed.). Teachers College Press.

Gee, K., Gonzalez, M., & Cooper, C. (2020). Outcomes of inclusive versus separate placements: A matched pairs comparison study. *Research and Practice for Persons with Severe Disabilities, 45*(4), 223–240.

Gerber, M., & Semmel, M. (1984). Teacher as imperfect test: Reconceptualizing the referral process. *Educational Psychologist, 19,* 137–148.

Gergen, K. J. (1994). *Realities and relationships: Soundings in social construction.* Harvard University Press.

Gillborn, D., & Youdell, D. (2000). *Rationing education: Policy, practice, reform and equity.* Open University Press.

Giroux, H. A., & McLaren, P. (1994). *Between borders: Pedagogy and the politics of cultural studies.* Routledge.

Glaser, B., & Strauss, A. (1967). *The discovery of grounded theory: Strategies for qualitative research.* Aldine.

Goffman, E. (1963). *Stigma: Notes on the management of spoiled identity.* Simon & Schuster.

González, N., Moll, L., & Amanti, C. (2005). *Funds of knowledge: Theorizing practices in households, communities and classrooms.* Routledge.

Gonzalez, V., Brusca-Vega, R., & Yawkey, T. (1997). *Assessment and instruction of culturally and linguistically diverse students with, or at-risk of learning problems*. Allyn & Bacon.

Gottlieb, J., Alter, M., Gottlieb, B. W., & Wishner, J. (1994). Special education in urban America: It's not justifiable for many. *Journal of Special Education, 27*(4), 453–465.

Gould, S. J. (1981). *The mismeasure of man*. Norton.

Gramsci, A. (1971). *Selections from the prison notebooks* (Q. Hoare & G. N. Smith, Eds.). International. (Original work published 1929–1935)

Graves, S., & Mitchell, A. (2011). Is the moratorium over? African American psychology professionals' views on intelligence testing in response to changes to federal policy. *Journal of Black Psychology, 37*(4), 407–425.

Gresham, F. M. (1993). "What's wrong with this picture?" Response to Motta et al.'s review of human figure drawings. *School Psychology Quarterly, 8*(3), 182–186.

Grindal, T., Schifter, L. A., Schwartz, G., & Hehir, T. (2019). Racial differences in special education identification and placement: Evidence across three states. *Harvard Educational Review, 89*(4), 525–553.

Guba, E., & Lincoln, Y. S. (2005). Paradigmatic controversies, contradictions, and emerging confluences. In N. K. Denzin & Y. S. Lincoln (Eds.), *The SAGE handbook of qualitative research* (3rd ed., pp. 191–216). SAGE.

Hardy, L. (1999). Building blocks of reform. *American School Board Journal, 186*(2), 16–21.

Harry, B. (1992). *Cultural diversity, families, and the special education system: Communication and empowerment*. Teachers College Press.

Harry, B. (2019). *Childhood disability, advocacy and inclusion in the Caribbean: A Trinidad and Tobago case study*. Palgrave MacMillan.

Harry, B., Allen, N., & McLaughlin, M. (1995). Communication versus compliance: African American parents' involvement in special education. *Exceptional Children, 61*, 364–377.

Harry, B., Hart, J., Klingner, J., Cramer, E., & Sturges, K. (2009). Response to Kauffman, Mock, and Simpson. *Behavioral Disorders, 34*, 164–171.

Harry, B., Kalyanpur, M., & Day, M. (1999). *Building cultural reciprocity with families: Case studies in special education*. Brookes.

Harry, B., & Klingner, J. (2006). *Why are so many minority students in special education? Understanding race and disability in schools*. Teachers College Press.

Harry, B., Klingner, J., & Cramer, E. (2007). *Case studies of minority student placement in special education*. Teachers College Press.

Harry, B., Klingner, J., & Hart, J. (2005). African American families under fire: Ethnographic views of family strengths. *Remedial and Special Education, 26*(2), 101–112.

Harry, B., Klingner, J., Sturges, K., & Moore, R. (2002). Of rocks and soft places: Using qualitative methods to investigate disproportionality. In D. J. Losen & G. Orfield (Eds.), *Racial inequity in special education* (pp. 71–92). Harvard.

Harry, B., & Ocasio-Stoutenburg, L. (2020). *Meeting families where they are: Building equity through advocacy with diverse schools and communities*. Teachers College Press.

Harry, B., Sturges, K., & Klingner, J. (2005). Mapping the process: An exemplar of process and challenge in grounded theory analysis. *Educational Researcher, 34*(2), 3–13.

Hart, J. E. (2003). *African American learners and 6-hour emotional disturbance: Investigating the roles of context, perception, and worldview, in the overrepresentation phenomenon* [Unpublished doctoral dissertation]. University of Miami.

Heller, K. A., Holtzman, W. H., & Messick, S. (1982). *Placing children in special education: A strategy for equity*. National Academy Press.

Hendricks, E. L., & Fuchs, D. (2020). Are individual differences in response to intervention influenced by the methods and measures used to define response? Implications for identifying children with learning disabilities. *Journal of Learning Disabilities, 53*(6) 428–443.

Hernandez, M. G., Lopez, D. M., & Swier, R. (2022). *Dismantling disproportionality: A culturally responsive and sustaining systems approach*. Teachers College Press.

Heubert, J. P., & Hauser, R. M. (Eds.). (1999). *High stakes: Testing for tracking, promotion, and graduation*. National Academy Press.

Hill, R. B. (1971). *The strengths of Black families*. Emerson Hall.

Hilliard, A. G., III. (1997). *Annotated selected bibliography and index for teaching African-American learners: Culturally responsive pedagogy project*. American Association of Colleges for Teacher Education.

Hilliard, A. G., III. (2000). Excellence in education versus high-stakes standardized testing. *Journal of Teacher Education, 51*, 293–304.

Hoover, J. J. (2010). Special education eligibility decision making in response to intervention models. *Theory Into Practice, 49*(4), 289–296.

Hoover, J. J., Erikson, J. R., Patton, J. R., Sacco, D. M., & Tran, L. M. (2018). Examining IEPs of English learners with learning disabilities for cultural and linguistic responsiveness. *Learning Disabilities Research and Practice, 34*(1), 14–22.

Hosp, J. L., & Reschly, D. J. (2002). Regional differences in school psychology practice. *School Psychology Review, 31*, 11–29.

Hruby, G., & Hynd, G. W. (2006). Decoding Shaywitz: The modular brain and its discontents. *Reading Research Quarterly 41*(4), 544–556.

Individuals with Disabilities Education Act, 20 U.S.C. § 1400 (2004).

Irvine, J. J. (1990). *Black students and school failure: Policies, practices, and prescriptions*. Praeger.

Jackson, S. A., Logsdon, D. M., & Taylor, N. E. (1983). Instructional leadership behaviors: Differentiating effective from ineffective low-income urban schools. *Urban Education, 18*, 59–70.

Jacobson, S. L. (1989). Change in entry-level salaries and its effect on recruitment. *Journal of Educational Finance, 14*, 449–465.

Jameson, J. M., Stegenga, S. M., Ryan, J., & Green, A. (2020). Free appropriate public education in the time of COVID-19. *Rural Special Education Quarterly, 39*(4), 181–192.

Johnston, P. H. (2011). Response to intervention in literacy: Problems and possibilities. *Elementary School Journal, 111*(4), 511–534.

Jussim, L., Eccles, J., & Madon, S. (1996). Social perception, social stereotypes, and teacher expectations: Accuracy and the quest for the powerful self-fulfilling prophecy. In M. P. Zanna (Ed.), *Advances in experimental social psychology*, (vol. 28, pp. 281–388). Academic Press.

Kalyanpur, M. (2022). *Development, education and learning disability in India*. Palgrave Macmillan.

Kalyanpur, M., & Harry, B. (2012). *Cultural reciprocity in special education: Building family-professional relationships*. Brookes.

Kauffman, J. M., & Hornby, G. (2020). Inclusive vision versus special education reality. *Education Sciences, 10*(258), 1–13.

Kauffman, J. M., Mock, D. R., & Simpson, R. L. (2007). Problems related to underservice of students with emotional or behavioral disorders. *Behavioral Disorders, 33*, 43–57.

Kavale, K. (1990). The effectiveness of special education. In T. B. Gutkin & C. R. Reynolds (Eds.), *The handbook of school psychology* (pp. 868–898). Wiley.

Kavale, K. A., & Flanagan, D. P. (2007). Ability—achievement discrepancy, response to intervention, and assessment of cognitive abilities/processes in specific learning disability identification: Toward a contemporary operational definition. In S. R. Jimerson, M. K. Burns, & A. M. VanDerHeyden (Eds.), *Handbook of response to intervention* (pp. 130–147). Springer.

Kellam, S. G., Ling, X., Merisca, R., Brown, C. H., & Ialongo, N. (1998). The effect of the level of aggression in the first grade classroom on the course and malleability of aggressive behavior into middle school. *Development and Psychopathology, 10*, 165–185.

Keogh, B. K. (2000). Risk, families, and schools. *Focus on Exceptional Children, 33*(4), 1–10.

Keogh, B. K., & Speece, D. L. (1996). Learning disabilities within the context of schooling. In D. L. Speece & B. K. Keogh (Eds.), *Research on classroom ecologies: Implications of inclusion of children with learning disabilities* (pp. 1–14). Lawrence Erlbaum.

Kirk, S. (1962). *Educating exceptional children.* Houghton-Mifflin.

Klingner, J., & Bianco, M. (2006). What is special about special education for culturally and linguistically diverse students with disabilities? In B. Cook & B. Schirmer (Eds.), *What is special about special education?* (pp. 37–53). PRO-ED.

Klingner, J., & Edwards, P. (2006). Cultural considerations with response to intervention models. *Reading Research Quarterly, 41*(1), 108–117.

Klingner, J. K., Ahwee, S., Van Garderen, D., & Hernandez, C. (2004). Closing the gap: Enhancing student outcomes in an urban professional development school. *Teacher Education and Special Education, 27*(3), 292–306.

Klingner, J. K., & Artiles, A. (2003). When should bilingual students be in special education? *Educational Leadership, 61*(2), 66–71.

Klingner, J. K., Cramer, E., & Harry, B. (2006). Challenges in the implementation of success for all by four urban schools. *Elementary School Journal, 106*(4), 333–350.

Knoff, H. M. (1993). The utility of human figure drawings in personality and intellectual assessment: Why ask why? *School Psychology Quarterly, 8*(3), 191–196.

Kohn, A. (2000). Burnt at the high stakes. *Journal of Teacher Education, 51,* 315–327.

Kozol, J. (1991). *Savage inequalities.* Crown.

Kozol, J. (2006). *The shame of the nation: The restoration of apartheid schooling in America.* Crown.

Kranzler, J. H., Yaraghchi, M., Matthews, K., & Otero-Valles, L. (2019). Does the Response-to-Intervention model fundamentally alter the traditional conceptualization of specific learning disability? *Contemporary School Psychology, 24,* 80–88.

Kratchowill, T. K., Clements, M. A., & Kalymon, K. M. (2007). Response to intervention: Conceptual and methodological issues in implementation. In S. R. Jimerson, M. K. Burns, & A. M. VanDerHeyden (Eds.). *Handbook of response to intervention: The science and practice of multi-tiered systems of support* (pp. 25–52). Springer.

Krei, M. S. (1998). Intensifying the barriers: The problem of inequitable teacher in low-income urban schools. *Urban Education, 33,* 71–94.

Krezimen, M. P., Leone, P. E., & Achilles, G. M. (2006) Suspension, race and disability: Analysis of statewide practices and reporting. *Journal of Emotional and Behavioral Disorders, 14*(4), 217–226.

Ladson-Billings, G. (1994). *The dream-keepers: Successful teachers of African American children.* Jossey-Bass.

Ladson-Billings, G. (2006). From the achievement gap to education debt: Understanding achievement in U.S. schools. *Educational Researcher 35*(7), 3–12.

Ladson-Billings, G. (2021). Critical race theory in education: A scholar's journey. Teachers College Press.

Ladson-Billings, G., & Tate, W. F., IV. (1995, Fall). Toward a critical race theory of education. *Teachers College Record, 97*(1), 47–68.

Lareau, A. (1989). *Home advantage: Social class and parental intervention in elementary education.* Falmer Press.

Lareau, A., & Horvat, E. M. (1999, January). Moments of social inclusion and exclusion: Race, class, and cultural capital in family-school relationships. *Sociology of Education, 72,* 37–53.

Larry P. v. Riles, 495 F. Supp. 926 (N. D. California 1979), aff'd, 793 F.2d 969 (9th Cir. 1984).

Lee, D. R. (1982). Exploring the construct of "opportunity to learn." *Integrated Education, 20*(1–2), 62–63.

Leonard, L. J. (2001). From indignation to indifference: Teacher concerns about externally imposed classroom interruptions. *Journal of Educational Research, 95,* 103–109.

Leone, P. E., Walter, M. B., & Wolford, B. I. (1990). Toward integrated responses to troubling behavior. In P. E. Leone (Ed.), *Understanding troubled and troubling youth* (pp. 290–298). SAGE.

Levine, M. (2002). Why invest in professional development schools? *Educational Leadership, 59*(6), 65–69.

Lincoln, Y., & Guba, E. G. (1986). *Naturalistic inquiry.* SAGE.

Liptak, G. S., Benzoni, L. B., Mruzek, D. W., Nolan, K. W., Thingvoll, M. A., Wade, C. M., & Fryer, G. E. (2008). Disparities in diagnosis and access to health services for children with autism: Data from the National Survey of Children's Health. *Journal of Developmental & Behavioral Pediatrics, 29*(3), 152–160.

Lomax, R. G., West, M. M., & Harmon, M. C. (1995). The impact of mandated standardized testing on minority students. *Journal of Negro Education, 64,* 171–185.

Losen, D., Dodson, C., Jongyeon, E., & Martinez, T. (2015). Disturbing inequities: Exploring the relationship between racial disparities in special education identification and discipline. *Journal of Applied Research on Children: Informing Policy for Children at Risk, 5*(2), 1–20.

MacMillan, D. L., Gresham, F. M., & Bocian, K. M. (1998). Discrepancy between definitions of learning disabilities and school practices: An empirical investigation. *Journal of Learning Disabilities, 31,* 314–326.

Maki, K. E., Barrett, A. A., Hajovsky, D. B., & Burns, M. K. (2020). An examination of the relationships between specific learning disabilities identification and growth rate, achievement, cognitive ability, and student demographics. *School Psychology, 35*(5), 343–352.

McDermott, R. (1993). Acquisition of a child by a learning disability. In S. Chaiklin & J. Lave (Eds.), *Understanding practice* (pp. 269–305). Cambridge University Press.

McDermott, R. P. (2010). The passions of learning in tight circumstances: Toward a political economy of the mind. *Yearbook of the National Society for the Study of Education, 109*(1), 144–159.

McIntosh, P. (1989). White privilege: Unpacking the invisible knapsack. *Peace and Freedom, 49*(4), 10–12.

McLeskey, J., Landers, E., Williamson, P., & Hoppey, D. (2012). Are we moving toward educating students with disabilities in less restrictive settings? *Journal of Special Education, 46*(3), 131–140.

McNeil, L., & Valenzuela, A. (2000). The harmful impact of the TAAS system of testing in Texas: Beneath the accountability rhetoric. In G. Orfield & M. L. Kornhaber (Eds.), *Raising standards or raising barriers? Inequality and high-stakes testing in public education* (pp. 127–150). Century Foundation Press.

Mehan, H., Hartwick, A., & Meihls, J. L. (1986). *Handicapping the handicapped: Decision making in students' educational careers.* Stanford University Press.

Mercer, J. R. (1973). *Labeling the mentally retarded.* University of California Press.

Merriam-Webster. (n.d.). BIPOC. In *Merriam-Webster.com dictionary.* Retrieved May 15, 2022, from https://www.merriam-webster.com/dictionary/BIPOC

Merton, R. (1948). The self-fulfilling prophecy. *Antioch Review, 8,* 193–210.

Miami–Dade County Public Schools. (2021). *Multi-tiered system of supports. Implementation guide 2021–2022.* osi.dadeschools.net

Miller, M., Strosnider, R., & Dooley, E. (2000). States' requirements for teachers' preparation for diversity. *Multicultural Education, 8*(2), 15–18.

Milner, H. R., IV. (2008). Critical race theory and interest convergence as analytic tools in teacher education policies and practices. *Journal of Teacher Education, 59,* 332–346.

Montague, M., & Rinaldi, C. (2001). Classroom dynamics and children at risk: A follow up. *Learning Disabilities Quarterly, 24,* 73–84.

Morgan, P. L., & Farkas, G. (2016). Evidence and implications of racial and ethnic disparities in emotional and behavioral disorders identification and treatment. *Behavioral Disorders, 41*(2), 122–131.

Morgan, P. L., Farkas, G., Cook, M., Strassfeld, N. M., Hillemeier, M. M., Pun, W. H., & Schussler, D. L. (2016). Are Black children disproportionately represented in special education? A best-evidence synthesis. *Exceptional Children, 83,* 181–198.

Morgan, P. L., Farkas, G., Hillemeier, M. M., Mattison, R., Maczuga, S., Li, H., & Cook, M. (2015). Minorities are disproportionately underrepresented in special education: Longitudinal evidence across five disability conditions. *Educational Researcher, 44*(5), 278–292.

Morningstar, M. E., Kurth, J. A., & Johnson, P. E. (2017). Examining national trends in educational placements for students with significant disabilities. *Remedial and Special Education, 38*(1), 3–12.

Morrier, M. J., & Hess, K. L. (2012). Ethnic differences in autism eligibility in the United States public schools. *Journal of Special Education, 46*(1), 49–63.

Motta, R. W., Little, S. G., & Tobin, M. I. (1993). The use and abuse of human figure drawings. *School Psychology Quarterly, 8*(3), 162–169.

Muller, E., & Markowitz, J. (2004). *Disability categories: State terminology, definitions, and eligibility criteria.* National Association of State Directors of Special Education.

Murphy, J. (1988). Equity as student opportunity to learn. *Theory into Practice, 27,* 145–151.

Murrell, P., Jr. (2000). Community teachers: A conceptual framework for preparing exemplary urban teachers. *Journal of Negro Education, 69,* 338–348.

National Academy of Sciences. (2002). *Unequal treatment: Confronting racial and ethnic disparities in health care.* National Academy of Sciences.

National Association of School Psychologists. (2020). *The pandemic's impact on special education evaluations and SLD identification* [Handout]. Author.

National Center for Learning Disabilities. (2020). *Significant disproportionality in special education: Trends among American Indian and Alaska Native students.* https://www.ncld.org/wp-content/uploads/2020/10/2020-NCLD-Disproportionality_-Native-Students_FINAL.pdf

National Center for Learning Disabilities. (2021). *Promising practices to accelerate learning for students with disabilities during COVID-19 and beyond—Introduction.* https://www.ncld.org/reports-studies/promising-practices-to-accelerate-learning-for-students-with-disabilities-during-covid-19-and-beyond/

National Research Center on Learning Disabilities. (2003). *National Research Center on Learning Disabilities RTI Symposium.* National Research Center on Learning Disabilities.

Neal, L. I., McCray, A. D., Webb-Johnson, G., & Bridgest, S. T. (2003). The effects of African American movement styles on teachers' perceptions and reactions. *Journal of Special Education, 37*(1), 49–57.

Nichols, P. L., & Chen, T.-C. (1981). *Minimal brain dysfunction.* Lawrence Erlbaum Associates.

Nieto, S. (1999). *The light in their eyes.* Teachers College Press.

No Child Left Behind (NCLB) Act of 2001, Pub. L. No. 107–110, § 115, Stat. 1425 (2002).

Oakes, J. (1985). *Keeping track: How schools structure inequality.* Yale University Press.

Oakes, J., Franke, M. L., Quartz, K. H., & Rogers, J. (2002). Research for high-quality urban teaching: Defining it, developing it, assessing it. *Journal of Teacher Education, 53,* 228–234.

Ocasio-Stoutenburg, L., & Harry, B. (2021). *Case studies in building equity through family advocacy in special education.* Teachers College Press.

Ochoa, S. H., Rivera, B. D., & Powell, M. P. (1997). Factors used to comply with the exclusionary clause with bilingual and limited-English-proficient pupils: Initial guidelines. *Learning Disabilities Research and Practice, 12*, 161–167.

O'Connor, C., & Fernandez, S. D. (2006). Race, class, and disproportionality: Reevaluating the relationship between poverty and special education placement. *Educational Researcher, 35*(6), 6–11.

Oelrich, N. M. (2012). A new "IDEA": Ending racial disparity in the identification of students with emotional disturbance. *South Dakota Law Review, 57*, 9–149.

Ogbu, J. U. (1987). Variability in minority school performance: A problem in search of an explanation. *Anthropology and Education Quarterly, 18*, 312–334.

Ong-Dean, C. (2009). *Distinguishing disability: Parents, privilege, and special education.* University of Chicago Press.

Orosco, M., & Klingner, J. K. (2010). One school's implementation of RTI with English language learners: "Referring into RTI." *Journal of Learning Disabilities, 43*, 269–288.

Ortiz, A. A. (1997). Learning disabilities occurring concomitantly with linguistic differences. *Journal of Learning Disabilities, 30*, 321–332.

Osterholm, K., Nash, W. R., & Kritsonis, W. A. (2007). Effects of labeling students "learning disabled": Emergent themes in the research literature 1970 through 2000. *Focus on Colleges, Universities and Schools, 1*(1), 1-11. http://www.nationalforum.com/Electronic%20Journal%20Volumes/Osterholm,%20Karen%20Effects%20of%20Labeling%20Students%20Learning%20Disabled.pdf

Oswald, D. P., Coutinho, M. J., Best, A. M., & Singh, N. N. (1999). Ethnic representation in special education: The influence of school-related economic and demographic variables. *Journal of Special Education, 32*, 194–206.

Paris, D., & Alim, S. (Eds.). (2017). *Culturally sustaining pedagogies: Teaching and learning for justice in a changing world.* Teachers College Press.

Parrish, T. B., Hikido, C. S., & Fowler, W. J., Jr. (1998). *Inequalities in public school district revenues.* National Center for Education Statistics, U.S. Department of Education.

Pflaum, S. W., & Abramson, T. (1990). Teacher assignment, hiring, and preparation: Minority teachers in New York City. *Urban Review, 22*, 17–31.

Pierce, C. (1970). Offensive mechanisms. In F. Barbour (Ed.), *In the black seventies* (pp. 265–282). Porter Sargent.

Portes, A., & Armony, A. C. (2018). *The global edge: Miami in the Twenty-first century.* University of California Press.

Portes, A., & Stepick, A. (1993). *City on the edge: The transformation of Miami.* University of California Press.

President's Commission on Excellence in Special Education. (2002). *A new era: Revitalizing special education for children and their families.* U.S. Department of Education.

Pugach, M. C. (1985). The limitations of federal special education policy: The role of classroom teachers in determining who is handicapped. *Journal of Special Education, 19*(1), 123–137.

Reid, K. R., & Valle, J. W. (2004). The discursive practice of learning disability: Implications for instruction and parent-school relations. *Journal of Learning Disabilities, 37*(6), 466–481.

Reschly, D. J. (2000). Assessment and eligibility determination in the Individuals with Disabilities Education Act of 1997. In C. F. Telzrow & M. Tankersley (Eds.), *IDEA Amendments of 1997: Practice guidelines for school-based teams* (pp. 65–104). National Association of School Psychologists.

Reschly, D. J. (2014). Response to intervention and the identification of specific learning disabilities. *Topics in Language Disorders, 34*(1), 39–58.

Reschly, D. J., Kicklighter, R. H., & McGee, P. (1988). Recent placement litigation, Part I, regular education grouping: Comparison of Marshall (1984, 1985) and Hobson (1967, 1969). *School Psychology Review, 17*, 9–21.

Rocha, R., & Hawes, D. (2009). Racial diversity, representative bureaucracy, and equity in multicultural districts. *Social Science Quarterly, 90*(2), 326–344.

Rodriguez, A., & Rodriguez, D. (2017). English learners with learning disabilities: What is the current state? *Insights on Learning Disabilities: From Prevailing Theories to Validated Practices,* vol. 14(1), 97–112. https://files.eric.ed.gov/fulltext/EJ1165743.pdf

Rogoff, B., & Chavajay, P. (1995). What's become of research on the cultural basis of cognitive development? *American Psychologist, 50*(10), 859–877.

Rosaldo, R. (1993). *Culture and truth: The remaking of social analysis.* Beacon Press.

Rosenblum, K. E., & Travis, T. C. (2000). *The meaning of difference: American constructions of race, sex and gender, social class, and sexual orientation.* McGraw-Hill.

Rosenthal, R., & Jacobson, L. (1968). *Pygmalion in the classroom.* Holt, Rhinehart & Winston.

Ross, S. W., & Lignugaris-Kraft, B. (2015). Multi-tiered systems of support preservice residency: A pilot undergraduate teacher preparation model. *Journals on Alternative Teaching Certification, 10*(1), 3–20.

Rothstein, R. (2017). *The color of law: A forgotten history of how our government segregated America.* Liveright Publishing.

Sacks, P. (2000). *Standardized minds: The high price of America's testing culture and what we can do to change it.* Perseus Books.

Sadler, J. Z. (Ed.). (2002). *Descriptions and prescriptions: Values, mental disorders, and the DSMs.* Johns Hopkins University Press.

Saeki, E., Jimerson, S. R., Earhart J., Hart, S. R., Renshaw, T., Singh, R. D., & Stewart, K. (2011). Response to intervention (RTI) in the social, emotional and behavioral domains: Current challenges and emerging possibilities. *Contemporary School Psychology, 15*, 43–52.

Sameroff, A. J., Seifer, R., Baldwin, A., & Baldwin, C. (1993). Stability of intelligence from preschool to adolescence: The influence of social and family risk factors. *Child Development, 64,* 80–97.

Scheurich, J. J. (1998). Highly successful and loving, public elementary schools populated by low-SES children of color: Core beliefs and cultural characteristics. *Urban Education, 33,* 451–491.

Schwartz, M. A., & Wiggins, O. P. (2002). The hegemony of the DSMs. In J. Z. Sadler (Ed.), *Descriptions and prescriptions: Values, mental disorders, and the DSMs* (pp. 199–209). Johns Hopkins University Press.

Serpell, R. (1994). The cultural construction of intelligence. In W. J. Lonner & R. S. Malpass (Eds.), *Readings in psychology and culture* (pp. 157–163). Allyn & Bacon.

Shaywitz, B. A., & Shaywitz, S. E. (2020). The American experience: Towards a 21st century definition of dyslexia. *Oxford Review of Education, 46*(4), 454–471. https://doi.org/10.1080/0305 4985.2020.1793545

Shell, E. M., Johnson, L. V., & Getch, Y. Q. (2019). Good intentions, poor outcomes: Centering culture and language diversity within response to intervention. *Journal of School Counseling, 17*(24), 1–35.

Shifrer, D., Muller, C., Callahan, R. (2010). Disproportionality and learning disabilities: Parsing apart race, socioeconomic status, and language. *Journal of Learning Disabilities, 44,* 246–257.

Shores, K., Kim, H. E., & Still, M. (2020). Categorical inequality in black and white: Linking disproportionality across multiple educational outcomes. *American Educational Research Journal, 57*(5), 2089–2131.

Skiba, R. J., Artiles, A. J., Kozleski, E. B., Losen, D. J., & Harry, E. G. (2015). Risks and consequences of oversimplifying educational inequities: A response to Morgan et al. *Educational Researcher, 45*(3), 221–225. https://doi.org/10.3102/0013189X16644606

Skiba, R. J., Chung, C., Trachok, M., Baker, T. L., Sheya, A., & Hughes, R. L. (2014). Parsing disciplinary disproportionality: Contributions of infraction, student, and school characteristics to out-of-school suspension and expulsion. *Research Journal, 51*(4), 640–670.

Skiba, R. J., & Peterson, R. L. (2000). School discipline at a crossroads: From zero tolerance to early response. *Exceptional Children, 66*(3), 335–346.

Skiba, R. J., Simmons, A. B., Ritter, S., Gibb, A. C., Rausch, N. K., Cuadrado, J., & Chung, C. (2008). Achieving equity in special education: History, status, and current challenges. *Exceptional Children, 74*(3), 264–288.

Skiba, R. J., Simmons, A. B., Ritter, A., Kohler, K., Henderson, M., & Wu, T. (2006). The context of minority disproportionality: Practitioner perspectives on special education referral. *Teachers College Record, 108*(7), 1424–1459.

Skrtic, T. M. (1991). The special education paradox: Equity as the way to excellence. *Harvard Educational Review, 61*(2), 148–206.

Skrtic, T. M. (2003). An organizational analysis of the overrepresentation of poor and minority students in special sducation. *Multiple Voices for Ethnically Diverse Exceptional Learners, 6*(1), 41–57.

Skrtic, T. M. (2005). A political economy of learning disabilities. *Learning Disability Quarterly, 28*(2), 149–155.

Skrtic, T. M., Saatcioglu, A., & Nichols, A. L. (2021). Disability as status competition: The role of race in classifying children. *Socius, 7.* DOI:10.1177/23780231211024398

Sleeter, C. (1986). Learning disabilities: The social construction of a special education category. *Exceptional Children, 53*, 46–54.

Sleeter, C. (2010). Why is there learning disabilities? A critical analysis of the birth of the field in its social context. *Disability Studies Quarterly, 30*(2), 210–237.

Sleeter, C. (2017). Critical race theory and the whiteness of teacher education. *Urban Education, 52*(2), 155–169.

Spencer, M. B. (1995). Old issues and new theorizing about African American youth: A phenomenological variant of ecological systems theory. In R. L. Taylor (Ed.), *Black youth: Perspectives on their status in the United States* (pp. 37–70). Praeger.

Spindler, G. D., & Spindler, L. S. (1990). *The American cultural dialogue and its transmission.* Falmer.

Spradley, J. (1979). *The ethnographic interview.* Holt, Rhinehart and Winston.

Spradley, J. (1980). *Participant observation.* Holt, Rhinehart and Winston.

Spring, Joel. (2016). *Deculturalization and the struggle for equality: A brief history of the education of dominated cultures in the United States* (8th ed.). McGraw-Hill.

SRI International. (1995). *National longitudinal transition study of students in special education.* Author.

SRI International. (2011). *National longitudinal transition study of students in special education.* Author.

Stanovich, K. E. (1991). Word recognition: Changing perspectives. In R. Barr, M. L. Kamil, P. Mosenthal, & P. D. Person (Eds.), *Handbook of reading research* (pp. 418–452). Erlbaum.

Steele, C. M. (1997). A threat in the air: How stereotypes shape intellectual identity and performance. *American Psychologist, 52*, 613–629.

Strauss, A., & Corbin, J. (1998). *Basics of qualitative research: Techniques and procedures for developing grounded theory* (2nd ed.). SAGE.

Sugai, G., & Horner, R. H. (2009). Responsiveness-to-intervention and school-wide positive behavior supports: Integration of multi-tiered approaches. *Exceptionality, 17*, 223–237.

Sullivan, A. L. (2011). Disproportionality in special education identification and placement of English language learners. *Exceptional Children, 77*(3), 317–334.

Sullivan, A. L., & Bal, A. (2013). Disproportionality in special education: Effects of individual and school variables on disability risk. *Exceptional Children, 79*(4), 475–494.

Sullivan, A. L., & Long, L. (2010). Examining the changing landscape of school psychology practice: A survey of school-based practitioners regarding response to intervention. *Psychology in the Schools, 47*, 1059–1070. https://doi.org/10.1002/pits.20524

Takaki, R. (1993). *A different mirror: A history of multicultural America*. Little-Brown & Co.

Tate, W. (2008). "Geography of opportunity": Poverty, place, and educational outcomes. *Educational Researcher 37*(7), 397–411. https://doi.org/10.3102/0013189X08326409

Tefera, A. A., & Fischman, G. E. (2020). How and why context matters in the study of racial disproportionality in special education: Toward a critical disability education policy approach. *Equity & Excellence, 53*(4), 433–448.

Terman, L. (1916). *The measurement of intelligence*. Houghton Mifflin.

Thorius, K. A. K., & Maxcy, B. D. (2015). Critical practice analysis of special education policy: An RTI example. *Remedial and Special Education, 36*(2), 116–124.

Townsend, B. L. (2002). "Testing while Black": Standards-based school reform and African American learners. *Remedial and Special Education, 23*, 222–230.

Townsend, B. L., & Patton, J. M. (2000). Reflecting on ethics, power, and privilege. *Teacher Education and Special Education, 23*, 32–33.

Travers, J., & Krezmien, M. (2018). Racial disparities in autism identification in the United States during 2014. *Exceptional Children, 84*(4), 403–419.

Trueba, H. T. (1989). *Raising silent voices: Educating the linguistic minority for the 21st century*. Newbury House.

Tuck, E. (2009). Suspending damage: A letter to communities. *Harvard Educational Review, 79*, 409–427.

Tyack, D. B. (1993). Constructing difference: Historical reflections on schooling and diversity. *Teachers College Record, 95*(1), 8–34.

U.S. Bureau of the Census, Shrider, E. A., Kollar, M., Chen, F., & Semega, J. (2021). *Income and poverty in the United States: 2020: Current population reports*. U.S. Government Publishing Office. https://cps.ipums.org/cps/resources/poverty/PovReport20.pdf

U.S. Department of Education. (2001). *The longitudinal evaluation of school change and performance in Title I schools: Final report*. Planning and Evaluation Service, Author.

U.S. Department of Education. (2009). *Race to the top program executive summary*. Government Printing Office. https://files.eric.ed.gov/fulltext/ED557422.pdf

U.S. Department of Education. (2015). *37th annual report to Congress on the implementation of the Individuals with Disabilities Act, 2015*. Office of Special Education and Rehabilitative Services, Office of Special Education Programs. https://files.eric.ed.gov/fulltext/ED572022.pdf

U.S. Department of Education. (2020). 41st Annual Report to Congress on the Implementation of the Individuals with Disabilities Education Act, 2019, Washington, D.C.

U.S. Government Accountability Office. (2013). *Individuals with Disabilities Education Act: Standards needed to improve identification of racial and ethnic overrepresentation in special education*. www.gao.gov/products/GAO-13-137

Utley, C. A., Kozleski, E. B., Smith, A., & Draper, I. (2002). Positive behavioral support: A proactive strategy for minimizing discipline and behavior problems in urban, multicultural youth. *Journal of Positive Behavior Supports, 4*, 196–207.

Valencia, R. R., & Villarreal, B. J. (2003). Improving students' reading performance via standards-based school reform: A critique. *Reading Teacher, 56*, 612–621.

Vaughn, S., & Fuchs, L. (2003). Redefining learning disabilities as inadequate response to instruction: The promise and potential problems. *Learning Disabilities: Research and Practice, 18*, 137–146.

Voulgarides, C. K. (2018). *Does compliance matter in special education? IDEA and the hidden inequities of practice.* Teachers College Press.

Voulgarides, C. K., Aylward, A., Tefera, A., Artiles, A. J., Alvarado, S. L., and Noguera, P. (2021). Unpacking the logic of compliance in special education: Contextual influences on discipline racial disparities in suburban schools. *Sociology of Education, 94*(3), 208–226.

Voulgarides, C. K., Fergus, E., & Thorius, K. A. K. (2017). Pursuing equity: Disproportionality in special education and the reframing of technical solutions to address systemic inequities. *Review of Research in Education, 41*, 61–87.

Waitoller, F. R., Artiles, A. J., & Cheney, D. A. (2010). The miner's canary: A review of overrepresentation research and explanations. *Journal of Special Education, 44*(29), 29–49.

Waitoller, F. R., & Lubienski, C. (2019). Disability, race, and the geography of school choice: Toward and intersectional analytical framework. *AERA Open, 5*(1), 1–12

Waitoller, F. R., & Radinsky, J. (2017). Geospatial perspectives on neoliberal education reform: Examining intersections of ability, race, and social class. In D. Morrison, S. Annamma, & D. Jackson (Eds.), *Critical race spatial analysis: Mapping to understand and address educational inequity* (pp. 147–164). Stylus.

Weber, G. (1971). *Inner-city children can be taught to read: Four successful schools.* Council for Basic Education.

Welch, K., & Payne, A. A. (2010). Racial threat and punitive school discipline. *Social Problems, 57*(1), 25–48.

Welner, K. G. (2001). *Legal rights, local wrongs: When community control collides with educational equity.* State University of New York Press.

White, J. M., Li, S., Ashby, C. E., Ferri, B., Wang, Q., Bern, P., & Cosier, M. (2019). Same as it ever was: The nexus of race, ability, and place in one urban school district. *Educational Studies, 55*(4), 453–472.

Wilkerson, I. (2010) *The warmth of other suns. The epic story of America's great migration.* Random House.

Willis, A. I. (2019). Race, response to intervention, and reading research. *Journal of Literacy Research, 51*(4), 394–419.

Wilson, W. J. (1998). The role of the environment in the Black-White test score gap. In C. Jencks & M. Phillips (Eds.), *The Black-White test score gap* (pp. 501–510). Brookings Institution Press.

World Health Organization. (2022, February 11). *WHO coronavirus (COVID-19) dashboard.* https://covid19.who.int/

Ysseldyke, J. (2001). Reflections on a research career: Generalizations from 25 years of research on assessment and instructional decision making. *Exceptional Children, 67*(3), 295–309.

Ysseldyke, J. E., Algozzine, B., & Thurlow, M. L. (1992). *Critical issues in special education* (2nd ed.). Houghton Mifflin.

Zirkel, P. (2019, October). *RTI and the law.* https://perryzirkel.files.wordpress.com/2019/10/zirkel-article-on-rti-and-the-law-2019-update.pdf

Zirkel, P., & Thomas, L. B. (2010a). State laws and guidelines for implementing RTI. *Teaching Exceptional Children, 43*(1), 60–73.

Zirkel, P., & Thomas, L. B. (2010b). State laws for RTI: An updated snapshot. *Teaching Exceptional Children, 42*(3), 56–63.

Zirkel, P. A., & Huang, T. (2018). State rates of 504-only students in K-12 public schools: An update. *West's Education Law Reporter—354 Ed. Law Rep. 621.*

Zirkel, P. A., & Weathers, J. M. (2015). Section 504-Only Students: National Incidence Data. *Journal of Disability Policy Studies, 26*(3), 184–193.

Index

Madon, S., 76
Mahotiere, M., 163
Marr, J. B., 24
Maxcy, B. D., 33
McNeil, L., 27
Mehan, H., 44, 45, 48, 122, 134
Meihls, J. L., 44, 45, 48, 122, 134
Menda, A., 163
Mercer, J. R., 6
Messick, S., 3
MTSS (Miami–Dade County Public
    Schools), 33–34

National Academy of Sciences (NAS),
    40–42, 43–45, 46, 47, 117
National Association of School
    Psychologists (NASP), 199, 200
National Center for Learning
    Disabilities, 199
National Longitudinal Transition Study
    (NLTS), 28, 29
Nature/nurture argument, 104–106
Nichols, P. L., 117
No Child Left Behind Act (NCLB), 26

Oakes, J., 58
Ochoa, S. H., 145
O'Connor, C., 46
Office for Special Education Programs
    (OSEP), 7, 40
Open coding, 224–225
Oswald, D. P., 47
Other Health Impaired (OHI), 7, 47,
    135, 181
Out-of-school suspension, 69–70
Overrepresentation, 6–7; and
    socioeconomic status, 124

Parental participation, 107–109
Parents: attitudes toward home
    language, 150–151; role in referral
    process, 149–151
Passive management style, 85–86
Patton, J. R., 145
Peer group, Learning Disability as
    relative to, 165–168
Peterson, R. L., 117
Placement patterns across schools,
    124–126

Portes, A., 34, 35
Powell, M. P., 145
Principals: selection of faculty, 64; and
    terminating ineffective teachers,
    66–67
Professional work, 136
Psychologists' philosophies, 135–137

Qualification, for special education:,
    133–140; classroom ecology, 134;
    psychologists' philosophies, 135–
    137; school personnel's impressions
    of family, 133; teachers' informal
    diagnoses, 134–135

Race, 5; and disability, 13; implications
    for research, 29–34
Race to the Top (RTTT) program,
    26
Racial bias, in classroom arrangements
    and referrals, 82–83
Racial/ethnic disproportionality in
    special education programs,
    39–56; constructing disabilities in
    schools, 42–45; process approach
    to understanding, 45–50; special
    education as support, 49–50
Racism, 45; embedded, 31; individual
    vs. institutional, 75; as structural
    issue, 75–79; systemic, 32–34
Rand, Y., 19
Rational model: English learners,
    143–145; identity construction,
    123–124
Referral fever, 128
Referrals: culture of, 126; guidelines for,
    126–127; process, parents' role in,
    149–151; race/ethnicity in, 83–86;
    teacher, 127–132; variable rates,
    148–149
Reschly, D. J., 22
Reschly, D. T., 24
Research methods, 213–235; data
    collection methods, 218–221; data
    collection phases and strategies,
    215–216; dialogue from research
    team meeting, 216–217; nature/
    purpose of research, 214–215;
    sample size, 217–218

About the Authors

Beth Harry is a professor of special education in the Department of Teaching and Learning at the University of Miami. Her research focuses on the intersection of culture, family, and disability. In 2002 she served as a member of the National Academy of Sciences' panel studying ethnic disproportionality in special education, and in 2003 she received a Fulbright award to study the education of minority children in Spain. She completed her secondary education at St. Andrew High School in Kingston, Jamaica, received her bachelor's and master's degrees at the University of Toronto, and received her PhD from Syracuse University. After teaching in general education in Canada and Trinidad, she entered the field of special education in response to the birth of her daughter, Melanie, who had cerebral palsy. Also in response to Melanie's needs, Beth founded the Immortelle Center for Special Education in Port of Spain, Trinidad.

Janette Klingner was a professor at the University of Colorado, Boulder. She was a bilingual special education teacher for 10 years before earning her PhD in reading and learning disabilities from the University of Miami. She was a coprincipal investigator for The National Center for Culturally Responsive Educational Systems and an investigator for the Center on Personnel Studies in Special Education. Her research interests included disproportionate representation and reading comprehension strategy instruction for diverse populations. She was the chairperson of AE976RA's Special Education Research SIG, a coeditor of AERA's *Review of Educational Research*, and an incoming Associate Editor for the *Journal of Learning Disabilities*. In 2004, she won AERA's Early Career Award.